Quality Management
and Benchmarking
in the Information Sector

Results of Recent Research

Also available in this series:

Quality Management and Benchmarking in the Information Sector

Results of Recent Research

John Brockman (Editor)
Philip Brooks
Peter Brophy
Kate Coulling
Penny Garrod
Margaret Kinnell
Eileen Milner
Don Revill
Tony Shelton
Bob Usherwood

BOWKER
SAUR ●

London • Melbourne • Munich • New Providence, NJ

British Library Cataloguing in Publication Data
A catalogue record for this book is available from the British Library.

Library of Congress Cataloging-in-Publication Data
A catalog record for this book is available from the Library of Congress.

Published by Bowker-Saur, a division of Reed Elsevier (UK) Limited
Maypole House, Maypole Road
East Grinstead, West Sussex RH19 1HU, UK
Tel: +44 (0) 1342 330100 Fax: +44 (0) 1342 330191
E-mail: lis@bowker-saur.com
Internet Website: http://www.bowker-saur.com/service/

Bowker-Saur is part of REED BUSINESS INFORMATION.

ISBN 1-85739-189-6

British Library Research and Innovation Report 47

Cover design by John Cole
Desktop published by Mary Feeney, The Data Workshop, Bury St Edmunds
Index compiled by Judy Batchelor
Printed on acid-free paper
Printed and bound in Great Britain by Antony Rowe Ltd, Chippenham, Wiltshire

Contents

The Authors

John Brockman (Editor) is the focal point for Total Quality Management (TQM) and benchmarking in the Ministry of Defence (MOD), with responsibility for providing the MOD, Armed Forces and Defence Agencies with advice on strategic and organizational aspects of these activities.

His career in information work spans the UK and Australia, and includes full-time research, teaching and consultancy. His distinctions include an Honorary Research Fellowship of University College London, a British Council Academic Links and Interchange Scheme Award, the Elsevier Research Award and a US Government International Visitor Program. He is Vice-Chairman of the Organisational Excellence Group of the International Federation for Information, Treasurer of the Quality Methods Association and has served as a Councillor of Aslib, the Association for Information Management. He is a part-time Principal Lecturer with the Quality Unit at Nottingham Trent University.

John Brockman is a business graduate of the Western Australian Institute of Technology, a Licentiate of the Institute of Quality Assurance and Fellow of the Library Association.

Philip Brooks is a Senior Lecturer in Psychology at Liverpool John Moores University. He has a BA in psychology and a PhD relating to the psychology of reasoning. He is an Associate Fellow of the British Psychological Society and a chartered psychologist.

He has been employed as a research assistant/fellow on several projects mainly relating to reasoning and statistical inference. Immediately prior to his present post, he was employed as a senior psychologist in the Personnel Psychology Division of the Army Personnel Research Establishment, UK. Recently he worked as consultant to the Home Office and Wirral Safer Cities Project, and has carried out survey work for the Liverpool Health Authority.

Philip Brooks is currently a joint grant holder of a Science and Engineering Research Council (SERC) research grant relating to the development and evaluation of a computerized marine pilotage system, and of an EPSRC Teaching Company grant to investigate image compression for human face recognition. He is also supervising three doctoral students.

Peter Brophy, a graduate of University College London, started his career as a Research Associate in the Library Research Unit at Lancaster University, working on computer-based simulations of library systems. In 1973 he went to Strathclyde University as Library Systems Officer, and then moved to Teesside Polytechnic, becoming Deputy Librarian in 1979. In 1983 he moved to Bristol Polytechnic as Polytechnic Librarian. He was appointed to his present post as University Librarian at the University of Central Lancashire in 1989.

He is a Fellow of the Library Association, a Fellow of the Institute of Information Scientists and a Fellow of the Royal Society of Arts.

Peter Brophy has published widely in the field of library and information management and has a particular interest in academic library management, the impact of information technology on library services and international librarianship.

Kate Coulling began her library career with Lancashire County Library in 1969 and subsequently worked at the Preston School of Nursing. She was appointed to the staff of the University of Central Lancashire Library in 1984.

In 1992 the decision was made for the University Library to seek registration to the quality assurance standards BS 5750/ISO 9000 and she was appointed Quality Co-ordinator responsible for implementing the quality management system. During this time she studied for Institute of Quality Assurance, Internal Auditor and Assessor of Quality Systems qualifications.

Following the Library's successful accreditation, she was appointed Research Fellow to the project on Quality Management in Libraries funded by the British Library Research and Development Department (now British Library Research and Innovation Centre), and co-authored a book on quality management. Upon completion of the project, she returned to her current post of Assistant Librarian and Quality Co-ordinator in the University Library.

Penny Garrod is Research Officer in the Academic Services Department at the University of Plymouth, where she is working on a project under the FIGIT (Follett Implementation Group on IT) programme.

Prior to this she worked as a researcher at the Department of Information and Library Studies, Loughborough University. Previous library experience includes managing a one-person research library and automated acquisitions. She has also served in HM Forces, the Civil Service and local government.

Margaret Kinnell (Evans) is Professor of Information and Library Studies and Head of the Department of Information and Library Studies at Loughborough University. She began her professional career in public libraries and has since researched extensively and been widely published in the fields of public library management, marketing and strategic decision-making in the public sector.

Eileen Milner is a Senior Lecturer in information management at the University of North London with particular research interests in employee involvement, organizational waste analysis and innovation. As a public sector training and management consultant she has worked with clients in both the UK and Ireland, specializing in quality management and marketing. A chartered librarian, her career experience has been gained within both the public library and education sectors in Cornwall and Hertfordshire.

Don Revill began his library career in Nottingham Public Libraries, followed by spells of National Service and Army Library Service. He was Lecturer, Senior Lecturer and then Principal Lecturer at Leeds Library School, before becoming Chief Librarian of Liverpool Polytechnic. He is currently Head of Learning Services at Liverpool John Moores University. His information service management interests include convergence, statistics, performance indicators, finance, building planning and quality issues.

Tony Shelton is a Senior Lecturer in the Centre for Psychology at Liverpool John Moores University with responsibilities for statistics, research methods and information technology. He has an extensive background in the research, development and evaluation of multimedia and artificial intelligence (AI) expert system technologies for higher education, training and sports coaching. Other interests include open learning and human computer interaction. Tony Shelton is on the editorial board of *Interacting with Computers* and in 1995 co-organized the

Third International Conference on Sport, Leisure and Ergonomics in the UK.

Bob Usherwood, Reader in Librarianship at Sheffield University's Department of Information Studies, is widely experienced in the practice and teaching of librarianship and information studies. Before joining his present department he was Chief Librarian in the London Borough of Lambeth, after a succession of posts in other public and academic library systems.

His international work has taken him to Singapore, India, Kenya, Ethiopia, Poland, Canada, Russia, Scandinavia, Swaziland and Hungary. In 1978 he received the Senior Librarian's Award, enabling him to investigate library public relations in the United States. Three years ago he was invited back to America to attend the White House Conference on Library and Information Services.

He is widely published and has served on many professional working parties and committees, including the Library Advisory Council for England and the Library Association Council. He was presented with an Honorary Fellowship of the Library Association in 1992 and was made a Fellow of the Institute of Information Scientists in 1993.

In 1992 he obtained his Doctorate as a result of research into the role of elected members in the operation of public library services. His other research interests include public policy issues, interpersonal skills, the role of Total Quality Management in public libraries and public library expenditure in the private sector. He was recently a member of the Aslib consultancy appointed by the Department of National Heritage to review the public library service in Great Britain.

Introduction and overview

John Brockman

Quality management, in the form of either Total Quality Management or the less holistic quality assurance, is probably the most dominant management theme to have emerged since the mid-1980s. How (or whether) it can (or need) be implemented will have exercised the minds of most of today's managers at some time or other, not least of all those in the information sector.

Although each of the four research projects described in this book focuses on a particular part of that sector, the methodological approaches adopted are far from introspective. The continuous search for best practice, regardless of whether it is to be found in one's own sector or industry, is a basic tenet of Total Quality Management. It is therefore appropriate that the case studies upon which much of this research has been based are drawn from both service and manufacturing activities, and both public and private sectors.

For example, Brophy and Coulling examine some of the working practices in Marks & Spencer shops and McDonalds fast food outlets, as well as in a small light engineering factory. Similarly, the twelve non-information sector case studies discussed by Kinnell, Usherwood and Milner include a law firm, an international freight handler and an airline. Significantly, one member of this project's Advisory Group was Head of the Employee Relations Group of the Confederation of British Industry.

It is probably true of any new management philosophy or technique that to attempt to implement it and fail can sometimes do an organization more harm than if it had not been tried in the first place. The appearance of this book is therefore particularly timely, because information sector managers are being pressed to reduce their costs, while simultaneously improving quality and becoming more customer-oriented. These latter objectives are achievable only through the structured application of specific tools and techniques used in a strategic way. Unfortunately, in both the information sector and elsewhere, these tools have frequently not been fully understood and have sometimes been adopted by managers who lack the necessary training and commitment, and who often fail to take a strategic view.

The studies complement one another by taking contrasting approaches to the topic of quality management in library and information services (LIS), and between them they cover the three major parts of the information services sector. The focus of the study by Brophy and Coulling is academic libraries; Kinnell, Usherwood and Milner look at public libraries; while Kinnell and Garrod largely base their benchmarking work on the special libraries sector. This last study, which investigates one of the key processes in quality management, complements that of Brooks, Revill and Shelton, who focus on another important process, that of measuring customers' perceptions of quality. Their research is based on evidence provided by the academic library user community.

Looking at each of the studies in more depth, Brophy and Coulling undertook their investigation into quality management at the Centre for Research in Library & Information Management of the University of Central Lancashire between April 1994 and June 1995. They set out to develop a generalized model or map of quality management which aims to illustrate how the key quality concepts relate to each other. They make the point that these concepts are often pursued separately, and in so doing there is a temptation to concentrate on a limited number of ideas, thereby running the risk of missing opportunities which might arise by taking the overall picture into account.

The concepts they have identified have been incorporated into a process model reflecting the broad areas of *inputs, processes* and *outputs*. These key concepts were derived from interviews with industrialists, service sector managers and LIS professionals, together with analyses of the quality management literature. The resulting map is then applied to the manufacturing, service and LIS sectors. By referring back to the map in each case, the aim is to illustrate the practical application of the model in terms of the principal activities, processes and features commonly encountered in each of these sectors.

Their emphasis throughout is on quality management as a holistic approach to delivering goods and services which satisfy customers' needs. The relationship between performance measurement, an area which has received particular attention from the LIS profession, and quality management is also discussed. Brophy and Coulling suggest in their conclusion that it has been the absence of adequate quality assurance and quality monitoring which has left the public sector so vulnerable to the present day barrage of external audits. This trend has, in turn, forced public services, including libraries, to develop a more customer-driven and customer-oriented approach.

Similarly, in the next study, the financial constraints and political change affecting the public library sector are seen as an incentive for its managers to adopt some of the tools of quality management. The potential benefits offered by these tools are assessed by Kinnell and Milner of the Department of Information and Library Studies at Loughborough University, in collaboration with Usherwood of Sheffield University's Department of Information Studies. This project, funded for the period from September 1994 to July 1995, investigated the take-up and practice of quality management philosophy, tools and techniques in the public libraries sector. The researchers also compared the convergence between approach and practice (or 'rhetoric' and 'reality') of quality management in this sector and in manufacturing, commerce and service sector businesses.

Data obtained from a survey of all UK public library authorities, interviews with information professionals and politicians, and an extensive literature search are used to demonstrate the different approaches to quality that have been used and the extent to which they have been adopted. A comparison based on case studies of twelve public libraries and twelve private sector organizations enabled the team to ascertain what approaches might be appropriate for use by public library authorities. Critical success factors and barriers to implementation found to be common in all sectors are identified. The data suggest that the incremental approach to implementation offers the greatest potential for success. Three approaches are identified for further evaluation in terms of their potential for the public library sector.

Kinnell, Milner and Usherwood conclude from their evidence that the general reluctance by public library managers to embrace quality management concepts more fully arose from their partial understanding of quality management and their expressed reluctance to adopt techniques which may not always be appropriate to a public service organization.

Rapid technological and organizational change, with dwindling resources, is increasing the need for objective feedback regarding library users' needs. The essence of the research carried out by Brooks, Revill and Shelton was to develop an instrument reflecting what university library users see as 'quality'. Most survey instruments tend to be derived largely from professional librarians' opinions, and those of other 'expert' authorities, and are therefore not value free. The investigation was undertaken by researchers based in the Centre for Psychology at the Liverpool John Moores University, and, with pilot work carried out in the libraries at Liverpool John Moores and Bristol Universities, the instrument was tested at six further university sites. The researchers began with a list of 85 statements describing the characteristics of 'good' and 'bad' academic libraries, generated by library user focus groups. Through successive pilot studies, and by using iterative statistical procedures, the researchers reduced this list to a single sheet containing 24 questions. These provide the means of gathering reliable and valid information on aspects of quality of university library services as perceived by consumers.

The researchers found evidence of a dichotomy between the level of quality expectations of library users and librarians' own perceptions of these users' expectations. As well as describing in detail the development of a multi-dimensional quality assessment measure and a cost-effective instrument, the administration of this instrument, scoring and the interpretation of survey results are also discussed.

The report discusses other approaches to quality measurement and helps the reader disentangle the concept of 'quality' from those of 'satisfaction', 'expectations' and users' actual experience of using libraries.

'If you can't measure it, you can't manage it', goes a current management cliché, and like most clichés it contains a large element of truth. This issue of measurement is addressed by Kinnell and Garrod of the Department of Information and Library Studies at Loughborough University.

Their report provides an evaluation of the use of best practice benchmarking as observed in two parts of the LIS sector: the academic and commercial areas. Research data were obtained through surveys, interviews, and a review of the literature, whilst action research, based on demonstrator organizations, provided data on the practical application of benchmarking techniques. A Workshop at the end of the project gave practitioners an opportunity to contribute to the development of guidelines on the use of benchmarking in the library and information sector, and to appraise the training needs of implementing quality methodologies.

Benchmarking is a process essential to quality management. As with the other three studies described in this book, it was necessary for Kinnell and Garrod to provide the context for their research by examining practices and attitudes relating to quality management within their survey sample. Their study found that barely 12 per cent of the services surveyed had formal written policies on quality, and about 7 per cent were involved in benchmarking activities. On the other hand, comparisons using Standing Conference on National and University Libraries (SCONUL) and Council of Polytechnic Librarians (COPOL) statistics were found to be widely used by LIS managers. The purpose of benchmarking is not to yield data for their own sake, but to reveal best working practices indicated by those data. Informal visits and networking were found to be a common means of sharing information and experiences.

Barriers to the implementation of quality management were found to include: dislike and distrust of the language and implications of quality management; the belief that quality methodologies are of more relevance to industry and commerce, particularly large organizations; and fears about the costs and time-consuming nature of implementation. A cross-sectoral analysis revealed that public libraries have higher levels of implementation than do the academic and industrial sectors.

Benchmarking techniques were tested by three demonstrator organizations drawn from LIS serving an academic institute, a pharmaceutical company and a National Health Service trust. The authors emphasize, however, that a critical mass in the adoption of quality management needs to be reached before benchmarking can be fully tested and evaluated. They offer suggestions for the way forward.

The pieces of research described in this book provide a basis upon which the philosophy and tools of quality management can be assessed in terms of their appropriateness for implementation in the information sector. There are many barriers to the use of these approaches, but all four studies have produced much evidence of the potential that they have for this sector, some of which would apply equally elsewhere.

These studies are four of a number of similar investigations being undertaken worldwide within the LIS sector, notably by Scandinavian researchers working under the aegis of Nordinfo and other European consortia involved with the European Commission funded European Quality in Information Programme (EQUIP). Particular mention should be made of another BLRIC funded study which is due to report shortly, namely that of Professor George Philip. Working at Queen's University Belfast, he is conducting an empirical study to measure the quality of LIS services for the Northern Ireland industrial and commercial sector. This involves structured interviews and a questionnaire survey of the business community's expectations of information services and its perceptions of the actual services received.

In concluding this introduction and overview consideration should be given to where this work is leading, and what the future research priorities should be. BLRIC's support in this area has largely been focused on descriptive and conceptual research, coupled with limited development of tools and methodologies. This work, represented by the projects described in this book, together with two earlier British Library sponsored surveys (Porter, 1993; Webb, 1995) probably take us as far is it is necessary to go with descriptive research, at least for the time being. Researchers should now be encouraged to enter the post-descriptive phase in which the focus should be on whether causal links between quality management practices and results, expressed in terms of strategic objectives, can be demonstrated. Do these practices lead to demonstrably and quantifiably superior LIS performance, and what is the impact of such performance on customers?

References

Porter, L. (1993) *Quality initiatives in British library and information services*. British Library R&D Report 6105. London: The British Library.

Webb, S.P. (1995) *Pursuing quality in special libraries: a study of current activities and developments in the United Kingdom*. British Library R&D Report 6214. London: The British Library.

QUALITY MANAGEMENT AND BENCHMARKING: BACKGROUND

Quality defined: the basic concepts[1]

Introduction

The literature of quality management is extremely widespread and contains large numbers of introductory texts as well as a corpus of evaluative and research literature. The former almost universally start with an exploration of what is meant by 'quality' and are at pains to provide clear definitions and explanations on which quality management as a discipline can be built. Although this is sometimes a rather dry approach it is particularly important in this area because the term 'quality' is used so widely in everyday speech. While the use of the expression 'the quality' to describe the upper classes has thankfully all but disappeared, a glance at any newspaper or magazine shows that every advertiser lays claim to 'quality' products or services even where this is patently not the case. A rigorous definition of quality is therefore essential if systematic steps are to be taken to improve the service or product which the customer receives.

Quality is not, however, an obscure concept, nor do definitions need to be theoretical or abstract. The ideas behind 'quality management' are essentially everyday concepts—applied common sense—and everyday actions help to illustrate the key ideas behind it. Perhaps the most important point is that meaningful assessments of quality can only be made by examining both the product or service in question *and* the use to which it is to be put. Each one of us makes a 'quality decision' many times each day. For example, we decide to take the train, or the car, or the bus, based on perceptions of how well each meets our various

---

1. In order to avoid overlap, the introductory material from three of the reports in this volume have been amalgamated to form this section—'Quality Management in Libraries', 'Quality Management and Public Library Services: the Right Approach?' and 'Towards Library Excellence: Best Practice Benchmarking in the Library and Information Sector'.

personal criteria of convenience, availability, cheapness and so on. In effect this is a 'quality assessment' exercise: in deciding which form of transport is most suitable to what we will be doing we are recognizing that *its* suitability is related to *our* purposes. That, in essence, is what quality means. Before we can legitimately give the tag 'quality' to anything, we have first to think through what it is that the product or service is to be used for. This is not to deny that there are generally accepted aspects of quality: a dirty bus is not generally regarded as providing a quality service, nor is one that is unpredictably late, but this is because few people regard dirt and lateness as desirable.

However, this brings in a second idea, allied to the quality–purpose linkage: quality for one person is not necessarily quality for another. One person may be delighted with a new bus service that calls at the end of the road, but the person who lives half a mile away and used to have almost a door-to-door service is unimpressed. Thus there is a quality–purpose–customer relationship underlying our definition of the term. Fundamentally, quality is concerned with meeting the wants and needs of individual customers.

Formal definitions of quality

It is through this kind of consideration that the early pioneers of quality management arrived at one of the key, enduring definitions of quality which can be found throughout the literature, and which permeates quality management practice across the world: 'Quality is fitness for purpose'. An alternative, again found very widely in the literature, is: 'Quality is conformance to requirements'. Provided that the requirements referred to are those agreed with the customer, these definitions are equivalent. Both emphasize that customer need is paramount.

Definitions assigned by formal quality organizations include that by the British Standards Institution for standard 4778, 1987 (and its international equivalent ISO 8402, 1986) (British Standards Institution, 1987):

> The totality of features and characteristics of a service that
> bear upon its ability to satisfy stated or implied needs.

and that of the American Federal Office of Management and Budget, where quality management is defined in the following terms (Milkovitch, 1990):

...a total organizational approach for meeting customer needs and expectations that involves all managers and employees in using quantitative (and other) methods to improve continuously the organization's processes, products and services.

A.V. Feigenbaum (1991), a key writer on quality management, provided this alternative:

[Quality is] the total composite product and service characteristics of marketing, engineering, manufacture, and maintenance through which the product and service in use will meet the expectation of the customer.

To drive the point home to its managers, the Ford Motor Company used the following definition (quoted in Lascelles and Dale, 1993):

Quality is defined by the customer. The customer wants products and services that throughout their life meet his or her needs and expectations at a cost that represents value.

In a paper concerned with the application of the ISO 9000 quality assurance standard to libraries, Tann (1993) suggested that fitness for purpose would include:

- knowing the customer's needs—stated and/or implied;
- designing a service to meet them on or off the premises;
- faultless delivery of service;
- suitable facilities—car park, cafe, library, crèche;
- good accommodation—seating, lighting, heating, toilets;
- good 'housekeeping';
- reliable equipment—computers, videos;
- efficient administration—welcome, queries answered efficiently and effectively;
- helpful, courteous staff;
- efficient back up service;

- monitoring and evaluation including customer expectations, complaints, recommendations for improvement; and
- feedback loops to build-in improvement procedures and or checking that improvements are put in place.

From these brief descriptions, it can be seen that the key issue is that quality becomes a meaningful concept only when it is indissolubly linked to the aim of *total customer satisfaction*. It does not matter whether the context is an industrial company involved in metal fabrication, a government department preparing legislation, a library lending books, a bus company offering inner-city travel, or a finance department operating internally within a local authority. All have to meet customer needs.

Quality and grade

Of course 'quality' is often used to mean 'better' in the sense of more luxurious or simply more expensive. To avoid confusion, the literature of quality management distinguishes between 'quality' and 'grade'. Quality management accepts that customers are frequently willing to pay more for a product with additional features or of more modern design, or for a premium service with enhanced characteristics (and this is the basis of many a successful business); this is defined as a *high grade* rather than a *quality* product. The quality product or service remains one which meets the specified requirements of the customer in a consistent fashion.

The distinction between grade and quality is very important because it emphasizes that while only some organizations can offer high grade products (Rolls Royce, Armani, etc.) every organization can strive for and achieve quality. The starting point is a clear definition of what the product or service is intended to achieve, agreement with the customers that this will meet their needs, and consistent delivery at the agreed price or cost. Very often, especially in public service, limitations may have to be placed on the service which is offered because not every customer need can be met: public libraries cannot necessarily expect to be book suppliers, information providers, child care agencies, schools, leisure centres, counselling services, video shops, restaurants and social services departments within the kind of resource base which they can normally command. The pursuit of quality very often means restricting the range of activity in order that what *is* done, is done well. Service level agreements have an important role to play in defining the services to be offered unambiguously and in such a way that quality can be pursued and achieved, and these are considered later in this volume.

Quality and standards

The relationship between *quality* and *standards* is also worth exploring. Standards are in effect statements of the minimum level or performance which is acceptable in a product or service. It is sometimes assumed (especially by governments!) that if an external body sets, and then raises, standards, then quality will be improved as if by magic. There is an element of truth in this insofar as the standards reflect the customers' requirements and are widely supported. Consumer power is very real and consumers' organizations have achieved a considerable amount over the years. An obvious example is that the quality of cars has been raised at least in part because of this consumer-led approach, with some manufacturers suffering serious loss of market share when their products were perceived to be defective—for example, prone to rust or simply dangerous. However, there are some dangers with the standards approach. Firstly, it assumes that standards do indeed reflect the needs of the customers, which is often very far from the case. Secondly, it assumes that the standards cannot be manipulated by the producers. The latter problem may be illustrated by the continuous rise in the proportion of first class honours degrees awarded by UK universities over the last few decades. There are two possible interpretations here: either that the quality of graduate achievement has improved; or that universities have reinterpreted the standard and now award first class degrees for work which previously would have received a lower classification. The political interpretation placed on such occurrences demonstrates the danger of a standards based approach, especially for complex services. The then Secretary of State for Education and Science, Kenneth Clarke (quoted in Harvey and Green, 1993), remarked:

> The statistics speak for themselves, with the proportion of graduates in PCFC (Polytechnic and Colleges Funding Council) sector institutions gaining first and upper seconds having risen alongside the surge in student numbers. There are plenty of examples from HMI (Her Majesty's Inspectorate) to show how increasing numbers need not adversely affect quality—quite the reverse.

It will be immediately apparent that the standards argument bears only a tangential relevance to the real issue of quality. Are higher education courses meeting student needs? Are employers able to rely on graduates having the necessary skills and knowledge? Have the courses been kept up to date in a rapidly changing world? Only insofar as the standards reflect the real needs of the customers do they have value. Oakland (1994) suggests that the real problem is that standards are imposed from outside the organization (and are therefore likely to be subverted to the organization's and individuals' own purposes). By contrast, quality management is a self-imposed discipline depending on the positive participation of the whole organization.

The evolution of quality management

In establishing an understanding of what is meant by the term 'quality management' in the 1990s, it is important to consider that as a management philosophy it has evolved over a period of some fifty years. Indeed, it could be argued that its historical origins date back at least to the medieval craft guilds, and isolated examples can be found much earlier. The Industrial Revolution saw a shift from the work of the highly skilled individual to mass production techniques, relying on final inspection to ensure the quality of the finished product. This approach continued into the twentieth century. Quality control took this a stage further, through use of more sophisticated methods and systems. The main thrust of quality control was error detection and elimination, which is sometimes referred to as 'fire-fighting' (Dale, 1994).

Quality assurance heralded a change in approach with prevention based systems replacing those of error detection. Instead of checking products for quality after production, the focus shifted to ensuring that quality is built in at the design stage. Quality assurance adumbrates the new philosophy of Total Quality Management (TQM); the approach is proactive, and requires a different type of thinking and a democratic style of management.

TQM requires quality management principles to be applied to all aspects of an organization's business, in what has been termed a 'core value chain', comprising customers, employees, suppliers, shareholders, and the community (Oakland, 1994). It is probably best thought of as a goal towards which an organization is continually striving, rather than a management system to be implemented and then left to operate. Tenner and De Toro (1992) suggest that TQM is based on:

One *objective*:	'continuous improvement'
Three *principles*:	'customer focus' 'process improvement' and 'total involvement'

and *six supporting elements*:   'leadership'
'education and training'
'a supportive structure'
'communications'
'reward and recognition' and
'measurement'

The main theorists

Quality management appears to be firmly established in the public mind as having close links with the development of Japanese business and industry. However, the philosophy that underpins the development of what is known today as quality management is, primarily, American in origin. During the Second World War engineers and statisticians in the USA and in the UK's Ministry of Defence pioneered work on quality control in the weapons industry. It was from the activities to improve the accuracy and reliability of armaments that quality management developed. However, the two key figures in this developmental work, W. Edwards Deming and Joseph Juran, were 'prophets' who achieved recognition in Japan some decades before their home nation recognized the importance of their work. The post-war boom in demand in the USA and Europe meant that manufacturing companies could sell almost anything regardless of its quality, and this mitigated against any serious consideration of the potential benefits offered by quality management.

In the UK, where there were no dominant theorists, the work begun during the Second World War continued to be developed, particularly in the field of quality assurance. The British Standard 5750 achieved post war dominance in the military, industrial and manufacturing sectors as being the primary mode of inspecting and assuring the quality of products and manufacturing processes (Jackson and Ashton, 1993). It is perhaps because of the way in which quality in the UK has, largely, developed along the inspection and measurement route set out in the British Standard, that its application in sectors where there is no tangible product has been more problematic. In recent years, the work of practitioners and academics including Pfeffer and Coote (1991), Stewart (1989), and Walsh and Davis (1993) has served to focus on the way in which a less inspection-oriented approach and more democratically open approach to quality could be successfully applied in public sector organizations. Indeed, Wilson and Game (1994) argue that a great deal of developmental work in the quality management field is to be found in local authorities, where the external pressures for change and realignment in service provision have proved powerful catalysts. Similarly, the National Health Service is presented by Williamson (1992) as being an active testing ground of methodologies associated with quality management.

The development of much of the underpinning philosophy of quality management can be traced to the aftermath of the Second World War when the USA effectively controlled Japan's reconstruction programme. Deming, in a pivotal role, taught the Japanese to focus on causes of variance, and to differentiate between special causes and common causes, in their fledgling manufacturing industries. Common causes he identified as being those which could not be assigned to local variations, but which stem from a flaw in the process design itself. He advocated the adoption of process development and control systems that were reliant upon harnessing the expertise of all employees who came into contact with them for their evolution and improvement.

Deming's approach was above all systematic and was formalized into what became known as the Deming Wheel—the Plan, Do, Check, Action cycle. His methodology extended beyond process control to include the customer as a central focus for quality improvement and development. His vision was one where customers were the most important part of the production line. It was not enough to aspire simply to satisfy their existing 'needs'. Improvement potential was perceived to come from broadening this focus to include a consideration of previously unexpressed perceptions and desires.

Although the bulk of his philosophy was developed in the 1950s, it was not until the early 1980s when the USA experienced a crisis of confidence in its traditional manufacturing base, that the lessons that had been learned so well by the Japanese achieved a resonance in the country of their origination. Deming, anxious to build upon the interest being expressed in his work, developed a 14 point approach, set out in the Appendix to this section, the adoption of which he regarded as being essential if Western business and industry were to compete on equal terms with their Eastern counterparts.

Mann (1989), in his comprehensive study of Deming's work, encapsulates his major achievements: 'Deming is the person who established Quality as the overriding management principle...'. Conway, formerly chairman of Nashua, and now head of his own major management consultancy, refers to Deming as the 'founder of the third wave of the industrial revolution' (Mann, 1989). The first wave, Conway explains, was the widespread mechanization that began with British textile factories in the eighteenth century. The second, he says, began in the USA early in the twentieth century with Taylorism and Fordism. These theories meant reducing a job to the simplest functions, applying efficiency programmes and producing in mass. The use of statistical analysis to solve the problems of both production and service and the attendant possibilities of customer and employee involvement, constitutes the third wave.

Joseph Juran, a contemporary of Deming, is the quality theorist most frequently linked with him in reviews of the development of this work. Central to Juran's approach was the message that quality does not happen by accident. It must be planned for and has three constituent parts: quality planning, quality control and quality improvement. His approach to the customer was that: '...customers are a moving target' (Juran, 1989). He expanded upon Deming's work, arguing that the customer is not simply the external purchaser of a product or service, but that the internal customer should also be valued. His emphasis upon the customer is reflected in the nine steps of his 'quality planning road map', shown in the Appendix.

The substitution of slogans and rhetoric in place of properly planned, substantial commitment to the principles of quality management were the reasons, he felt, why so much that was labelled 'quality' had little or no credible impact on organizations into which it was introduced. The importance of training and education for all employees was another factor felt by Juran to be critical to the success of quality management, a factor which on the whole was not approached with sufficient understanding and commitment by organizations in the West.

Feigenbaum (1991), another of the early American exponents of quality management, differed from Juran and Deming inasmuch as he spent the greater proportion of his career actually working in the USA. His main interest was in the use of statistical methods to improve all aspects of quality control. However, he emphasized that this could only ever be one element in the overall philosophy that is quality management. In the 1980s and 1990s he added to his original concepts a need for there to be a properly constructed approach to human resource management, as well as giving some importance to attempts to measure customers' perceptions of quality. It was his interest in linking many different aspects of quality management that caused Feigenbaum to be identified as one of the earliest proponents of Total Quality Management. It is interesting to note that he was also vociferous in arguing that the 'costs' of quality should be seen as an integral part of any definition and approach to the subject. The ten benchmarks identified by Feigenbaum as being critical to the success of quality management in the 1990s are shown in the Appendix.

Philip Crosby completes the grouping of what might be termed the 'classical' philosophers responsible for developing the bedrock of current quality management thinking and practice. His influence upon the more evangelical proponents of the subject, such as Tom Peters and Robert Waterman Jr., has been immense. Crosby's guiding principle is that of the importance of organizations in striving towards 'zero defects'. Whilst recognizing that any process that involves a human being can never completely avoid mistakes, a margin for error which sends out the message that errors and waste are expected should never be built into any system. Much of his work also forcefully puts across the point that failures attributed to quality problems and difficulties are almost always attributable to poor management and that the only way of rectifying them is ultimately to improve the management skills contained within an organization (Crosby, 1979). Crosby is interested in the degree to which conformance or non-conformance takes place, the importance of which is outlined in his 14 steps for quality, shown in the Appendix.

The concept of conformance and non-conformance is an important one in any consideration of quality management and is an amalgam of the work and influence of Deming, Juran and Crosby, with the latter having had perhaps the greatest influence in popularizing the theory. The costs associated with ensuring conformance and rectifying non-conformance are offered by Crosby as being the primary reason for organizations in all sectors to consider their systems and procedures within a quality framework (Crosby, 1979). Within the public sector, Peacock (1995) identifies the difficulty of assigning a 'cost' to non-conformance as being a significant barrier to the widespread adoption of this approach. Drawing on some of the anecdotal evidence offered, he cites the example of a hospital trust that attempted to calculate the 'costs' of a failure to meet specified criteria for the testing of blood in a cardiology unit where the significant research input accrued considerable costs. He arrived at conclusions rejected by the medical staff. Some public library authorities, including Clwyd and Wiltshire, have undertaken investigations of non-conformances in specified areas such as requested materials, with a view to improving service to the end user, rather than assigning a specific 'cost' to instances of failure.

Peters and Waterman, writing in the 1990s, acknowledge that their original view of quality management has moved forward. Leadership and the need for organizations to be flexible form the basis of their later works. Peters, reviewing his earlier works, now promotes the concept of 'liberation' management, recognizing that there will be times when organizations will need to look beyond the needs of the customer (Peters, 1992). Middle management, in the culture of empowerment and greater employee involvement, is, he claims, effectively 'dead'. It remains to be seen if this will be true in the somewhat different circumstances of the 1990s. Peters' 12 attributes of 'quality revolution' are outlined in the Appendix.

Another emerging view in the continuing debate on and evolution of quality management is that of Oren Harari (1993). His work, and that of other academics in the USA and Europe, has questioned whether the widespread adoption of TQM has achieved any significant or even tangible improvements in quality, productivity, competitiveness or financial returns. Managers, he asserts, are beginning to realize that TQM is not necessarily synonymous with the successful adoption and practice of quality management. Whilst the latter is essential for organizational success and competitive advantage, TQM is only one of many possible means to attain quality.

David Freemantle (1993), a leading consultant in the area of quality management who advises and practises in a wide range of sectors in the UK, argues forcefully that customer focus remains a neglected area for many practitioners of quality. They concentrate too much on the internal processes to the virtual exclusion of an examination of the interaction between the customer and the organization. He states:

> Customer service is the final test. You can get everything else right...but unless you complete the process with incredibly good customer service you run the risk of losing business or even going out of business.

Quality management today

The quality programmes of today can be seen as a response to the current business and technological ethos. The emphasis is on cost-cutting, national and global competition, value for money, and increased use of IT to speed up supply chains and process complex data. The needs and wants of the customer are paramount in the race to retain and increase market share. Quality management practices represent a radical shift of focus away from the organization and its needs, and towards consumers (of goods and services), and *their* needs. The mechanistic view of the workplace—as typified by Taylorism and Fordism, with its emphasis on inspection and work study—has been superseded by a more organic and holistic approach. This is concomitant with the decline of manufacturing based industry and the rise of service industry. Management approaches now acknowledge the importance of the human interface, recognizing employees as autonomous, self-motivated individuals, who are capable of making decisions and influencing the success of the company. The philosophy of quality management is therefore based on what are accepted as sound management principles, and most organizations recognize that putting it into practice can, and should, be beneficial in terms of stakeholder satisfaction, increased effectiveness and success against competitors.

The volume of literature on TQM has grown steadily since about 1988 (Brockman, 1992), which has led to increased awareness of, and interest in, the issues which surround quality methodologies. However, as Line (1995) has noted, there is a tendency to 'work to death' these 'new' concepts, although he acknowledges that TQM is a large topic which warrants extensive treatment. Perhaps the saturation coverage of management topics such as TQM, and the tendency of some proponents to take an evangelical stance towards one particular methodology, has resulted in increasing management resistance to the implementation of quality practices. When resources are tight is it not more sensible to do nothing, rather than adopt an approach which might be both costly and ineffective, and where there is no consensus on what constitutes a right approach? Once again Line (1995), whilst ostensibly dealing with the quality of the literature on TQM, accurately pinpoints the reason for the gap between the practice of TQM, and the interest professed in it:

> The spirit behind TQM may be admirable, but it soon gets reduced to a set of techniques, prescriptions and formulae: the spirit is lost in the letter (a great many letters).

The trend, so far, has been for theory to proliferate, whilst practice lags behind. There is much talk, but action seems to be confined to large companies in the with–profit sector—the obvious examples being Marks & Spencer and Sainsbury's, where quality levels have been sustained over long periods. There is also widespread use of quality systems such as BS5750 (now BS EN ISO 9000: 1994). In the UK over 20,000 firms have attained the standard (British Standards Institution, 1995). However, a report of 1992 states that many UK organizations were having problems with TQM implementation, and that the task was not an easy one (Cruise O'Brien and Voss, 1992). Another report, appearing in the same year, suggests that 80 per cent of TQM programmes fail (Kearney, 1992).

Benchmarking, as part of this quality thrust, has been found to be widely used in top companies in the commercial sector (Coopers & Lybrand, 1994; Coopers & Lybrand/CBI, 1993), and more recently its use has extended to the public sector, in particular to the National Health Service (NHS), where the work of the NHS Benchmarking Reference Centre[2] has been influential (Bullivant, 1994). Benchmarking clubs and organizations are being established, and they seem to offer a practical way into the benchmarking process. One example is the Benchmarking Centre in Hemel Hempstead which, according to an article in August 1994, had 40 member companies—including SmithKline Beecham, TSB, IBM and ICL (Houlder, 1994). In the library and information sector there is increasing interest in benchmarking techniques, and an acknowledgement that much can be learnt from other organizations. In the public library sector four library authorities are embarking on a benchmarking project to compare their enquiry services (*Library Association Record*, 1995). The outcomes of this exercise will be of interest to all LIS managers, irrespective of sector.

---

2. NHS Benchmarking Reference Centre, Croesnewydd Hall, Wrexham Tehnology Park, Wrexham, Clwyd.

The quality environment

Quality management in the service and public sectors

Throughout its history quality management has been synonymous with industry and manufacturing. However, in the 1980s quality management moved from its original constituency to gain widespread adoption in a range of service sector businesses, including the hotel and hospitality industry, private healthcare, transport and financial services. State owned enterprises in the UK, most notably British Airways and British Rail, began to adopt quality management into their cultures from the mid 1980s. British Airways, once in a position where it was losing some £200 per minute of every day of the year, introduced through the leadership of their Chief Executive, Sir Colin Marshall, a focus on importance of the customer and of encouraging greater employee involvement (BA, 1995). By the end of the decade, the airline was amongst the most profitable in the world. As quality management entered the vocabulary of the service sector, Ascher (1987) identifies how politicians, particularly in the USA and the UK, began to express an interest in seeing quality management adopted in a wide range of functions of government and other public sector services.

In the UK, the pressure to move towards quality in the public sector could be said to emanate from five distinct areas:

- Competitive tendering
- An emphasis on measuring performance
- Constraints on spending
- A process of continual comparison with private sector practice
- Customer focus

However, when considering those factors which contributed towards the raising of awareness of the potential offered by quality management, it is important to keep in mind Pollit's caution: '...managing public services is different' (Pollit and Harrison, 1992).

Possibly the greatest problem when considering the application of quality management in public sector organizations is the degree of scepticism shown by those who view it simply as a methodology for improvement, designed by and for use by those in, the manufacturing and industrial sectors. The intrinsic link that quality management has with the production of a tangible product has, Stebbing suggests, led many public sector managers to reject it immediately (Stebbing, 1990). Crosby's often quoted phrase of 'getting it right first time, every time,' does not sit comfortably with organizations such as hospitals, schools, benefits offices and public libraries, where the interactions that employees have with customers, both internal and external, can be subject to considerable variance. In this context it should also be noted that this is not a problem unique to public sector organizations, but is also identified by Drummond (1992) as being an important consideration in certain service sector businesses, including banking, finance and medical insurance. However, it could be argued that the principle of making a response based upon the actual needs of the customer in front of you, or on the telephone, is nothing else if not 'getting it right'. In the public sector, however, it is important to consider the potential conflict between the needs of the individual customer and the community as a whole.

Kieron Walsh gives a perspective on the progress of quality management in this sector (Walsh and Davis, 1993):

> Quality is now a key focus of local authority discussion. The tendency, so far, has been to focus on quality assurance, particularly as expressed in BS5750 (ISO 9000). In the longer term, as the overall nature of local authority services changes, there is a need to consider more deeply what is meant by quality, and how different concepts and approaches can be balanced.

Walsh identifies the adoption pattern for quality management that could be charted across the UK in public sector organizations during the 1990s. In health services and education, the two areas of greatest change during this period, the Government's claim to increase levels of public accountability led many senior managers to focus almost entirely on ensuring the reliability of internal processes, with external accreditation, such as that awarded by the British Standards Institution and the International Standards Organization, being the goal of many organizations (Walsh and Davis, 1993). However, as in many profit making businesses in the service sector, formal standards that had been developed for use primarily in manufacturing industry were found to be unlikely to deliver the essential organizational shift of culture that a more holistic approach to quality management offered (Law Society Training and Education Group, 1994). This evolution of theory and practice within the whole of the service sector provides the background to the local government change factors in the UK discussed below.

In this context, benchmarking is seen as relevant to the public sector because it fulfils the demand that public services be more businesslike in their operations. Staff, users, auditors, the press, politicians and public accounts committees, have all levelled criticism at public services, and expect them to offer value for money and be competitive (Bullivant, 1994). However, it has been argued that benchmarking offers little that is new, as the techniques it employs are familiar ones: pareto charts, empowerment and customer focus are all part of the standard toolkit of a quality approach. Benchmarking's usefulness lies in its ability to support the management of change (Bullivant, 1994).

Local government change factors in the UK

Throughout the life of the Conservative administration in the UK, local government and the services that it provides have often been criticized by the Government as wasteful and lacking in full public accountability (Leach, 1993). This agenda has been addressed by:

- Subjecting publicly provided services to market testing and con-tracting out exercises. The underlying belief is that competitive pressures from rival suppliers will mean that organizations who have hitherto operated in a protected environment must improve their services and reduce costs if they are to retain the right to provide the service, or to become 'enablers' of fully contracted out services.

- The examination of the structures of local government in the UK through a comprehensive review initiated by the Local Govern-ment Act 1992. Over an initial two-year period the variety of pattern of provision in England, Wales and Scotland was inves-tigated, with an emphasis being placed upon facilitating public consultation. The pace for change in Wales and Scotland was in advance of that in England, with new authorities due to come into being in 1996. In England the recommendations made by the review body were by no means as far reaching as had been originally envisaged, with most of the County and District coun-cils apparently remaining. However, at the time of writing the position remains fluid, while for several authorities there is now the certainty that the fragmentation of their services has to be implemented during 1996/7.

In seeking to create a 'market' environment in the provision of public services, Wilson and Game (1994) identify central government as having created an entirely new management vocabulary for public sector employees. Terms such as 'competitive tendering', 'contracting out' and 'market testing' are identified as having entered the public sector lexicon. With a total amount of revenue involved in the whole of the public sector likely to exceed £25 billion, existing public service personnel have often found themselves in competition with the private sector to retain the work which was traditionally theirs (Barker, 1994). Public sector management, until the mid-1980s a profession that had required little knowledge of competition, found itself pitted against seasoned commercial sector operators. Walsh suggests that managers in many local authorities met this challenge of change and competition with some success (Walsh and Davis, 1993).

The first areas of service to be contracted out were in many ways the 'softest' options—refuse collection, cleaning, building, highways construction and maintenance, and housing management. As Walsh highlights, contracts were almost always awarded to those offering the lowest tender (Walsh and Davis, 1993). The actual savings made, in terms of direct and efficiency savings, vary widely, with Cubbin estimating that in refuse services alone the average saving was some 22 per cent (Cubbin *et al.*, 1986). This apparently contradicted a survey carried out in the *Local Government Chronicle*, in 1990, following the first year of competition, which found average savings of some 5.6 per cent (*Local Government Chronicle*, 1990). In the USA, where there has been a far longer tradition of contracting out services, arguments abound as to whether over the long term the savings achieved are anything more than negligible, a point argued forcefully by Kettl (1993).

The issue of competition is, however, firmly on the agenda for those in local government. The culture and mode of operation have shifted considerably in just a few years but as the agenda widens—for example, legal services are currently being contracted out in many authorities—all locally provided services are now being subjected to the scrutiny of the market. The potential problems that lie ahead are raised by Walsh (Walsh and Davis, 1993):

The market for public services is at an early stage and the long term effects of competition are likely to depend upon the nature of competition for particular services. In simple, repetitive services, such as cleaning, it is easy for providers to enter the market. The effects are likely to be quite different in professional services. Markets are likely to develop more slowly, and the effects are much less predictable.

Although the review of Local Government Commission in England has not resulted in the overarching changes once envisaged, in Scotland and Wales, where decisions on reorganization were made without the same recourse to public consultation, the changes are much more sweeping, with, in the main, much smaller 'unitary' authorities appearing to take on the powers once shared between County and District councils. Leach (1993), in his consideration of the purpose of the review, argues that a 'cynical' approach to the motives of central government may be appropriate:

Is the aim to create a sharply divided climate within local government in which large amounts of organizational energy are being spent on battles with the 'other tier' to maximize the chances of survival? It is certainly plausible to suggest that, even if this scenario was not conspiratorially planned, it is certainly coming to fruition. Reorganization is making it easier for the Government to push local government in a direction as yet obscure, but which is clearly not to local government's advantage!

Whilst the underpinning vision of reorganization may indeed be obscure, what the review of Local Government appears to have achieved (and this is borne out in the research data presented later) was to focus the efforts of local authorities on reviewing their existing service provision in terms of its efficiency, effectiveness and 'quality'. If quality management was something of a shadowy spectre prior to local government review, it gained an increasing importance and prominence as authorities organized themselves for the challenges ahead.

The central government 'quality' agenda

The Government claims that quality of service and value for money have been the guiding principles behind its approach to change in all aspects of public service, health, education, the armed forces, social security, the civil service and local government. Increasingly, however, it is important to note that quality of service and value for money in the delivery of public sector services are also cornerstones of the policies of the two major opposition parties.

The publication in 1991 of the Citizen's Charter was said to reinforce the doctrine of public accountability and the rights of the 'citizen' as a customer of publicly provided services (Great Britain, 1991a). The placing of the term 'customer' in the public context was to act as a catalyst for the considerable changes that the Government wished to see in all aspects of public service provision. Their vision for the years ahead was set out in the White Paper, *Competing for quality*, published in 1991 (Great Britain, 1991b):

> The Citizen's Charter sets out a comprehensive pro-
> gramme to improve the quality of public services. Central
> to this programme is the setting of rigorous standards for
> each service, and the development of ever better methods
> of delivering those standards. Where the Government
> takes the citizen's money through taxation and buys serv-
> ices on the citizen's behalf, there is a heavy obligation to
> ensure that the services provide the highest quality and
> best value that can be sought with that money.

> Competition is the best guarantee of quality and value for
> money. In the 1980s, the Government's policy of increas-
> ing competition gave a new dynamism to the British
> economy. We mean to extend those policies in the 1990s.
> We will expand the frontiers of competition outwards,
> bring new benefits to all those who use or work in public
> services. Activities close to the heart of government will
> be market tested.

Quality, competition and flexibility are the features that the Govern-
ment has seen as moulding the shape of public service for the future. Hospital trusts, agencies of government such as those dealing with benefits, child support and vehicle registration, grant maintained

schools, community care and local government bodies increasingly acting as enablers rather than direct providers of service, are now the reality of public service in the 1990s. Quality management has been influential in shaping the current pattern of provision. Its emphasis on assuring that what is delivered is consistent, is continuously reviewed in the light of the potential for improvement, and has a focus upon the customer, sits comfortably with Government policy. The question remains whether it can exist comfortably with the delivery of public services.

Drummond (1992) suggests that quality management has established a considerable degree of interest in the public sector in the UK. Peacock (1995) has also argued that this sector has become the most advanced in Europe in its adoption and patterns of practice. However, despite the legislation and pace of change affecting local government, Wilson and Game (1994) put forward the argument that sufficient time has not yet elapsed to allow the organizational embedding of 'quality' that is evident in many private sector organizations. There has undoubtedly been a considerable cultural shift in local authorities and over time it is likely that the specific tools and techniques of quality management may achieve an even higher profile. The desired result is something that Aristotle identified many centuries before Deming and Juran had theorized: 'Excellence is not an act, but a habit' (Logothetis, 1992).

The Confederation of British Industry (CBI)

The CBI states that it is 'completely independent...both commercially and politically' (Ashmore, 1994). However, this organization, with its 350 strong national Council, has an influential role in Government policy, and was instrumental in the formation of the Investors in People (IiP) initiative, which has been embraced by many organizations, including universities. To conform to IiP, organizations must be able to show clear evidence that staff training and staff development are accorded a high priority and that all staff are involved actively. Sir Bryan Nicholson, a former President of the CBI, advocates the use of benchmarking in the battle to gain competitive advantage in world markets (Ashmore, 1994).

The European Union

The European Union also plays a key role in the promotion of best management practice. The European Commission's White Paper,

Growth, competitiveness, employment, specifies that it intends to develop 'a European policy' for the promotion of quality. This will aim to 'reinforce the European industrial fabric and to exploit the competitive advantages connected with the demilitarization of the economy' (*EC supports European quality management,* 1995).

The European Foundation for Quality Management (EFQM) has 416 members,[3] and is supported by the European Union (Silva Mendes, 1994). The EFQM has devised a European Business Excellence Model which places considerable emphasis on customer satisfaction, and on the importance of the human interface to the successful organization. The model has been received with interest, and its potential for use in the public and service sectors, via the self-assessment route to quality, has been noted. The European Quality Award, which was devised by EFQM with the support of the European Organization for Quality (EOQ), is awarded to companies that demonstrate excellence in the management of quality. The objective for 1996 is to extend the award to small and medium-sized enterprises (SMEs) and to the public sector (Silva Mendes, 1994).

Library and information services (LIS)

In an historical review, covering the period 1970 to 1988, of the literature on performance measurement in LIS (Goodall, 1988), the scenario described then is little different from the situation in respect of quality management today: there is a plethora of literature, but little evidence of progress. There was, at that time, a tendency to stick to traditional, easily obtainable, library statistics. Such penetrating criticisms hold true for the library profession today. These include the fact that much research has been of a circular nature, and is 'collateral rather than cumulative'. The literature of quality management pertaining to the library and information sector today tends to reiterate that quality is a good thing, that it takes time, that it should be integrated into strategic plans, and, above all, that quality techniques need to be modified, or adapted, to suit the information sector in order to be workable. The title of one article sums up the situation: *Quality assurance: going round in circles* (Porter, 1992). Articles often have titles which indicate the dilemma facing the library

3. European Foundation for Quality Management (EFQM) List of members, 1 May 1995.

professional when confronted with quality management methodologies: *Quality in academic libraries: how shall we know it?* (Irving, 1992); and *Just another management fad? The implications of TQM for library and information services* (Brockman, 1992). Although the aim of these articles is to promote the cause of quality management, the authors' tone suggests that they too have doubts about the efficacy of their thesis, but feel that quality management must be implemented, if only to demonstrate that LIS are business-oriented and firmly in touch with current trends. The prevailing ambivalence is two-fold: first, there is dislike of 'commercial' activities and a belief that the public sector/educational ethos is being undermined by rampant commercialism; and, secondly, there is fear that if the profession does not embrace these new methodologies, both it and its service will be dispensed with (Lawes, 1993):

> It is said that to survive and thrive in the 1990s, performance and profitability must be the primary focus in our organizations. This concept runs contrary to many of our profession's long-held aspirations and beliefs.

However, there is a positive side to this emphasis on performance and profitability—it is a chance to tackle long-standing problems. The British Library Research and Innovation Centre has provided support in this area over a long period, ranging from work on 'interlibrary comparisons' in the late 1970s and early 1980s to the current programme of research into the issues surrounding quality management in the LIS sector. Benchmarking is seen as impacting directly on services and has the potential to improve them further. However, attitudes and beliefs relating to benchmarking within the LIS profession mirror those in the private sector: there is little consensus on what it involves or how best to do it. Awareness of, and interest in, quality may be spreading but this is not being translated into action. The problem seems to be both perpetual and difficult to overcome.

References and bibliography

Ascher, K. (1987) *The politics of privatisation*. London: Macmillan.

Ashmore, C. (1994) A man with a competitive mission. *Engineering Management Journal*, December, 257.

BA (1995) *British Airways benchmarking day*. London, April.

Barker, L. (1994) *Competing for quality*. Harlow: Longman.

British Standards Institution (1987) *British Standard 4778*. London: BSI.

British Standards Institution (1995) *A customer's guide to BSI*. London: BSI.

Brockman, J. (1992) Just another management fad? The implications of TQM for library and information services. *Aslib Proceedings*, 44(7/8), July/August, 283-288.

Bullivant, J. (1994) *Benchmarking for continuous improvement in the public sector*. Harlow: Longman.

Coopers & Lybrand (1994) *Survey of benchmarking in Europe 1994*. London: Coopers & Lybrand. (For information contact Sue Cannon or Richard Archer on 0171 2133845).

Coopers & Lybrand/CBI (1993) *Survey of benchmarking in the UK*. London: Coopers & Lybrand and the Confederation of British Industry. (For information contact Sue Cannon or Richard Archer on 0171 2133845).

Crosby, P. (1979) *Quality is free*. New York: McGraw Hill.

Cruise O'Brien, R. and Voss, C. (1992) *In search of quality. An assessment of 42 British organizations using the criteria of the Baldridge Quality Award. Executive summary*. London Business School Operations Management Paper 92/02, March. London: London Business School.

Cubbin, J., Bomberger, S., and Meadowcroft, S. (1986) Competitive tendering and refuse collection: identifying the sources of efficiency gains. *Fiscal Studies*, 8(3), 69-87.

Dale, B. (ed.) (1994) *Managing quality.* 2nd edn. Hemel Hempstead: Prentice Hall.

Deming, W. (1988) *Out of the crisis.* Cambridge: Cambridge University Press.

Drummond, H. (1992) *The quality movement.* London: Kogan Page.

EC supports European quality movement, (1995) *Quality Link,* 7(35), January/February, 11.

Feigenbaum, A.V. (1991) *Total quality control.* 3rd edn. New York; McGraw Hill.

Freemantle, D. (1993) *Incredible customer service.* London: McGraw Hill.

Goodall, D. (1988) Performance measurement: a historical perspective. *Journal of Librarianship*, 20(2), April, 128-143.

Great Britain (1991a). *The Citizen's Charter—raising the standard.* London: HMSO.

Great Britain (1991b) *Competing for quality.* London: HMSO.

Harari, O. (1993) Ten reasons why TQM doesn't work. *Management Review,* January, 33-38.

Harvey, L. and Green, D. (1993) Defining quality. *Assessment and Evaluation in Higher Education*, 18(1).

Houlder, V. (1994) Measuring up to success. *Financial Times*, 1 August, 8.

Irving, A. (1992) Quality in academic libraries: how shall we know it? Aslib Information, 20(6), June, 244-246.

Jackson, P. and Ashton, D. (1993) *Implementing quality through BS5750 (ISO 9000).* London: Kogan Page.

Juran, J. (1988) *Juran on planning for quality.* New York: Free Press.

Juran, J. (1989) *Juran on leadership for quality.* New York: Free Press.

Kearney, A.T. (1992) *Total quality: time to take off the rose-tinted spectacles.* The results of a survey conducted by A.T. Kearney in association with *The TQM Magazine.* Bradford, West Yorkshire: MCB University Press.

Kettl, D.F. (1993) *Sharing power: public governance and private markets.* Washington DC: Brookings Institution.

Lascelles, D.M. and Dale, B.G. (1993) *The road to quality.* Bedford: IFS Ltd.

Law Society Training and Education Group (1994) *Presentations and discussions at Law Society Training and Education Group meeting,* held in Sheffield, December.

Lawes, A. (1993) The benefits of quality management to the library and information services profession. *Special Libraries,* 84(3), Summer, 142-146.

Leach, S. (1993) Local government reorganisation in England. *Local Government Policy Making,* 19(4), 35.

Library Association Record (1995) Inquiries tests. *Library Association Record,* 97(9), September, 477.

Line, M. (1995) Needed: a pathway through the swamp of management literature. *Library Management,* 16(1), 36.

Local Government Chronicle (1990) Supplement. 6 July.

Logothetis, N. (1992) *Managing for total quality.* London: Prentice Hall.

Mann, N. (1989) *The keys to excellence: the Deming philosophy.* Salisbury: Mercury Books.

Milkovitch, M. (1990) Total Quality Management for public sector productivity improvement. *Public Productivity and Management Review,* 9(1), 209.

Oakland, J. (1994) *Total Quality Management.* 2nd edn. Oxford: Butterworth Heinemann.

Peacock, R. (1995) *Organisational self-assessment.* A presentation to the Institute of Electrical Engineers,London, 9 June, 1995.

Peters, T. (1989) *Thriving on chaos.* London: Macmillan.

Peters, T. (1992) *Liberation management*. London: Macmillan.

Peters, T. and Waterman, R.H. (1982) *In search of excellence: lessons from America's best-run companies*. New York: Harper & Row.

Pfeffer, N. and Coote, A. (1991) *Is quality good for you?* London: Institute for Public Policy Research.

Pollit, C. and Harrison, S. (eds.) (1992) *Handbook of public services management*. Oxford: Blackwell.

Porter, L. (1992) Quality assurance: going round in circles. *Aslib Information*, 20(6), June, 240-241.

Silva Mendes, A. (1994) European policy for the promotion of quality. *European Quality. 1994 European Quality Award Official Publication*. London: European Quality Publications Ltd., 8.

Stebbing, L. (1990) *Quality management in the service industry*. London: Ellis Horwood.

Stewart, J. (1989) *The future of local government*. Basingstoke: Macmillan Education.

Tann, J. (1993) Dimensions of quality in a library setting. In *Quality management: towards BS5750*. Proceedings of a seminar held in Stamford, Lincolnshire, UK on 21 April 1993, ed. M. Ashcroft and D. Barton. Stamford, Lincs: CPI.

Tenner, A.R. and DeToro, I.J. (1992) *Total Quality Management: three steps to continuous improvement*. Reading, Mass.: Addison-Wesley.

Walsh, K. and Davis H. (1993) *Competition and service: the impact of the Local Government Act 1988*. London: HMSO.

Williamson, C. (1992) *Whose standards?* Buckingham: Open University Press.

Wilson, D. and Game, C. (1994) *Local Government in the United Kingdom*. Basingstoke: Macmillan.

Appendix

Deming's 14 Points

1. Create constancy of purpose to improve product and service.
2. Adopt new philosophy for a new economic age by management learning responsibilities and taking on leadership for change.
3. Cease dependence on inspection to achieve quality; eliminate the need for mass inspection by building quality into the product.
4. End awarding business on price, instead minimize total cost and move towards single suppliers for items.
5. Improve constantly and forever the system of production and service to improve quality and productivity and to decrease costs.
6. Institute training on the job.
7. Institute leadership.
8. Drive out fear so that all may work effectively for the organization.
9. Break down barriers between departments.
10. Eliminate slogans, exhortations and numerical targets for the workforce.
11. Eliminate quotas or work standards and management by objectives or numerical goals; substitute leadership.
12. Remove barriers that rob people of their right to pride in their work.
13. Institute a vigorous education and improvement programme.
14. Put everyone in the organization to work to accomplish the transformation.

From Deming, W. *Out of the crisis*. Cambridge: Cambridge University Press, 1988.

Juran's 'Quality Planning Road Map'

1. Identify who are the customers.
2. Determine the needs of the customers.
3. Translate their needs into our language.
4. Develop a product which can respond to these needs.
5. Optimize the product features so as to meet our needs as well as our customers' needs.
6. Develop a process which is able to produce the product.
7. Optimize the process.
8. Prove that the process can produce the product under operating conditions.

From Juran, J. *Juran on planning for quality*. New York: Free Press, 1988.

Feigenbaum's 10 benchmarks for total quality success

1. Quality is an organization wide process.
2. Quality is what the customer says it is.
3. Quality and cost are a sum not a difference.
4. Quality requires both individual and team zealotry.
5. Quality is a way of managing.
6. Quality and innovation are mutually dependent.
7. Quality is an ethic.
8. Quality requires continuous improvement.
9. Quality is the most cost-effective, least capital intensive route to productivity.
10. Quality is implemented with a total system connected with customers and suppliers.

From Feigenbaum, A.V. *Total quality control.* New York: McGraw Hill, 1991.

Crosby's 14 steps to quality improvement

1. Make it clear that management is committed to quality.
2. Form quality improvement teams with senior representatives from each department.
3. Measure processes to determine where current and potential problems lie.
4. Evaluate the cost of quality and use it as a management tool.
5. Raise the quality awareness and personal concern of all employees.
6. Take actions to correct problems identified through previous steps.
7. Establish progress monitoring for the improvement process.
8. Train supervisors to actively carry out their part in the quality improvement programme.
9. Hold a 'zero defects day' to let everyone know that there has been a change and to reaffirm management commitment.
10. Encourage individuals to establish improvement goals for themselves and their groups.
11. Encourage individuals to communicate to management the obstacles they face in attaining their improvement goals.
12. Recognize and appreciate those who participate.
13. Establish quality councils to communicate on a regular basis.
14. Do it all over again to emphasize that the quality improvement programme never ends.

From Crosby, P. *Quality is free.* New York: McGraw Hill, 1979.

Peters' 12 attributes of a quality revolution

1. Management obsession with quality—this obsession to find expression in practical action to back up and emotional commitment.

2. Passionate systems—failure will occur if there is a system without passion or *vice versa* and an ideology is important, though not one necessarily based on a particular guru.

3. Measurement of quality—this should be a feature from the start, enacted by everybody, and the results of it widely displayed.

4. Quality is rewarded—recognizing quality achievement with tangible rewards provides the incentive to bring about breakthroughs in attitude.

5. Everyone is trained for quality—extensive training should apply to all in the organization, and this should encompass instruction in cause and effect analysis, statistical process control, and group interaction.

6. Multi-function teams—teams which span the traditional organizational structures should be introduced: quality circles, or to be more recommended, cross-functional teams.

7. Small is beautiful—there is significance in every change and no such thing as a small improvement.

8. Create endless 'Hawthorne' effects—new events are the antidote to flagging interest in quality.

9. Parallel structure devoted to quality improvement—this describes the creation of shadow quality teams and emphasizes that it is a route to improvement.

10. Everyone is involved—the quality process is comprehensive embracing suppliers, distributors and customers.

11. When quality goes up, costs go down, quality improvement is the primary source of cost reduction. The elementary force at work is simplification—of design, process or procedures.

12. Quality improvement is a never ending journey—all quality is relative, it does not still.

From Peters, T. *Thriving on chaos*. London: Macmillan, 1989.

QUALITY MANAGEMENT IN LIBRARIES

Peter Brophy
Kate Coulling

Introduction

*It is almost an intellectual impossibility to assess the real
needs of users.* (Johannsen, 1992)

Quality management

Interest in quality management is widespread across all types of organization. References occur frequently in the literature of management and of most professions. Government and senior managers demand continuous improvements in quality. Advertisers back up their claims to be offering 'high quality' products by reference to BS 5750, ISO 9000 and the results of supposedly independent tests and trials. Quality is 'in'.

But what exactly do these disparate and sometimes opposing voices mean by 'quality'? Why have so many organizations climbed on the 'quality bandwagon', and how is the rather bemused onlooker to distinguish between the rhetoric and the real thing? Does quality management—which so often seems to betray its origins in manufacturing industry—really apply to services such as libraries and information providers, especially those in the non profit-making sector? And if it does, how are professional librarians and information scientists to distinguish the useful and valuable from among the morass of quality management concepts and techniques?

The answers to these questions are not straightforward, but what is clear is that government, funding bodies and, most of all, service users are demanding not only that quality be delivered but that it be demonstrated. It is part of the value-for-money equation which looms so large in most organizations, and certainly in public services. The days when consumers could be given any kind of product or service and be expected to put up with its shortcomings are long gone—consumer power is here to stay. There is an imperative to make every effort to satisfy customers' requirements, and indeed to go beyond customer satisfaction to 'customer delight', the kind of reaction to a service which leads the customer to come back again and again, and to become a lifetime supporter.

The shift to market economies throughout the world has likewise helped to provide a focus on delivering products and services which the market (i.e. the customers) want. Viewed in this light, quality management could be seen as a realignment of the marketing function, but in fact it is much more, involving every managerial and operational function of the organization. In the public sector, developments such as market testing, compulsory competitive tendering and the Citizen's Charter have all helped to move services towards a focus on quality management. Such shifts are set to continue.

Quality and libraries

Libraries have not been immune from the changes in the wider organizational climate and the literature of librarianship and information science, as we shall demonstrate, depicts an increasing use of quality management terminology. Public libraries have been in the forefront of the adoption of the Citizen's Charter and a number have been awarded the Charter Mark; academic libraries have been involved in institutional quality assurance processes, have been influential in the Higher Education Funding Councils' deliberations on the assessment of quality, and have developed sophisticated statistical measures of performance; special libraries have played their part in their organizations' drive towards quality management, and a number have achieved accreditation to the international quality assurance standard, ISO 9000.

Alongside this avowedly quality management activity, and indeed pre-dating it, libraries have developed approaches based on many years' work on performance measurement, on a tradition of customer care (albeit under other names), and on a track record of customer satisfaction. While the terminology may be changing, much quality management in libraries and information services is thus built on the solid foundation of past achievement. Because of this it is often difficult to gauge the extent to which libraries have adopted quality management. Porter (1992), reporting on a survey carried out in 1992, summarized the results as showing that only 17 per cent of academic and public libraries had no quality initiatives under way, although it was clear that terminology was a major problem in the work. More recent work at Loughborough University appears to show that 67 per cent of public libraries have no written quality policy. Such bare statistics, however, clearly need considerable interpretation.

The Quality Management in Libraries project

The Quality Management in Libraries project at the Centre for Research in Library & Information Management of the University of Central Lancashire examined the concepts, techniques, tools and applications of quality management. The aim was to provide a conceptual framework for the adoption of quality management by library and information services (LIS), to interpret the main approaches taken by LIS, and to explore the relationship between quality management and library performance measurement. Most of the work was desk-based research, supplemented by interviews with key players and direct observation, as described below.

A literature search provided insight into the concepts, definitions and applications of quality management as understood in manufacturing and service industries, including LIS. Key concepts were identified and linked to traditional LIS practices through visits and interviews with managers from a selection of LIS and other organizations. These concepts were then 'mapped' to show how the jargon of quality management linked up to form a holistic picture of a quality organization. A checklist based on the mapping exercise was taken on visits to another selection of LIS, to test its efficacy as a tool for judging a quality organization. Finally, a set of case studies was developed of LIS organizations which have implemented quality management techniques. The strands of the investigation were drawn together to write this final report and to produce a prototype system for exploring LIS practices and their measures within a quality management concepts framework.

This report offers LIS managers an opportunity to assess current practices for their position within current quality management philosophy. It should also indicate where attention might be focused to move forward from one position to the next cluster of concepts and techniques, towards the implementation of Total Quality Management (TQM). Whilst it is true to say that most organizations are now attuned to the need to identify, meet and monitor customer requirements, how to undertake this, how to turn evidence into purposeful change and how to achieve continuous improvement, and then demonstrate success to funding bodies or others, all require further attention. Reductions in LIS funding, especially in the public sector, provide clear evidence of our need to make a better case, both culturally and economically.

The work reported here complements a number of other projects, many also funded by the British Library Research and Innovation Centre, as has already been described by John Brockman in the Introduction to this volume. In addition, John Brockman and Alan Gilchrist have been examining TQM and its relationship to corporate excellence, and have developed excellent contacts with Japanese quality management experts (Brockman and Gilchrist, 1995). A particular focus is on information networks as part of the total quality approach, for example in facilitating communication and the sharing of good practice. Another project, based on research funded directly by the University of Central Lancashire, has resulted in a book which describes all the major theories of quality management, the relevant international standards and awards, and the ideas of the main writers on quality management (Brophy and Coulling, 1996). These complementary projects consolidate much of the theory and practice of LIS-based quality management to provide managers in all types of LIS with a framework for incorporating quality management into strategic planning and into the operational management of their services.

Quality and the organizational environment

The process model

There are many different approaches to understanding organizations, and many different models have been used in management theory. It is notable, however, that the literature of quality management relies very heavily on the systems or process model which views an organization as a means of transferring inputs via processes into outputs, which then have outcomes. The organization exists in an environment which affects it and which it affects, and there are various feedback loops by which inputs and processes and outputs are redefined and changed over time as the organization seeks to adjust to its environment and to improve its effectiveness. Figure 1 shows this model in its simplest form.

Figure 1: The Process Model

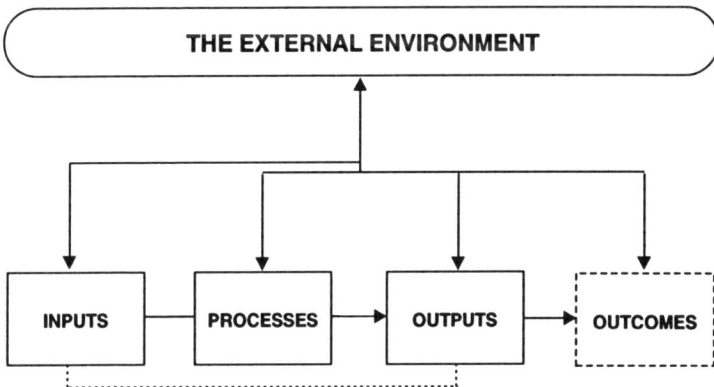

An organization uses *inputs* and applies *processes* to produce *outputs* which, when used, have *outcomes*. The *external environment* both influences all these elements, and is itself influenced by them (including inputs, for example where raw materials are being mined). While the process model may bring to mind an image of manufacturing industry, the approach is also fairly familiar in library and information science. The approach was described in Brophy (1986) and is used in Abbott (1994), although many other references will be found in the literature of librarianship and information science.

The process model is the basis for most of the established and widely implemented quality systems such as ISO 9000 and the European Quality Award (EQA), both of which have been applied to manufacturing and service industries. For example, the European Business Excellence Model is defined as shown in Figure 2.

Figure 2: The European Business Excellence Model

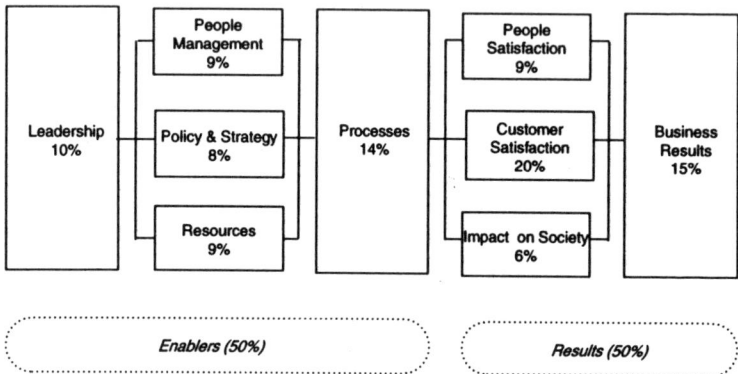

Leadership 10%	People Management 9%	Processes 14%	People Satisfaction 9%	Business Results 15%
	Policy & Strategy 8%		Customer Satisfaction 20%	
	Resources 9%		Impact on Society 6%	

Enablers (50%)   Results (50%)

It is useful to concentrate on the EQA since it is both widely accepted as a basis for assessing quality management systems and widely used as a model by organizations seeking to implement quality management or improve their existing systems.

The criteria for the EQA are grouped into *enablers* (which enable the organization to produce something, whether it is a physical product or a service) and *results* (which are what impact on customers). Each of the nine criteria used in making an assessment for the Award is given a weighting, as follows (and reading from right to left across the diagram in Figure 2):

- *Business Results* (15 per cent), which compares the actual achievement of the organization with the targets it set;

- *People Satisfaction* (9 per cent), being an assessment of the organization's own staff's views and experiences of the implementation of quality management;

- *Customer Satisfaction* (20 per cent), which is an assessment of the views of the organization's customers on whether their needs are being met;

- *Impact on Society* (6 per cent), a recognition that organizations do not exist in a vacuum but must be responsible within the wider local, national and global environment;

- *Processes* (14 per cent), which looks at the management of the organization's internal processes;

- *People Management* (9 per cent), focusing on the way in which human resources are managed;

- *Policy & Strategy* (8 per cent), which seeks evidence of mission, vision, and strategic thinking;

- *Resources* (9 per cent), looking at the way in which the organization uses its financial, technological, information and other resources;

- *Leadership* (10 per cent), examining the evidence for clear leadership being exercised throughout the organization.

The EQA is not the only model available, of course, but it was developed after the perhaps better known Deming Prize[1] and Baldrige Award,[2] and probably better reflects the European and British cultural environment. It is, of course, possible to view organizations from many different perspectives and different models could provide useful insights. Soft systems methodology, for example, could be used to elucidate the quality chain and the roles of stakeholders. While useful research could be carried out in this area, it is beyond the scope of this Report.

Developing practice

Current practice with regard to quality varies from organization to organization. Libraries and information services are probably no different from other sectors in this regard, although Webb (1995) presents some evidence that they lag behind their parent organizations. Some libraries have a high profile with a well documented quality initiative; some are using a few of the techniques as they feel appropriate or as they feel they can afford; some are doing nothing, as quality management is seen as inappropriate or too expensive to implement (or perhaps is simply ignored). Yet the latter are almost certainly using aspects of quality management, albeit under other names.

In addition to the survey by Porter (1992) mentioned above, and Webb's more recent work, a considerable body of literature testifies to the increasing use of quality management practice by libraries and information services of all kinds. Lester (1994) reported on the use of quality management in the sector across Europe, providing a wider perspective (although a number of UK examples were included), and there is a considerable body of American LIS literature on the topic (see, for example, Jurow and Barnard, 1993). A series of contributions to the

---

1. The Deming prize was established in 1950 by the Union of Japanese Scientists and Engineers, and is closely linked to business excellence achieved through the use of Statistical Process Control (SPC) and development of SPC techniques.
2. The Baldrige Quality Award is awarded annually in the USA and uses seven categories: Leadership; Strategic Planning; Customer & Market Focus; Information and Analysis; Human Resource Development & Management; Process Management; Business Results. Many American companies have modelled their quality management on the Award, even though they had no intention of applying for it. Information is available on the World Wide Web at http://www.quality.nist.gov/

TQM conference at the 1992 Library Technology Fair covered all the main sectors (HERTIS, 1992). Professional groups have contributed through surveys, conferences and guidelines—see, for example, Library Association (1993). Particular aspects of quality management have received detailed attention—examples are Pluse (1994) on 'Investors in People', Ellis and Norton (1993) on ISO 9000 and Curtis *et al.* (1993) on stakeholders. A fuller account of the literature can be found in Brophy and Coulling (1996).

In interviewing practitioners we found that applying quality management to existing practice is often perceived as the most problematic aspect of this whole issue. Problems voiced by library staff interviewed during this project included:

- apparent *incoherence* due to the number of concepts, many of which appear to be in conflict;

- confusing *definitions* and approaches;

- the *transfer* of quality management to service industry contexts from its manufacturing industry base;

- the lack of *training* in quality management techniques;

- little *advice* on where to start;

- the apparently high *cost* of implementing quality initiatives;

- the difficulty of *measuring* quality in libraries;

- the *'bad press'* arising from texts which present it as a 'cure-all', when it is patently obvious that it is a 'long haul';

- the idea that quality management is *a passing fad*, so that it can be ignored.

If there is a range of opinion about quality management itself, there is equal divergence regarding the 'best way' of implementing it. It can be argued that there is no single way of implementing quality management concepts in all organizations: implementation must be tailored to the needs of the individual library and its customers. Perhaps implementation is a misleading idea, for 'proper' quality management pervades service thinking and is not something which can be added on.

However, what is apparent both from the literature and from our interviews is that there is considerable interest among professional librarians and information scientists in quality management; that a considerable number of successes have been experienced when it has been applied; that the external pressures to improve quality are expected to continue and indeed increase; and that, above all, there is confidence that careful application of quality management can and will lead to benefits to the end-users. Our discussions and interviews with practitioners in the field confirm the literature, and give weight to the primary motivation for the work reported herein, namely to provide a map of quality management, both as a whole and as the sum of its parts, within the organizational setting. In the following Chapter we present the general map or model that we have developed. This map is then illustrated in the next Chapter by examples from manufacturing, services in general, and library and information services in particular.

Mapping quality concepts

Introduction

From the literature, it is not always clear which are the important concepts of quality management, which tools and techniques are relevant, and how seemingly disparate concepts and tools are related. Indeed, systems, tools and techniques sometimes seem to be ends in themselves with little relevance to the specialized needs of organizations such as LIS. For example, the focus of ISO 9000 is on procedures for achieving quality and not the achievement of quality itself (as we note later). Yet such distinctions are often unclear in the writings of quality 'experts' and thus difficult to perceive in the LIS field.

The core of quality management is a group of fundamental concepts, with other concepts and ideas as subsets of the major ones. BS EN ISO 9004–1 (British Standards Institution, 1994b) suggests that the requirements of the customer are the focal point of the three key aspects of quality management:

- Management responsibility;
- The management of personnel and material resources; and
- The quality system structure.

Although quality concepts relate to, and indeed depend upon, coherence, they are often pursued separately. In implementing quality management the temptation may be to concentrate on a limited number of ideas, yet there is always the danger that in so doing the big picture is missed.

To illustrate how key quality concepts relate to each other we have taken the process model of *inputs, process,* and *outputs,* together with *review and improvement* and grouped the key concepts into an overall map of quality management. This idea is then developed further in the next Chapter to illustrate how the main elements fit together to form models of quality management for different sectors.

Figure 3: The basic map of quality management concepts

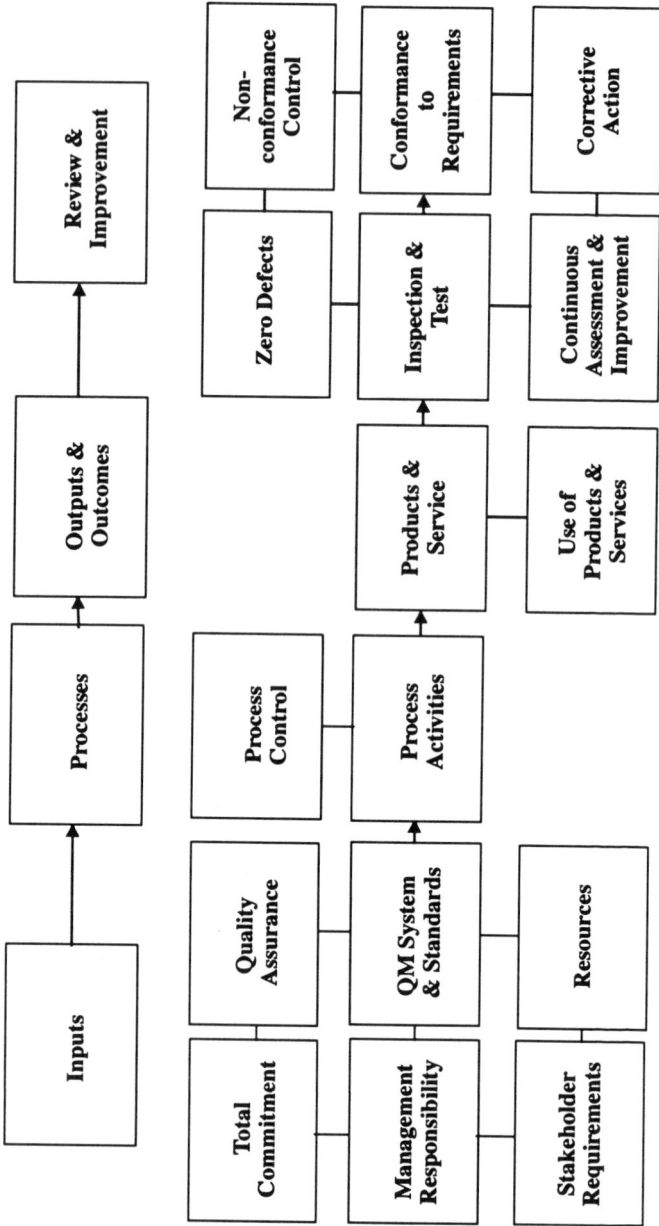

Figure 4: Quality management concepts illustrated by example

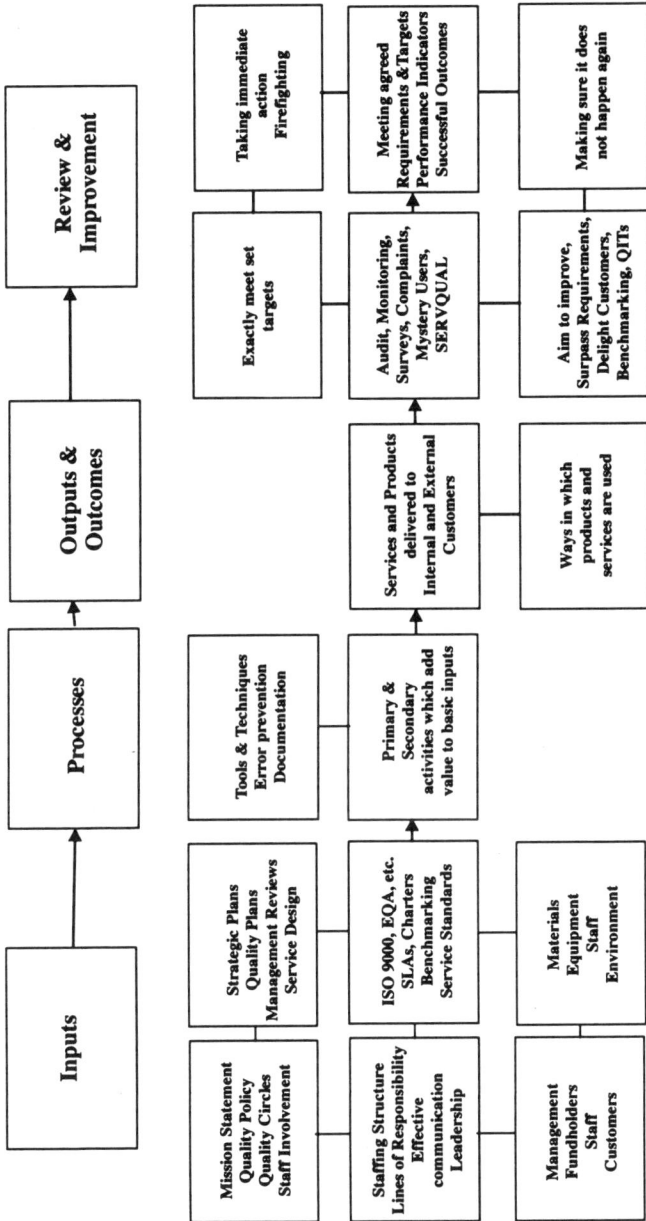

Inputs	Processes	Outputs & Outcomes	Review & Improvement

Mission Statement
Quality Policy
Quality Circles
Staff Involvement

Strategic Plans
Quality Plans
Management Reviews
Service Design

Tools & Techniques
Error prevention
Documentation

Taking immediate action
Firefighting

Staffing Structure
Lines of Responsibility
Effective communication
Leadership

ISO 9000, EQA, etc.
SLAs, Charters
Benchmarking
Service Standards

Primary & Secondary activities which add value to basic inputs

Services and Products delivered to Internal and External Customers

Exactly meet set targets

Audit, Monitoring, Surveys, Complaints, Mystery Users, SERVQUAL

Meeting agreed Requirements & Targets
Performance Indicators
Successful Outcomes

Management
Fundholders
Staff
Customers

Materials
Equipment
Staff
Environment

Ways in which products and services are used

Aim to improve, Surpass Requirements, Delight Customers, Benchmarking, QITs

Making sure it does not happen again

Concepts explained

On the following pages, the basic concepts of quality management are described with reference to the map of Figure 3. Figure 4 provides some examples which are used to interpret those basic concepts. To gain the full effect the two figures should be read together. Readers may find it useful to make a copy of Figure 3, preferably on some transparent material such as acetate, which can then be placed over Figure 4 as an overlay.

The basic map draws on the process model of organizations, and links quality management to *inputs, processes, outputs and outcomes* and *review and improvement*. For the purposes of the map each of the elements is taken independently, but it cannot be stressed too highly that quality management is holistic—the lines which join elements together are as important as the elements themselves. Again, as an aid to navigation, readers will find it useful to keep a copy of Figure 3 to hand in order to relate the text to the model itself.

Inputs

The importance of inputs to the quality of the finished product or service is sometimes expressed in clichéd terms but is basically commonsense. 'Garbage in, garbage out', goes the expression in computing; 'getting the ingredients right' might be an equivalent in catering. The dependable quality of the items sold at Marks & Spencer is an important factor in the company's success, which is why so much emphasis is placed on making sure that the quality of inputs to its stores is consistently excellent, and why even a single failure on the part of a supplier can result in whole orders being cancelled. A successful outcome to any activity depends to a major extent upon the quality of the inputs. In library terms definitions of input extend to include the *commitment* and *skills* of all staff from senior management to the most junior, and an understanding of the needs of all the *library users*, as well as having the right library stock or access to appropriate databases.

Success depends upon a *chain of quality*, the organization being only as strong as the weakest link. The quality chain in libraries extends from library suppliers (who are themselves increasingly aware of quality initiatives), through each stage of library activities until the user leaves the library with his or her information. The *interaction of staff* with the library user is an inseparable part of the process, repeated each time a service is used. Each transaction is a unique occurrence and the user's perceptions of the library service can be determined at that instant. A library may provide an excellent service on most occasions, but users who receive even one isolated unsatisfactory experience may have their perceptions of the library determined at that moment. Staff and staff training are as important a part of the inputs into the library facilities as the most expensive item in the library stock.

Total commitment

The drive for quality starts with *commitment* and *leadership*, beginning with the chief executive and extending throughout the organization. The importance of effective *leadership* is recognized by the organizers of all the major quality awards—the Deming Prize, the Baldrige Quality Award and the European Quality Award—who include it as part of the assessment criteria. Deming (1988) and Juran (1988) both stress the vital role of management and identify the responsibility of management for quality problems within the organization. Total commitment and effective leadership are elusive concepts to identify and measure, yet without them any quality initiative is doomed to failure. Line (1993) points out that there is no single, correct style of leadership but identifies desirable characteristics such as vision, optimism and enthusiasm which leaders are able to communicate to their staff.

Management responsibility

Total Quality Management is defined in BS 7850: *Total Quality Management* (British Standards Institution, 1992b) as 'Management philosophy and company practices that aim to harness the human and material resources of an organization in the most effective way to achieve the objectives of the organization', a philosophy echoing Ishikawa (1985) on the need for grassroots workers to understand and practise quality. This is particularly important in service industries because it is not only the delivery of the service which affects customers' perceptions of quality but also *how* the service is delivered.

Commitment throughout the organization must be management-led and reflected at all levels. Morgan and Murgatroyd (1994) identify 'a radical shift' in the way that responsibility for quality is viewed within many organizations. For many years it was only those at the top of the organizational pyramid who were charged with a general responsibility for quality, with only quality controllers inspecting the post-production product having additional quality responsibilities. This attitude dates back to the Industrial Revolution, when the process owner who performed the task was not seen as having responsibility for the final quality of the product.

The quality literature stresses that *process owners* are in the best position to identify problems and make quality improvements. They should, therefore, be given the authority to make them. This is the thinking behind the *quality circles* movement championed by Ishikawa (1985). A number of libraries have established quality circles among their staff as a way of empowering junior staff to make improvements in working practice. The most successful of these have provided circle members with training and access to information and ensured that action is taken on recommendations wherever possible.

Stakeholder requirements

An understanding of customer requirements is one of the fundamental concepts in quality management and is embodied in standards such as BS 7850 : Part 1: 1992. Customers are the recipients of the results of a process or activity. Whilst there may be a need to balance the needs of stakeholders (see below), the external customer (the end-user of the service) is invariably viewed as the most important element in the equation. Customer requirements may be stated or implied, and identified internally or externally. Requirements can be identified through a customer stating what is needed or by means of market research/surveys of user opinions. Library users might not, however, articulate their wants into demands for a number of reasons. Green (1990) examines the question of who should be responsible for defining user needs and suggests criteria for assessing user needs which can be used for evaluation and planning.

Customer requirements, or the organization's perceptions of those requirements, underpin the standards, specifications and procedures used to provide the service. Quality planning starts with customer requirements. Juran (1988) described the trilogy of quality: quality *planning*, quality *control* and quality *improvement*.

Customer assessment of whether requirements are met is 'the ultimate measure of the quality of a service' (British Standards Institution, 1991).

A service organization may think that it is providing a good service, but the user may disagree. Comparison needs to be made of the user's perceptions and assessment of the service with the organization's own perceptions and assessment. The magnitude of any gaps which occur are a measure of the quality of the service (Zeithaml *et al.*, 1990).

The philosophy of Total Quality Management suggests that the customer-driven organization should aim to *surpass* consumer requirements and expectations in a cycle of never-ending improvement. The goal of customer satisfaction should be replaced by one of 'delighting' the customer (Morgan and Murgatroyd, 1994). This need not mean extra resources: the extra which raises the satisfaction of expectations to the area of delight may be small (for example, a recent visitor to one library was delighted to find that not only was a car parking space available but the attendant on duty escorted her to the space and greeted her by name). This supports Atkinson's (1990) observation that quality does not depend upon spending alone but is about attitude and organizational culture.

The shift in attention from customers to stakeholders suggested a refinement in understanding the TQM process. Customers are those who 'purchase' the goods or services provided, and who shape their development. The stakeholder is anyone with an interest in the provisions. For example, the elected members in a local authority may not be customers of the public library service but they have an interest in it. Most organizations have multiple stakeholders with multiple requirements which may at times appear to be conflicting. Whilst customers have their own expectations and perceptions of their needs, the organization has to reconcile the demands of a variety of interested parties. Calvert (1994) identified three groups of stakeholders in public libraries—staff, users and fund-holders—and this same diversity can be seen in other LIS organizations. In an academic library a whole range of stakeholders can be identified: students; academic, administrative and support staff; library staff of different grades and functions; the organization's management; national government; the local community; and so on.

Within manufacturing industry the identification of the requirements of stakeholders might seem to be a fairly simple matter as company goals are assumed to be financial and the number of stakeholders involved is more limited. In a service industry the requirements of one group of stakeholders may act as a constraint on the voiced needs of another: the users' plea for multiple copies of items in heavy demand may conflict with management's views on cost-effectiveness. Whatever the organization, however, the identification of stakeholder requirements and the reconciliation of possibly conflicting interests are the starting points for the identification of organizational goals.

This leads to other problems of definition; for example, who are the customers in the quality managed library? This may seem obvious at first: the library users, the individuals who borrow the books, read the newspapers, use the photocopiers. However, quality management also stresses the needs of the *internal customer*. This concept can clearly be seen in the operation of most libraries where each department acts as both supplier and customer to the others. Equally, others who do not physically use the library may have an interest in it, as, for example, when governments or the European Union use public libraries to disseminate information on their activities. Equally, society as a whole has an interest in the development of a library system, so the needs of 'posterity' may have to be considered. The idea of *stakeholders* is to take into account and hold in balance the legitimate needs and interests of all who have a stake in the organization.

Quality assurance

The primary aim of quality assurance, as opposed to quality control, is the prevention of error. The BS 4778 definition of quality assurance is: 'all those planned and systematic actions necessary to provide adequate confidence that a product or service will satisfy given requirements for quality' (British Standards Institution, 1987). Every effort should be made to identify potential problems *before* users are affected.

Quality techniques used in manufacturing industries for error prevention, which can equally be applied to a service industry environment, include quality planning, training, documented work instructions, and monitoring. These have long been used by library managers. The importance of planning in the quality process is stressed by Feigenbaum (1983), who suggests a systematic or total approach to quality, involving all functions, with quality built in an early stage. Morgan and Murgatroyd (1994) have examined the application of TQM to service industries and conclude that a quality culture is one of *preventing failure*. It is the job of library management to design procedures which minimize the risk of error and give users and staff the confidence that the service will run as smoothly as possible.

Quality management systems and standards

The definition of a quality system according to BS 4778 is 'the organizational structure, responsibilities, procedures, processes and resources for implementing quality management' (British Standards Institution, 1987). It is a way of ensuring that organizational quality goals are met. The aim of a quality management standard is primarily to prevent problems with quality activities and to use an established system model to achieve customer satisfaction. In a service, such a system provides the opportunity for improved performance and customer satisfaction by managing the processes involved.

Quality management systems such as ISO 9000 are sometimes seen as being incompatible with Total Quality Management: see, for example, Gillman (1992). This view is not shared by Oakland (1994), a leading British expert on Total Quality Management, who stresses that a company must organize itself in such a way that the human, administrative and technical factors will be under control, and who sees the function of quality management systems as the means of establishing that control. The British Standard for Total Quality Management, BS 7850, also recognizes the need for a system along with supporting tools and techniques to make the best use of organizational resources and achieve customer satisfaction (British Standards Institution, 1992b).

The concept of synergy in quality management, that the whole can be greater than the sum of the parts taken in isolation, was advocated by the quality 'guru' Feigenbaum (1991). He claimed that most management systems are haphazard, having simply evolved piecemeal without thought to the overall system. However, they can be effectively engineered and managed into total quality systems which will then provide major improvements in company quality. He also stated that a planned, structured system is far more than just a number of interacting activities and will produce 'full customer quality satisfaction ... with optimum speed, human harmony and motivation, economy and overall control of action'. That is not to say that all systems have to be absolutely identical: if key activities are covered, the system can be tailored to a company's requirements, resources and goals.

A quality management system thus provides both a management framework for effective operation and a baseline for quality improvement. Oakland (1994) sees a quality management system as a means of putting Deming's Plan, Do, Check, Act cycle into operation, by building a system which is a *quality loop*:

- Write down what you do (written procedures)

- Justify what you do (meet the requirements of a good international standard)

- Record what you do (keep quality records and statistics)

- Review what you do (management review of system)

- Revise what you do (quality planning)

The system is designed so that desired quality standards can be met, whether they are for nuts and bolts or for customer services.

Standards describe a consistent level of service which meets customer requirements. Standards may be stated or implied, visible to the external user or used internally, complex or simple. Different types of standards can be identified: company or organizational standards drawn up to satisfy the needs of a particular group of customers (e.g. a library or group of libraries); industrial, or in the case of LIS, professional standards (e.g. from the Library Association); national standards (e.g. government standards/charters), international standards (e.g. ISO or Open Systems Interconnection (OSI) standards). The ISO 9000 quality management systems series do not specify standards of performance (and are often criticized on this point) but there are mandatory requirements (e.g. staff responsibilities must be clearly defined, there must be a system for analyzing customer complaints and taking action to prevent recurrence). The work of Dale and Oakland (1991) demonstrates how standards can be used to improve quality within manufacturing and service industry environments.

Resources

In considering the resources available to the organization, quality management moves away from the original 'inputs' element of the process model in industry, which concentrated almost entirely on physical resources such as machinery and raw materials, to a recognition that every resource which an organization uses must be considered and managed. Thus resources include staff, information (hence the importance of information management to the quality organization), raw materials, finance, buildings, information technology, the environment and even intangibles such as reputation. Because organizations depend on others for their inputs, especially for raw materials, supplier assessment is important in quality management: procedures for ensuring that the materials the organization uses in delivering its product or service are of acceptable standard. Again, the recognition of the importance of staff leads into training commitments such as regular customer care programmes, and into broader initiatives such as Investors in People.[3]

Processes

For the purpose of mapping quality management it is useful to distinguish between the activities which an organization undertakes and the way in which those activities are controlled and managed. We therefore differentiate between *process activities* and *process control* in this section.

Process activities

For many people, the word 'process' brings to mind a factory environment, and the use of such terminology may be a barrier to the understanding of quality management concepts by LIS staff. When one library implemented ISO 9000 its managers found that the language of the standard, speaking of process and process control, was difficult to interpret for library staff. It may even be difficult to identify what a process is in library terms. Oakland (1994) offers the standard definition of process as the 'transformation of a set of inputs, which can include actions, methods and operations, into outputs that satisfy customer needs and expectations'. Clearly, this definition covers the key activities of any library service. A process is a value-adding activity and, at the point of delivery to the library user, is inseparable from the final testing of the process. Service delivery is part of process, with participation from the customer. The library user can therefore be seen as a co-producer, almost as an unpaid employee of the library. The importance of the customer's contribution is illustrated by the Library Charter of a small college library which sets out the library user's entitlements on one page and the library service obligations on the facing page (see Figure 5 overleaf).

---

3. The Investors in People scheme is a UK Government initiative which povides a national standard for staff training and development practices, linked to organizational needs. An unpublished report from the Institute for Employment Studies estimated that 1,200 companies had reached the standard by Spring 1995, with over 12,000 more having committed themselves to it.

Figure 5: A College Library Charter [Reproduced by permission]

THE LIBRARY CHARTER

Everyone using the library at Newton Rigg College is encouraged to make full use of all the facilities. The library's main aim is to provide a wide range of information resources and services and help all users to get the maximum benefit from the services. To help achieve these aims the library charter has been introduced to clarify your entitlements from the library and your obligation to it:

What the library will do for you (your entitlements).
The library operates within available resources to achieve its aims including to:

- educate students in the use of the library and in the availability and use of learning resources,
- provide advice and guidance in identifying, finding and using appropriate resources
- provide an environment appropriate for study

In order to give you the best possible access to the resources we:

- lend items for specific periods
- renew items if they are not required by other people
- make special arrangements for items which are in heavy demand
- purchase new items as appropriate to support courses
- where appropriate, borrow items from other libraries

What we expect you to do (your obligations).
In the library we expect you:

- to treat the library as a place of study and behave accordingly
- to allow others to study undisturbed by noise, unnecessary conversation or any other distraction
- not to damage or deface any resources, furniture, notices or other items
- to keep bags and personal belongings safely and not to leave unattended
- not to eat, drink or smoke
- not to remove any items from the library unless they have been issued to you

In order to borrow items from the library we expect you:

- to complete a registration form and inform library staff of any change of address
- not to keep items on loan beyond the date due for return
- to keep your borrower tickets safely and not allow anyone else to use them
- to pay for any items you may lose, damage or fail to return to the library for whatever reason.

In order to survive in a competitive world, industrial processes need to be efficient, economic, accurate and reliable—factors which can equally be applied to library activities. Public libraries are subject to compulsory competitive tendering for services, pressure to indicate performance measures and success, and increasing customer awareness of service standards. Process is a key factor in creating overall perceptions of satisfaction.

Within any organization there is always a chain of processes—in libraries it might run from ordering items to shelving and the circulation desk. The internal customers become the process owners as they receive results of one process, add value and pass it on to the next customers in the chain, until the outputs reach the library user. The system must be well designed and managed by senior staff, but the running of each 'mini' process belongs to the staff performing that particular activity. In the quality organization process ownership enables employees to have a degree of control over their work.

It is sometimes useful to sub-divide into key (or critical) processes and support processes, so that effort can be concentrated on those areas crucial to the achievement of the library's mission.

Process control

Control of all process activities begins with planning. In theory, if all the elements of a process have been well planned there would be no need for any sort of in-process or post-process checking. In practice, however, there are a number of causes which can introduce unplanned variability into a product or service. Process control, according to Ishikawa (1985), attempts to discover the 'factors that hinder the smooth functioning of the process'. With process control, he argues, quality, cost and productivity can all benefit. The Statistical Process Control method was founded by the American statistician Shewart and developed by Deming as a means to enable the effective operation of control during a process as an alternative to checking the quality of the finished product.

Despite the terminology, the concept of process control applies to services where it is not always feasible to check the quality of the completed result of an activity. Within a service environment, it is seldom possible to perform material testing in the same way that most manufactured articles can be checked. It may be that products cannot be sampled without destroying the samples themselves; for example, hamburgers would need to be tasted and then cannot be sold on to the customer (and this raises the additional question of how to control an element as subjective as taste). Such 'special processes', as they are termed, need to be controlled in other ways, such as through the provision of detailed instructions and the devising of criteria for workmanship. The quality management system itself becomes a means of controlling the variability of the process. Oakland (1994) suggests that the key to this is in planning and in the recruitment and training of staff. This is especially true in libraries where an important factor in service provision is the experience and skills of staff.

Outputs and outcomes

Products and services

For the reasons given above it is useful in the quality management map to differentiate between the product or service itself and the use to which that product is put. Quality management recognizes that the delivery of products and services which accord with agreed requirements is all important, but goes further and suggests that the quality organization will investigate how those products and services are actually being used, so as to better meet customer needs and to identify new market opportunities. Even when the organization cannot directly influence outcomes (e.g. where a library sees one of the outcomes of use of its services as increased personal knowledge), it can tune its services by understanding what characterizes desirable outcomes and changing its delivery to facilitate them.

Use of products and services

Traditionally, the *output* of a process has been a tangible product, which is then used by a customer in order to bring about an *outcome*. This remains true in some service contexts, so that, as noted above, the service output of providing a library user with a book may be regarded as leading to the outcome of a better informed individual. In the language of quality, however, the distinction becomes less well-defined. If organizations espouse quality management they accept that it is the customers' needs which have to be met, and that customers are primarily interested in outcomes. A successful outcome is *conformance to* (the customers') *requirements*. A successful outcome occurs, not as the result of chance, but following planned activities: Disneyland measures successful outcomes by viewing people as they leave and counting the number of smiling faces. An example in library terms might be a successful transaction: not merely a library user with a book, but *the* book he or she particularly wanted (a link with conventional librarianship can perhaps be seen here—Ranganathan's 'every reader his book'). However, it is not uncommon for libraries to measure outputs rather than outcomes, producing statistical information which gives, for example, the number of 'seat hours' available each week. Whilst such information has a value, for example as management information for controlling resource allocation, in a manufacturing equivalent it is rather like counting the number of screws produced, regardless of whether they are faulty or of acceptable quality or, indeed, of the size the customer really wanted. The counting of outputs can only be meaningful if what is being counted has been the result of meeting identified stakeholder requirements.

Review and improvement

Librarians are familiar with the idea of regular review, if only through the requirements of funding bodies. Fundamentally, however, review and improvement are what turns the simple process model of organizations into quality management. Nothing is done in the quality managed firm without its outcome being reviewed. The aim of review is not self-congratulation or self-assurance, but simply to grasp opportunities for improvement. Continuous improvement is thus the watchword of quality management.

Inspection and test

Summative evaluation used to be the main approach to performance measurement: is it right at the end? Quality theorists now indicate that quality measurement must be a *continuous process*, rather than a series of samples of final performance taken over time. In manufacturing, this means building and operating *a procedure to monitor performance* frequently enough to capture non-conformance and prevent recurrence. The incidence of error must be prevented, and no percentage figure for failure can be considered acceptable. This is the principle of zero defects discussed below.

In service industries, this is again unusual. Most organizations take a sample to check conformity, by time, by customer, or by aspect of the service.

Zero defects

Crosby (1979) states that the only absolute standard which must be applied is that of zero defects. In LIS, time and customer sampling has been the norm when assessing whether or not a service specification is met. The application of the concept of continuous conformance can only be achieved when customer requirements are checked on every occasion, or procedures are designed to eliminate error to achieve zero defects. LIS are increasingly applying themselves to the needs of ISO 9000 in the area of quality assurance systems—a step towards the achievement of zero defects.

Continuous assessment and improvement

Quality *improvement* is a never-ending process—a concept repeated by many writers in numerous ways, such as the *quality loop* and the *Continuous Improvement Wheel.*

Continuous improvement is an integral part of the TQM culture: Tenner and De Toro (1992) suggest that it is the primary objective of TQM. It is perceived as equally important by Lascelles and Dale (1993) who see it as a way of life. Deming's cycle of continuous improvement (Plan, Do, Check, Act) is fundamental to his approach to quality management.

The Japanese word *kaizen* has entered the vocabulary of quality to describe the small, cumulative steps which improve quality. Whether they are small steps or large, continuous improvements in customer service is what differentiates the 'quality library' from the rest. Such improvements need not be expensive changes, but to be meaningful, they must be based on stakeholder requirements. A continuous improvement programme requires a range of measures: a focus on quality, focus on the customer, a 'right first time' mentality, prevention of error, measurement of performance. Above all it must be management-led.

Conformance to requirements

The critical indicator of quality is conformance to requirements (almost literally from the basic definitions). Its opposite is nonconformance. Either a product or service conforms, or it does not conform; there is no mid-way point.

In the LIS field, asking whether or not a service or an aspect of a service conforms precisely to requirements is unusual. We are more content with shades of performance. This application of conformance is shared by other service industries. A meal may be cooked well, but not to the level of perfection. However, it would still conform to customer requirements because those requirements are less absolute. This approach is reflected in the expressions of intent embodied in the various charters and service level agreements. One would expect to see a statement which indicates that for x per cent of the time the requirement will be met. The British Rail Passenger's Charter shows how this works in practice, with 90 per cent of Intercity trains aiming to arrive within ten minutes of scheduled time. To be meaningful, standards have to be set at an attainable level. For example, the standard for punctuality of Regional Railways' short distance routes is that 90 per cent of trains will arrive within five minutes of scheduled arrival time. However, this figure drops to 80 per cent on the congested Network SouthEast lines.

Conversely, in manufacturing, the conformance is precise: a component must be exact if it is to fit into and perform a specific function inside a mechanism.

Nonconformance control

Nonconformance, according to BS 4778:1987, is the 'nonfulfilment of specified requirements' and can range from the absence of just one minor element or characteristic of the product to something which is totally unacceptable (British Standards Institution, 1987). Feigenbaum (1983) classified nonconformances according to the severity of their consequences, from the 'critical', which would result in loss of life or property, to the 'incidental', which have no unsatisfactory effect on customer quality but which nevertheless have a detrimental result on operational effectiveness and costs.

It has been claimed that service industries waste 35 per cent of their revenue as a result of preventable problems (Crosby, 1979). The aim of nonconformance control is to contain such problems, by identifying what is faulty, separating out the nonconforming products, and so to prevent accidental or continued use. In quality management this alone is insufficient, since long-term corrective action (see below) needs to be taken to prevent recurrence.

Corrective action

Corrective action on problems and faults is far more than the immediate resolution of problems. It is not a 'firefighting' approach but a systematic method to prevent problems. BS 7850: Part 2 defines this as 'action taken to eliminate the causes of an existing nonconformity, or other undesirable situation to prevent recurrence' (British Standards Institution, 1992b). *Correction* and *corrective action* are seen as two different things: correction is to repair an existing problem, whereas corrective action is the elimination of the cause. Caplen (1988) states that if planning and execution were perfect, there would be no errors and therefore no need for corrective action. Since perfection is hardly ever achieved the system must provide for the identification and correction of errors.

The need to identify and report problems is the duty or responsibility of each individual within the organization. When an error is discovered action must be taken to record, analyze and correct it. This should be a two-stage process: immediate action to satisfy the needs of the user, followed by an investigation into the underlying cause of the problem so that action may be taken to prevent recurrence. This does not mean finding a scapegoat, but taking a positive step towards error prevention and consequently service improvement. James (1989) suggests the use of *encounter analysis* in public services as a framework for corrective action: finding out what has gone wrong, whether from lack of training, lack of resources or poor management. It provides one way of working out how to improve services and enables an input from all stakeholders.

The quality management model in practice

The concepts map (Figure 3) shows the relationship between key quality concepts. The detailed models presented in this Chapter show how the concepts can be applied in different types of organizations—manufacturing companies, service industries, libraries and information services.

The models are not intended to be used in isolation—so that, for example, library staff could turn to a 'library' model—as it is important to copy ideas and techniques from other sectors. The best way to use the models is to assemble a range of complementary elements to support any particular concept (rather like building with Meccano or Lego kits which contain blocks, cogs and connectors). A kit part is of little practical use unless it is combined with others to form small structures which, in turn, can make up a greater whole. A single part can support, and have an effect upon, more than one internal structure; and if a key part is taken away, the overall appearance of the construction may not change a great deal, but the system will not operate effectively. To take one example: a 'commitment to quality' needs to be linked to 'identification and satisfaction of stakeholder requirements' and the 'availability and effective use of available resources'. A structure of quality concepts and elements can be built up as required. Whilst guidelines for doing this may be useful, structures will differ among services because each is geared to its own stakeholders' requirements. Examples of current practice have been used wherever possible in the following pages, to illustrate how quality management works in practice. Examples are drawn from the published literature, discussions with manufacturing and service industry staff, library managers and staff, and visits (sometimes anonymous) made during this research project.

On the following pages Figures 6, 7 and 8 illustrate the model applied in manufacturing, in services in general, and in library and information services. As in the previous Chapter, these Figures should be read in conjunction with the basic map provided in Figure 3.

Figure 6: Quality management model: manufacturing

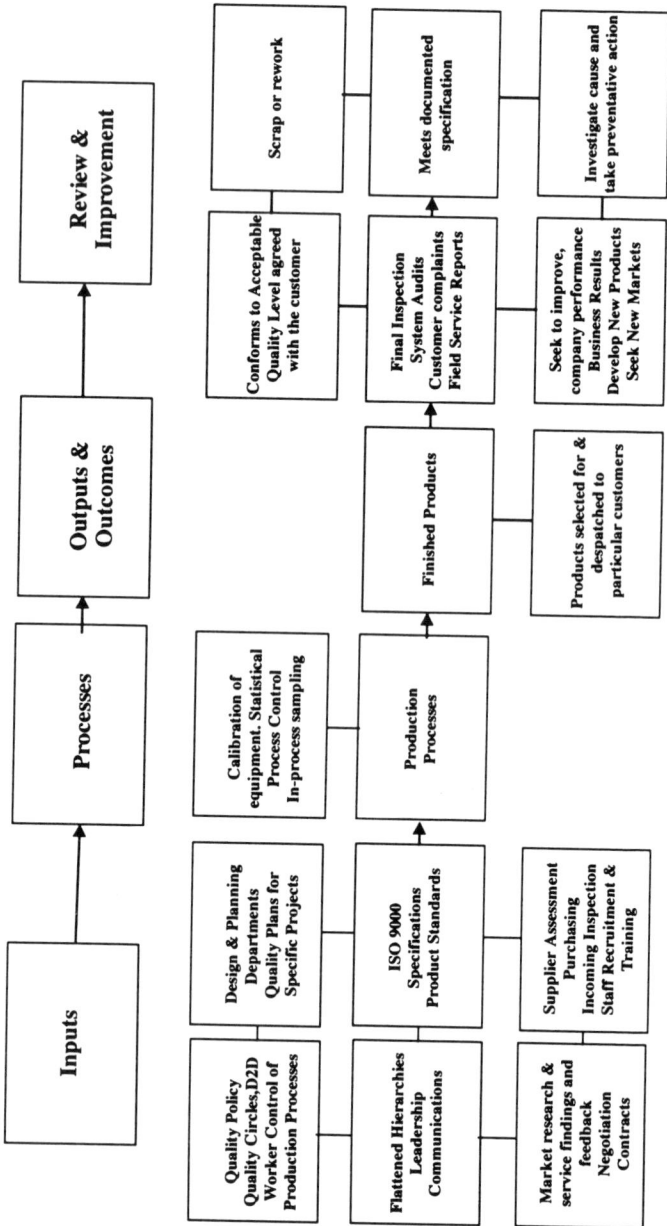

Figure 7: Quality management model: services

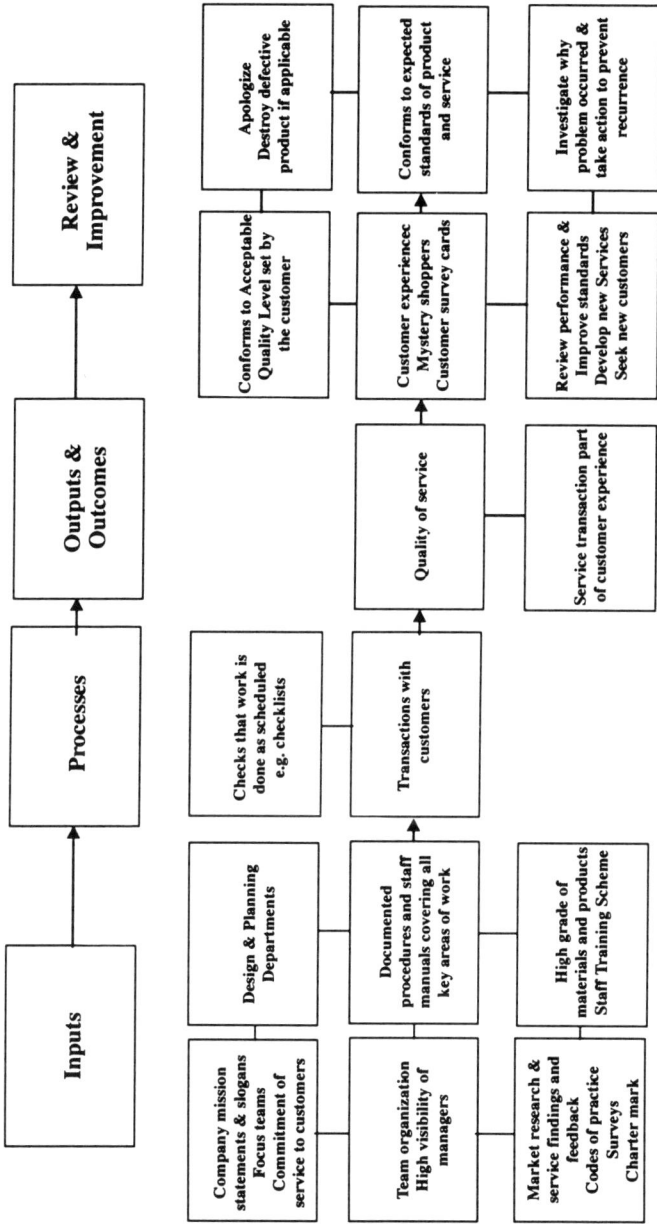

Inputs	Processes	Outputs & Outcomes	Review & Improvement

Company mission statements & slogans
Focus teams
Commitment of service to customers

Team organization
High visibility of managers

Market research & service findings and feedback
Codes of practice
Surveys
Charter mark

Design & Planning Departments

Documented procedures and staff manuals covering all key areas of work

High grade of materials and products
Staff Training Scheme

Checks that work is done as scheduled e.g. checklists

Transactions with customers

Quality of service

Service transaction part of customer experience

Conforms to Acceptable Quality Level set by the customer

Customer experiences
Mystery shoppers
Customer survey cards

Review performance & Improve standards
Develop new Services
Seek new customers

Apologize
Destroy defective product if applicable

Conforms to expected standards of product and service

Investigate why problem occurred & take action to prevent recurrence

Figure 8: Quality management model: library and information services

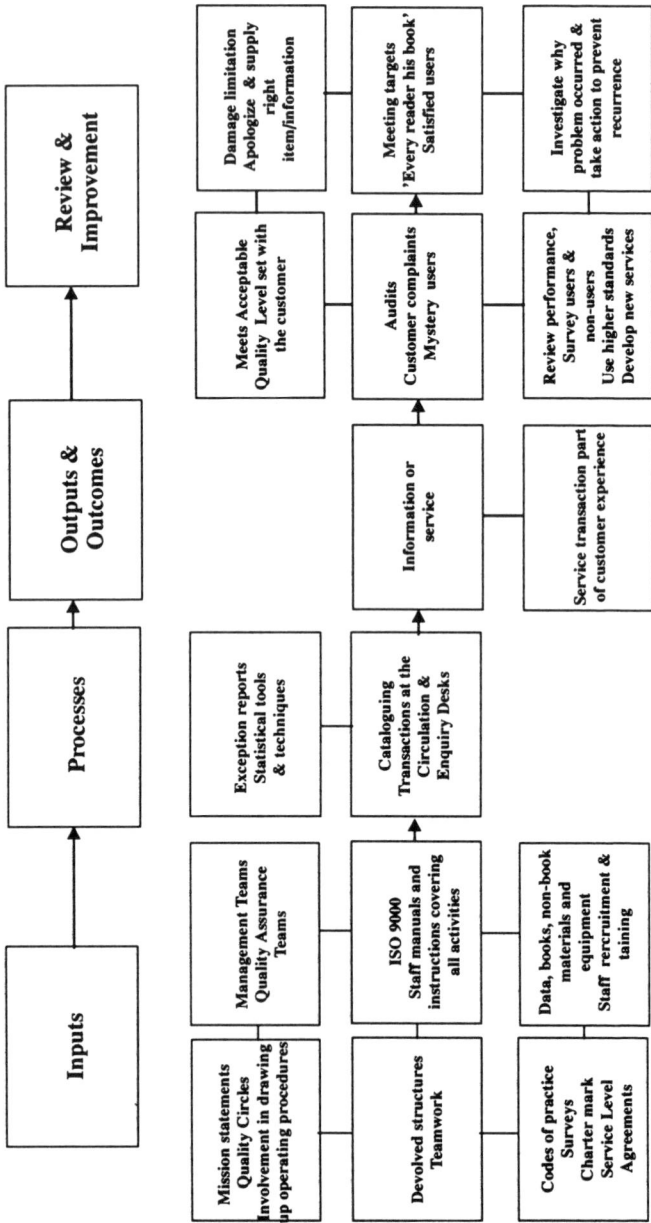

Inputs	Processes	Outputs & Outcomes	Review & Improvement

Mission statements Quality Circles Involvement in drawing up operating procedures			
Management Teams Quality Assurance Teams	Exception reports Statistical tools & techniques		Meets Acceptable Quality Level set with the customer	Damage limitation Apologize & supply right item/information
ISO 9000 Staff manuals and instructions covering all activities	Cataloguing Transactions at the Circulation & Enquiry Desks	Information or service	Audits Customer complaints Mystery users	Meeting targets 'Every reader his book' Satisfied users
Data, books, non-book materials and equipment Staff rercruitment & taining		Service transaction part of customer experience	Review performance, Survey users & non-users Use higher standards Develop new services	Investigate why problem occurred & take action to prevent recurrence
Devolved structures Teamwork			
Codes of practice Surveys Charter mark Service Level Agreements			

CONCEPT: Total commitment

Manufacturing

It is almost a truism that the only proof of management commitment is action, but evidence such as mission statements or quality policies based on customer requirement and backed up by results provide a useful surrogate. During this project we looked at a number of manufacturing companies with a written commitment to quality—including British Aerospace, GEC, Guardscan Ltd.—as examples of quality management in action.

One of the best examples in the manufacturing sector is the textiles company Milliken Europe, whose approach to quality is summed up by the Managing Director's statement that 'Excellence is a direction, not a destination; the road to excellence is still being plotted and built'. Milliken's strategy has evolved over the past fourteen years, each stage building on the last, from improving product quality, acting on consultations with customers, applying quality improvement techniques, to customer-focused Total Quality.

Total commitment from the whole organization is more difficult to measure, especially when cultural differences are taken into account. Japanese industry is legendary for the commitment of its workforces, but this commitment appears to be fostered by a paternalistic attitude of management which is unacceptable in other cultures. However, in the best manufacturing organizations there is a commitment to the production of high quality products—reminiscent of the professional pride in skills which is often cited as typical of an earlier age, such as the work of the craftsman in medieval times or the skilled artisan of the eighteenth century. In the twentieth century this might take the form of workers on the production line who refuse to let substandard parts leave their section.

Other indicators of management commitment which are often cited are the entrusting of control of production to workers, giving time to attend quality circle meetings, providing staff training and offering the resources and training needed to implement the solutions which workers have identified. The commitment of staff can take the form of voluntary participation in work teams and quality circles or in the design and documentation of improved operating procedures. However, this commitment of staff is not always easy to achieve in British industry. A manager at one industrial plant visited during the project had found some

CONCEPT: Total commitment

suspicion at first when introducing quality management techniques, but noted increasing participation as what he termed a 'change in culture' took place. In part this was achieved when staff realized that participation was not a means of slimming down the workforce: inevitably this took considerable time. This finding is supported by the literature which stresses that quality management is not a 'quick-fix' solution but one which takes time to implement fully. Ishikawa (1985) claimed that successful implementation of quality management could take two or three years and that this is desirable: 'Practice ... for 2–3 years, and you will then know the taste and appreciate it'.

Service industries

Mission statements and simple slogans are often found in service companies which have implemented quality management, although they can be used simply as 'window dressing'. Two of the best-known in the UK are those advertised by Marks & Spencer and McDonalds. Marks & Spencer have adopted the slogan 'Quality—Value—Service', while McDonalds uses the slogan '100% Total Customer Satisfaction'. Both organizations enable their workforces to contribute to the quality of the service. Marks & Spencer set up 'Focus Teams' as a deliberate attempt to empower staff and find ways of delivering a more efficient service. McDonalds uses the rather less staid terminology of 'Rap Meetings' to involve staff in identifying problems and finding solutions that will increase customer satisfaction. Both are voluntary, but both were identified by the staff we interviewed as being an effective way to harness enthusiasm and encourage commitment to customer service.

The attitude of staff is an integral element in service delivery and therefore their commitment is essential in a quality organization. If services are delivered in a mechanical way, giving the customer the impression that the staff are simply not interested, then it is difficult to see how customer expectations can ever be lifted from satisfaction to delight. The quality culture within services demands a high level of commitment from staff if 'have a nice day' is to sound genuine.

Enthusiasm alone, however, is not enough. One anecdote tells of the parcel service which scored very highly when it came to staff friendliness, but poorly in customer satisfaction. The reason was simple enough: the delivery driver was cheerfully delivering the wrong parcels! Staff

CONCEPT: Total commitment

may work hard, yet the effort is wasted if commitment is not supported by other elements in the quality management model.

Libraries and information services

Libraries and information services often make public statements of commitment to quality of service. The Public Libraries 'Quality Forum' conducted a survey in May 1994 which revealed that 54 public library authorities had issued a customer service charter and another eight were currently preparing one. Libraries have increasingly used mission statements to demonstrate their total commitment to user-driven services: a study of library mission statements revealed that the user-driven model of library service was dominant (Brophy, 1991). Phrases such as 'to serve the needs of users' were commonplace. Whatever the motivations for developing a mission statement (and it has to be admitted that some are developed more under institutional pressure than for the library's own purposes), they are an attempt to set out the direction in which the library intends to develop and to provide all stakeholders with an agreed common purpose. As such, they are a starting point for gaining the commitment of all stakeholders. The process of developing the mission statement, if it is participative, provides a strong methodology for involving stakeholders and finding common ground.

As in manufacturing and services, these observations have to be handled with some care. The study noted above was based on input from senior library managers. When interviewed for the current project, library managers from both public and academic libraries claimed to have a commitment to quality, but this was not always reflected in views of junior staff. Management enthusiasm and commitment may not be reflected in the attitude of some of the staff who seemed disillusioned by shrinking resources.

Quality circles, an idea from the manufacturing sector, may help to harness staff commitment. Quality circles are used in a number of public and academic libraries, e.g. Liverpool John Moores University, Berkshire County, University of Central Lancashire, Lancashire County. Libraries which are successfully implementing quality assurance programmes have involved library staff at all levels in drawing up the standards, documenting procedures and instructions which they will

CONCEPT: Total commitment

work to, and empowering them to make improvements in the way that the library service is delivered.

From the external customer's viewpoint, the best demonstration of total commitment within a library is the quality of the service delivered. Given the premise that a service meets the minimum level to satisfy the users' requirements (e.g. finding the books they wanted), it can be the commitment of staff that adds the 'quality' to the basic service. The commitment of staff can be seen in attitudes to the handling of transactions. In project visits to both a busy reference library and a commercial library enquiry desk staff were seen to give the extra effort to the service by showing users how to operate a piece of equipment, by escorting them to the shelf to find the information needed, by checking that it was what was required, and so on. This is good library practice, and relies on the commitment of staff. It can be seen as an illustration of a quality management concept in action.

CONCEPT: Management responsibility

Manufacturing

The quality management system standard ISO 9000 requires that management responsibilities for quality are defined from the top executive throughout the organization. In practice this means that management is responsible for establishing a policy to meet company goals, including the meeting of stakeholder requirements, and for making sure that the policy is implemented effectively. Management must also ensure that the policy is understood by all staff. This might be achieved in a simple way by publicizing the policy throughout the workplace. For example, one manufacturing company places copies on walls, and has stickers printed with the slogan attached to internal telephones.

Management has also to ensure that quality policy is put into practice throughout the company, a somewhat more difficult enterprise. Staff responsibilities for a finished product may be documented in a quality manual or an organization chart. Management has a responsibility to design a structure and system to implement policy and achieve objectives, and ensure the effective use of resources. According to TQM

CONCEPT: Management responsibility

philosophy, the most effective staffing structure is a flattened hierarchy, with responsibility for quality distributed throughout the organization. Lines of communication run through and across the company.

Managers in a quality-managed company will ensure that they are aware of how the company operates. This may mean having offices close to the main operations and/or 'walking the talk' on the shop floor to see things in action.

Service industries

Effective management in a service environment will also be committed to the effective operation of company policy in line with its quality objectives. At McDonalds the importance of customers and role of staff in each team ('crew') in providing customer service is stressed during induction, training and customer care sessions. A training booklet is given to all staff (with the company slogan on the front). Systems are designed to operate as efficiently as possible to deliver what the customer wants. McDonalds aims to provide food which is freshly cooked and speedily served in a friendly and efficient manner. To enable this to happen, crew members are organized to work as a team—which includes all levels of staff. For example, shift and floor managers will help on the front counter during busy periods. A similar ethos is found at Marks & Spencer where the store manager will come into the shop to talk to staff, observe how customers are being served, check how policies are being put into practice and resolve any problems which may have arisen.

Libraries and information services

The proliferation of charters in public and academic libraries demonstrates management commitment and responsibility. Staff structures have changed: team organization is now the norm with the aim of empowering all levels of staff. For example, some public libraries have given control of budgets to local library managers. In others, branch managers work in a team with junior staff. This rarely extends to more senior staff, although one project interviewee enjoyed occasional enquiry desk duties. His staff, however, told him that he was more of a hindrance than a help! It was noticed at one central library that manage-

CONCEPT: Management responsibility

ment arranged for additional staff to help when the queue at the service desk reached three people. Other evidence of management responsibility in action at this particular library included the use of names when answering the telephone, a 'Your library manager today is ...' sign, and name badges for all library staff.

CONCEPT: Stakeholder requirements

Manufacturing

'Stakeholder' is a relatively new concept: a search of various management abstracts for the 1980s revealed no references to stakeholders, but the 1994 *ABI Inform* lists 181. The stakeholders in manufacturing industries include individual members of staff, managers, people living near the factory and external shareholders. In the aerospace industry, stakeholders include the shareholders and directors who want to see a profit, along with local businesses and national government who are not only customers, wanting to buy the best aeroplanes at the lowest cost, but also have a financial interest in profits and are perhaps equally concerned about unemployment prospects which must be balanced with costs and profitability.

Market research may be used to ascertain what the customer wants, but negotiation with the external customer is needed when drawing up a contract to an agreed specification which will enable those requirements to be met. It is of little use, for example, to promise to build an aeroplane quickly which will carry out every manoeuvre the customer might wish to see, if the materials cannot be procured in time, if the machinery and tools are not available at acceptable cost, if the workforce would have to work unacceptably long hours to produce the goods in time, or if there would be unacceptable pollution of the environment, and so on.

Negotiation and compromise are needed if one group of stakeholder requirements is likely to cause problems for others. A large manufacturing company has its own travel department whose goal is to work as efficiently as possible and save money for the company. By booking company executives onto cheaper international flights at inconvenient times or airports, the department can meet its objectives. However, this

CONCEPT: Stakeholder requirements

can result in highly paid executives wasting valuable time travelling, waiting for meetings or arriving at meetings exhausted and risking losing the company huge amounts in lost sales.

Manufacturing industry's impact on the environment is beginning to receive formal attention and the British Standards Institution has established the Environmental Standard, BS 7750. However, at the time of writing only four companies have achieved registration. A responsible attitude to the environment and society is encouraged by the European Foundation for Quality Management who include 'Impact on Society' as one of the scoring criteria for the European Quality Award.

Services

Similar groups of stakeholders are to be found in service industries, and this means taking a holistic approach to the reconciliation of conflicting requirements which considers the needs of the system as a whole.

The multiple stakeholder problem is also common in service industries. Marks & Spencer is renowned for its attention not only to customers and staff, but also to shareholders: it remains very profitable. The company also achieves customer participation by techniques such as focus groups, using these to assist in the design and layout of new stores and to make suggestions about the range of goods and services to be provided.

External customers are possibly the most important factor in the stakeholder equation. A quality system is designed around them and identifying who they are is of paramount importance. Successful service organizations are clear about who their customers are and what they are prepared to pay: diners at the Savoy will expect their meals to be cooked exactly to their individual requirements, and are willing to pay a substantial amount for the privilege. Other organizations will design a product to meet the requirements of as large and varied a customer base as possible, but the variations permissible are much fewer. McDonalds and, to a lesser extent, Marks & Spencer operate on an international basis, and both have multiple outlets and numerous customers with different tastes, expectations and requirements. Some variation and flexibility is possible; you can have your Big Mac without lettuce if you wish, but the

CONCEPT: Stakeholder requirements

bun will still be toasted in the same way and the dressing used will be standard, as the product is designed to appeal to the majority.

It is also possible for stakeholders to take different roles at different times. McDonalds staff work in different areas of the restaurant, so that they are, in turn, both supplier and internal customer. One day a crew member may be working at the front counter, another day in the kitchen, another day in the restaurant area among the diners, and during a break he or she may eat a McDonalds meal or bring family and friends to the restaurant. This gives staff an insight into a variety of requirements.

Some organizations publish a code of practice as a guide to some of their stakeholder priorities. Others publish service charters, and the Citizen's Charter movement explicitly encourages public bodies to do this. In such cases, the organization is making explicit the results of its analysis of stakeholder requirements and its efforts to balance those of internal and external customers while taking into account available resources.

Libraries and information services

Libraries and information services have undertaken an enormous amount of research (albeit much of it repetitive) into the needs of end-users and a large number of studies have been published. Individual services likewise have profiled their user populations, and some have used sophisticated instruments (such as geographic information systems for public libraries) to establish the characteristics of discrete groups. A research project at Glasgow Caledonian University, for example, is seeking to establish a methodology for assessing the views and priorities of all the stakeholders of academic libraries.

The interests of the end-users are not always as dominant among public sector services such as libraries as they are in commercial organizations. One of the reasons for this is that other stakeholders' interests can take priority, especially where the end-user is not paying directly for the service received. For a public library, therefore, the interests of elected members (who may not even be library users) have to be given considerable weight. Buckland (1988) has referred to the 'double feedback loop' whereby the influence of users, and the level of demand, may operate only indirectly on the system. In academic libraries there is the complication that the students' interests are often mediated by teaching staff, and library staff then have to balance the demands placed on them by the two different groups: if academics' knowledge of student reading habits were perfect there would be fewer problems!

Government and funders also make their presence felt in a variety of ways. The Public Library Act, for example, can be seen as the statement by a major stakeholder (the Government, acting for society) of its requirements on the public library system. The recent Follett Report (HEFCE,1993), once adopted by the Higher Education Funding Councils, became a powerful statement of the funding bodies' expectations of university libraries.

CONCEPT: Quality assurance

Manufacturing

Quality assurance originated in the manufacturing industries and a great deal can be learned about it from that sector. Three manufacturing companies, ranging from large multi-site operations to a small light engineering firm, were studied as part of this project. All three were found to have quality assurance staff with specialized training or qualifications. In addition, a number of shop floor operatives had been given training in quality management techniques, such as the use of control charts, to monitor the performance of the processes they were working on.

All three implemented quality assurance in a similar fashion: by planning for quality and controlling each stage of the operation from the ordering to final despatch of the finished products. All had systematic training programmes, not only for specific tasks, but also in quality awareness including the company quality policy. Other quality assurance techniques in use included equipment maintenance and calibration (which ensures the accuracy of measuring equipment), and work instructions available for staff to use. At one company, a copy of the instructions was clipped to the side of each machine so they could be retrieved quickly by operatives. At the same company, activities were recorded to identify not only that work had been done but when and by whom; however,

CONCEPT: Quality assurance

managers were keen to stress that this was done not to check up on individual workers, but rather to ensure that work was being done correctly and that queries could be traced back. There was widespread use of identification and traceability principles, including labels on parts to identify what things were and what had been done to them, to ensure that stages were performed in the right order, that nothing was missed, and to indicate where they had come from and where they were going. The purpose of the system was to ensure that the company ran smoothly and that the final customers received a product which met their requirements.

Services

Marks & Spencer's approach to quality assurance begins with the marketing and design teams. The company's success is founded on identifying what the customer wants and then planning the best way of producing it. The way in which Marks & Spencer has traditionally operated, ensuring that the quality of the products sold matches the customers' expectations, pre-dates the concept of quality management in service industries. Marks & Spencer's policy on procurement, for example, dates back to 1926 when company management started to design their own products and specify exactly how they were to be produced.

Planning for quality is carried down to the smallest detail, including safety considerations, and results in a very detailed specification on, for example, the depth of hems on children's clothes to prevent children trapping their feet in them, and extensive testing of prototype and production-line items at suppliers. The result is that the customer can have confidence that items purchased will be of the grade expected. However, it also results in a very long lead time from initial design to items appearing in their shops.

The quality and reputation of the organization depend to a large extent on the staff, a factor recognized by Marks & Spencer which has supplemented care for the welfare of its employees with a drive to improve the way in which the service is delivered. The company now has a specialized Quality Management Team who are centrally based and are available to train and advise staff on quality issues at all the stores.

CONCEPT: Quality assurance

Libraries and information services

The key to quality assurance in services is *planned and systematic activities*, supported by *information and data*. The elements include marketing, the setting of standards based on the identification of user requirements and the design of a service and system to achieve these consistently without error.

Interest in quality management and quality assurance in LIS is evident from a glance through the *Library Association Record*, and we have already referred to the extensive literature which has developed around the subject. More specific examples of quality assurance approaches include: the development of staff manuals on a systematic basis; training initiatives based around the ideas of quality assurance (e.g. in customer care); exception reporting, where problems are dealt with in a systematic way; and the monitoring of services. This last has been widespread in libraries for some time and it can be argued that much of the quality assurance effort observed so far has centred around statistical reporting and analysis. In the next Chapter we consider performance measurement in more detail because of the importance and extent of activity which has been undertaken in this area. The essence of quality assurance, however, lies in the prevention of error through good planning and design (i.e. designing quality in rather than adding it later), so close attention needs to be paid to the planning and redesign processes. How do we build quality into library processes, and how do we use feedback to redesign those processes so as to achieve systematic improvement?

The Library Association is undertaking a number of quality assurance related initiatives, including the maintenance of a file of information on quality issues and the provision of comprehensive training programmes to familiarize librarians with quality concepts and techniques. To supplement training courses, information on suitable publications is available. The Association has issued a model charter for libraries and is producing a similar document on standards. An extract of the model charter is reproduced overleaf.

CONCEPT: Quality assurance

*Figure 9: The Library Association's 'Model Charter' (extract).
Reproduced with acknowledgement.*

A Charter for Public Libraries (Extract)

1   Local Authorities in England, Scotland and Wales and the Education and Library Boards in Northern Ireland have a legal duty to give you a full and efficient library service.

2   Your local library service (insert name) has an important role in the community. We give everyone access to books, information and works of creative imagination which will:

  * encourage them to take part in cultural, democratic and economic activities;

  * educate them, either formally or informally;

  * help them make good use of their free time;

  * promote reading as a basic skill for life; and

  * make them aware of the value of information and encourage them to use it.

We serve local communities. We meet the needs of particular groups within communities, while also giving access to wider resources through regional and national library networks.

3   Charter Statement

We will provide a high quality service. We will give value for money and will meet your needs.

3.1   Elected councillors, the local community and library staff will work together to decide what these needs are. We will involve the community by:

  * speaking regularly to our users, local organisations and voluntary groups;

  * giving you a way to make suggestions and complaints; and

  * making regular surveys of people who use and do not use the library. We will publish the results of these as quickly as possible.

3.2   We will give special attention to those who need special facilities and services because of their education or ethnic origin or any disability.

CONCEPT: Quality management system and standards

Manufacturing

A quality management system brings together a range of elements of quality management, to put quality policy into action. There is a control and feedback system for managing inputs through to final output and a review of performance, all of which must be documented and recorded. The most commonly used model for a quality management system in the UK is ISO 9000, although in the USA the Baldrige Award criteria are frequently used instead.

Both large and small manufacturing companies have formal quality management systems, although the complexity and amount of documentation vary according to company. The small engineering firm we visited had a single document covering both the company quality policy and how to carry out activities, with simple instructions for using machinery issued separately. Common practice in multi-site or multi-national companies is to have a set format for the quality management system and procedures so that staff can move from one site to another without the need to retrain.

There is no obligation to have the quality management system accredited by a third party, although it ensures that all elements of the chosen standard have been covered, that there is continuing compliance and that the system does not slide into disuse. If large companies are to be accredited it seems more practical to have individual accreditation for sites than to implement and audit a single system at all sites situated throughout a county or country. This pattern has been followed by GEC and in the service industry by some bank and building society branches.

Services

A true quality system, as described in BS EN ISO 9004–1: 1994, covers the structure of the organization and all the procedures, processes and resources needed to implement quality management, suitably tailored to the organization's type of business (British Standards Institution, 1994b). It is therefore more than a procedures manual which alone cannot guarantee quality of service.

CONCEPT: Quality management system and standards

A number of service companies, from medical practices to estate agencies, are using the ISO 9000 quality management system model. In the public services sector the Oasis Leisure Centre run by Thamesdown Borough Council has an accredited quality management system, as does the Barnsley Job Centre in South Yorkshire. McDonalds' documented procedures run into several volumes and cover not only work instructions for crew members but also all the aspects of the operation of a restaurant. Likewise, Marks & Spencer have an extensive documented system which, they estimate, exceeds ISO 9000 requirements.

Libraries and information services

A quality management system is a step beyond the traditional staff manual. It is more comprehensive, covering both policy and organization structure. It may, however, be tailored to suit the needs of a particular library. It can take the form of an extensive structured and controlled staff manual to support library activities; it can be automated; it can be written in very formal or informal terms; and it may also include service standards and policies. Professional standards and responsibilities are an important part of library work and can be built into a quality management system. For example, standards for cataloguing or the training requirement and experience needed for specified tasks can be explicitly stated in procedure documents.

The approach to formal quality management systems and standards in LIS varies widely. A limited number of libraries are currently using ISO 9000. One university library, the University of Central Lancashire, has been accredited to ISO 9000 on its own behalf, while another, the University of Wolverhampton, operates within the broader registration of the University as a whole. During the project we visited one small college library which is drawing up a documented quality management system based on the clauses of the ISO 9000 standard but will not be seeking accreditation at present; instead it is using it to ensure a consistent service, as an aid to staff training and as a means of empowering junior staff to write procedures and influence how work is performed. A number of special libraries within commercial companies have had to comply with their parent organizations' policies on ISO 9000.

CONCEPT: Quality management system and standards

Beyond ISO 9000 requirements, the need for libraries to adopt their parent organizations' quality management systems is widespread. It occurs in academic institutions, where libraries draw on and contribute to the main university and national higher education quality assurance systems, such as course validation procedures and HEFC quality assessments. Public libraries equally operate within a larger organization, and local authorities' approaches to quality assurance systems will be a major factor in influencing the libraries' own practices. National influences, such as the Citizen's Charter, will also be important in designing the quality assurance system.

CONCEPT: Resources

Manufacturing

The use of inferior resources can have consequences ranging from the annoying to the disastrous. Metal which has an inherent fault or is of an unsuitable grade could cause failure of a component or the whole item. Faulty components used in aircraft manufacture or safety equipment can result in the loss of company reputation, profits, life, or all three of these. Because of this, manufacturing companies take as many steps as possible to ensure that the resources used are suitable for the final product produced. Techniques include:

- *Vendor appraisal:* Suppliers are selected by reputation, or following evaluative visits to the supplier, or by using third party accreditation. The last is increasingly common as industries may use dozens of different suppliers, and need a way of identifying those which meet basic standards and have proper management systems in place. Two out of the three manufacturing companies examined during this project used only ISO 9000 accredited suppliers unless there was no alternative.

- *Vendor rating:* Where a number of existing suppliers are able to supply the same product, they may be scored by reference to performance criteria weighted according to importance. Criteria

CONCEPT: Resources

might include a quality rating (to include conformance to specification, reliability, etc.), a price rating (bearing in mind that price may not always be crucial for key components) and a delivery rating (possibly linked to 'Just In Time' delivery systems).

- *Purchasing documents:*These describe exactly what is required in the minutest detail and permit more open competition between suppliers, but are always coupled with very tight contracts often with penalty clauses.

- *Isolating input resources*: Inspection is carried out before items are put to use with process activities. One company allowed use 'under concession' as long as the part could be traced if the batch was found on inspection to be faulty. Inspection at this stage was invariably on a sampling basis—it is hardly practicable to check every nut and bolt if thousands are being used.

Services

Local branches of Marks & Spencer do not use incoming inspection but instead rely upon the production of a very detailed product specification and control of their suppliers, including spot visits to the suppliers' premises. Likewise, McDonalds set very high specifications for their ingredients and packaging. For example, the company specifies the precise cuts of meat to be used for their hamburgers (use of additives or fillers is not allowed) and insists that every consignment of meat undergoes 36 separate quality control checks. Even the cardboard used to pack products en route to the restaurants has to be pre-chilled.

Staff are often the key resource in service industries, and their 'processing' takes the form of training and development. In Marks & Spencer even part-time seasonal staff are given five days' initial training before they work with the public. Training enables staff to do their jobs more efficiently, to cope with any problems which might arise, and to develop their own skills. Some service industries, including W.H. Smith, have adopted the Investors in People initiative as a means of meeting the needs of their staff.

CONCEPT: Resources

Libraries and information services

In LIS, not only are staff important to service delivery, but often they are the product itself. In academic libraries, the specialist subject librarian is 'delivered' to academic faculties through meetings, committees, information skills activities, current awareness programmes and individual contacts in departments and the library. The Open University pioneered the strategy of including librarians in academic course development teams, and this model can also be found in many other universities, colleges and schools. Some industrial information staff also work in teams with research scientists. Turning all of these into quality workforces—the key service resource—is, unlike in manufacturing industry, more of a shared responsibility between employers, professional associations and educational institutions. Most of the players have collaborated on the development of sector-wide standards for education and training (note the role of National Vocational Qualifications (NVQs) here). Most employers therefore have some guarantees of workforce quality, so that the human resources are both broadly comparable and adequate.

LIS equipment is usually ordered from specialist suppliers, who are themselves increasingly aware of the importance of quality. Even very well known library suppliers (such as Askews and Holt Jackson) have implemented quality management systems to give an extra assurance of the quality of the products and services they supply to LIS.

Formal supplier assessment can be used in LIS as well as other industries. One academic library studied used a limited number of library suppliers. In selecting suppliers, certain criteria for assessment were laid down, including:
- reliability
- accuracy of library processing
- delivery times
- action taken to correct mistakes
- helpfulness of staff

The academic library monitored the performance of selected suppliers, with an annual review to decide whether to continue using them or change to others.

CONCEPT: Resources

A much more challenging resource for quality management in LIS is the ubiquitous database. Whilst there are widely-adopted standards for book production, making the monitoring of physical quality a relatively minor task, databases have grown and changed considerably over the last twenty years. Initially, they were 'published' by reputable organizations, compiled by well-trained and qualified staff, and held data which had been checked for accuracy. Now there are many compilers and suppliers marketing their goods with neither the traditional refereeing systems which control the quality of the majority of books and journals, nor the checks added by the publishing industry on the products which would become resources for LIS. The Centre for Information Quality Management (CIQM) is proposing to address this problem on behalf of both the LIS community and end-users by introducing a 'database labelling' system.

CONCEPT: Process activities

Manufacturing

Manufacturing takes raw materials or parts and uses tools and machinery, plus the skills of the operator, to produce finished items for the use of the customer—the nuts and bolts of industry. The library process takes information and materials and uses equipment (machinery) and the personal and professional skills of library staff (tools) to produce a service for the library users.

To make sure that the product is fit for its purpose and that the process runs as efficiently as possible, controls are built in. Prevention is the best form of control: if work has been planned to occur in the right order, if equipment used is checked and maintained, if the operative is equipped with the skills and knowledge needed, and if there is suitable documentation available where it is needed, the chances of problems occurring are reduced.

Although the factory owners or shareholders may own the equipment, and the finished item will be owned by the customer, while the process is under way that process is the property of the person carrying out the task. Modern quality management thinking suggests that monitoring the

CONCEPT: Process activities

process, keeping checks on whether the process is working correctly, and making corrections as the process is in progress, is best done by that worker, the process owner.

Sometimes problems with the process and the resulting product are detected immediately; it is fairly obvious if a part which is supposed to be square suddenly comes out round. However, if the part begins to change shape slowly, by becoming gradually more distorted, nothing may be noticed until the problem becomes significant and a whole batch might have to be scrapped. To prevent this happening, industrial processes are constantly monitored and the results analyzed using a variety of statistical techniques—Statistical Process Control—so that errors can be detected as early as possible. Statistical Process Control can be adopted by libraries to monitor and analyze the *operation* of their service and identify a situation which may be gradually worsening.

Services

In a service context the primary process is the *transaction* with the customer, which may use a certain amount of equipment but which relies heavily upon the skills of staff. There may be a number of sub-processes required before this process can take place, all of which have inputs and outputs and which require controls in the same way as the major process. As in manufacturing industry, controls make it possible to spot problems which are immediately visible or which may be the result of a gradually worsening situation which has been undetected by staff.

Marks & Spencer control the quality of service to the customer by extensive staff training and the use of documented instructions. To ensure that routine tasks are always performed a series of checklists were devised by staff. Items on the checklist are signed off as they are completed and the lists are checked weekly. It was stressed that this is done to improve the efficiency of the service and identify problems, not as a way of disciplining staff. If someone is unable to carry out the checklisted work, it may be that there is an underlying problem with the system, or that insufficient training has been given. Staff are encouraged to watch out for problems during the day and record them on a special-purpose form, together with what was done about them. The forms provide an aid to the identification and resolution of future errors.

CONCEPT: Process activities

Libraries and information services

There are a number of 'processes' which take place in libraries: record creation, cataloguing, circulation services, and the answering of enquiries all take place as the result of a number of inputs. Value is added by the skills of library staff to produce a service which aims to satisfy user requirements. Unlike manufacturing processes, results of library activities may be intangible. The training, expertise and experience of library staff is an important element in the 'process'. This can be supplemented by staff manuals of varying detail, and is a means of 'process control', although few staff describe it as such.

CONCEPT: Process control

Manufacturing

Process control has generally been seen as the focus of most quality management activity in industry. The tasks that are commonly undertaken include the identification of individual processes, followed by detailed planning of how they are to be carried out. This may result from findings of a review, where the need for a new process has been identified. Once the process has been designed and the production activity set up, work instructions are issued and procedures set up to enable monitoring and calibration to be carried out. Criteria will be established so that the monitoring data can be used to control the process. For example, at what tolerance should screws be manufactured so that a decision to close down manufacture for recalibration can be taken before an impact on the conformance of the end product to customer requirements is found?

Many large industrial companies have their own specialized manuals on process control (Bank (1992) refers to IBM's 'Process Control, Capability and Improvement' and Ford's 'Potential Failure Mode and Effects Analysis'). Statistical Process Control itself includes flow charts, run charts, control charts and histograms amongst its armoury.

CONCEPT: Process control

Services

The control of processes in services is complicated by the fact that the actual output of the process activity is an interaction with a customer. Control has therefore to be sensitive to this direct integration between processes and outputs/outcomes. The National Girobank faced this problem when trying to reduce errors made at Post Offices, which handle a high proportion of its transactions. It was estimated that errors on documentation were costing £1.3 million a year (Dale, 1994). The Bank set up a project team, who arranged for all errors to be recorded by type, volume and source (i.e. originating Post Office), and the information was used both to redesign forms and to feed back to the Office concerned. Over three years, the estimated cost of errors was reduced to £0.9 million while customer complaints fell by over a half.

Libraries and information services

One academic library records all incidents and problems at the issue desk, in similar fashion to Marks & Spencer, and also gives library users opportunities to record problems via suggestions and complaints schemes. Others keep statistics of all main LIS activities, such as cataloguing and processing throughputs, queue lengths, waiting times and shelving times, as an aid to detecting any gradual changes to service quality. Aston University, for example, uses control charts adapted from industry for this purpose, as does the British Library Document Supply Centre. Apart from their use in process control, such charts can also boost staff morale.

Libraries make wide use of performance measures and performance indicators in managing their processes. As this is such a highly developed area in LIS, it is referred to separately in the next Chapter.

CONCEPT: Products and services

Manufacturing

The results of manufacturing processes are tangible; they can be seen and touched, and thus it is easy to understand the process mechanism of

CONCEPT: Products and services

input–process–output in this context. Manufacturing companies may be relatively simple in organization, taking one set of inputs and producing a single product. In practice, however, even small companies have a number of assembly processes producing a partially finished product which then moves forward to the next stage, so that the departments within the company become, in turn, customers and producers until the finished item reaches the external customer. There may well be several different units in production at a factory which are assembled at a final stage.

Services

Services are somewhat hybrid creatures in the 'product' that they produce. Customers in the burger bar will come away with a tangible product which, they hope, will meet their expectations. The way in which they were served—the 'total service experience'—is a factor which may influence their decision on whether they want to return. This aspect of the product is created at the time of delivery and cannot be recalled; it may be made up of a number of identifiable points, such as how long they had to wait in the queue, but also includes less easily measured elements, such as the friendliness of the staff. The appropriate amount of friendliness is a subjective element—what is friendly to one person may be unwelcome to another. An article in the *Independent on Sunday* (22 January 1995) reveals the degree of irritation felt by the journalist who disliked the 'frightful breeziness' of the 'most friendly young man in history' at the store checkout.

Libraries and information services

As in other services, some of the products of library processes are tangible, in the form of items and information that can be touched, heard or read—the right book supplied, a correct citation given, etc. Others are intangibles. For example, supplying the result of a reference enquiry does not test the efficacy of the item supplied until the customer has applied this to his/her problem (see below on the related question of liability).

The full portfolio of services offered by any one library is rarely used by every customer. Services may be targeted at particular groups, so that, for instance in an academic library, the majority of interlibrary loan

CONCEPT: Products and services

requests are made by academic staff. The 'product mix' becomes important, and the aim must be to ensure a correct balance for each stakeholder group in a situation where not all demands, nor even all legitimate demands, can be met.

As we have seen, politeness, friendliness and other factors are important parts of service delivery. These need to be considered as part of the equation (i.e., *how* the service is delivered as well as *what* is delivered).

CONCEPT: Use of products and services

Manufacturing

Clearly there is a strong link between the product itself and the use to which it is to be put in any quality managed company. However, in the best companies this is extended beyond producing items which meet the customer's stated requirements to investigating how products are used so as to be able to provide improvements in the future. The accident which killed the seven Challenger astronauts in 1986 was caused, ultimately, by management failures, but had the company which produced the faulty 'O-rings' been more closely involved with assessing the conditions under which they would actually be used (rather than simply following the specification for the product), perhaps the accident could have been averted.

Services

As we have seen, in the service sector the actual delivery of a service and its use tend to occur at the same time. However, companies such as McDonalds do put considerable effort into understanding how the customer wants to use the service as well as into the basic fast food itself. Drive-through restaurants were an innovation which relied on insights into the *use* of the service rather than its *nature*. Video stores have to be aware of the use to which their loan stock might be put, and have to abide by licence requirements regarding the age of borrowers. Retail stores similarly must not sell cigarettes to under-age children because of the

CONCEPT: Use of products and services

use to which they might be put (even when the explanation is 'they're for my dad/mum...'!).

Libraries and information services

One example of the use of services beyond delivery in the LIS field occurs with the supply of health and medical information. If we treat doctors and health workers as part of the information industry, we can see that information they impart is actually used by patients outside the service delivery point. Issues of liability have been raised which make it clear that information service providers need to take into account what customers are likely to do with the information they are given.

CONCEPT: Inspection and test

Manufacturing

In manufacturing industries the product is checked against the specification at a number of points and for a number of reasons. It is usual to carry out a 'first-off' inspection to ensure that machinery has been set up correctly and that the design and planning process will result in a suitable product. It is a waste of resources and time to wait until all the items have been manufactured and then check them to find that they are all incorrect.

Assuming that the process has been well designed and set up correctly, samples are taken at intervals so that action can be taken if problems begin to emerge. This obviously has a resultant cost which must be balanced against the possible cost if faulty items are produced. To reduce the chance of flawed products finding their way to the customer a certain amount of final testing is carried out before the products are released for sale. The amount of testing which is needed is deemed to be in inverse proportion to the amount of preventative action which has been undertaken. Expenditure on prevention techniques reduces the amount of final inspection needed and lessens the cost of dealing with nonconforming items.

Inspection of the manufactured product does not end with final despatch. The external customer has the final word on whether the

CONCEPT: Inspection and test

product meets the specification. The inspection and test process can be seen to continue as the customer first receives and then uses the finished item. Feedback from customers and field service staff provides evidence of the performance of the item in use.

Services

As in the manufacturing sector, there are a number of checks which can take place during service provision. Checking that the service process is operating according to plan is not limited to quality management teaching but is simply good management practice. Planning and prevention are particularly important in service as it is almost impossible to halt a service once under way and start making adjustments whilst the customer waits. Nevertheless, a certain amount of in-process monitoring can be used in services. For example, having established by surveys that the majority of customers dislike having to queue at supermarket checkouts, both Tesco and Sainsbury's keep a check on the length of queues. Inspection alone is insufficient without action so both stores guarantee to open additional tills when any queue reaches a maximum of three people until all the tills are open.

Testing the quality of the service offered is more difficult than checking that nuts and bolts are the correct size. A number of methods are to be found in operation in services. Marks & Spencer, in common with other service providers such as brewery chains, employ 'mystery shoppers' who observe whether company standards of service are being met. McDonalds use a similar system whereby each restaurant is visited anonymously four times a year and scored against criteria which include cleanliness, speed and accuracy of order taking, and friendliness of service.

The customer provides a final test on the quality of the product and service by comparing what has been received with expectations and what the company has promised to provide. A number of companies are printing their guarantees on receipts given to the customer; one from McDonalds states that the company aims to provide hot, fresh food, 100 per cent order accuracy, and fast and friendly service. To back up the guarantee, the manager's telephone number is given. In addition the company, along with numerous others, invites customer comments by displaying customer survey cards in its restaurants.

CONCEPT: Inspection and test

Libraries and information services

Inspection and testing of library services can take place in a number of formal and informal ways. To a considerable extent, the customers themselves test the service at every transaction. In a busy library this can result in literally thousands of tests carried out each day by the users rather than, as in industry, on a sampling basis by staff. Also unlike most of the testing carried out in industry, the results of such tests will not necessarily be reported back to library staff and managers.

As a way of harnessing customers' 'inspection reports', libraries have traditionally used surveys of both users and non-users and analyses of written suggestions and complaints. In a closed academic or business community it is possible to ask library users their opinions directly through formal meetings and course reviews. Research (as yet unpublished) into the library needs of students on franchized courses carried out at the University of Central Lancashire used focus groups as a way of identifying user perceptions about the library service.

Formal audits by third parties are in use at academic libraries as part of the Higher Education Quality Council (HEQC) assessment exercise where tangible aspects of a service, such as subject coverage to support courses, are part of assessment criteria, alongside discussions with academic teaching staff. A group working under the aegis of the Higher Education Funding Councils has recently produced a document entitled 'The Effective Academic Library', which, although broader in scope than purely inspection and test, covers much of this area as it could be applied with the Councils' quality assessment processes (HEFCE, 1995). Libraries which are accredited under ISO 9000 are subject to ongoing surveillance, although it should be noted that it is the suitability of the system which is being assessed and not the level of service provided. Internal monitoring, and checks and audits of the system or service standards promised are used in a number of libraries—for example, Westminster Public Libraries, Leeds Metropolitan University and the University of Central Lancashire.

An alternative approach, suggested by the American Baldrige Award criteria, is for frontline service staff to ask for customer opinion as a matter of course. The Baldrige Award also suggests that feedback on incidents and problems encountered by staff is a way of checking whether services meet requirements and of identifying areas for improvement.

CONCEPT: Conformance to requirements

Manufacturing

Industrial systems and processes are geared to produce finished articles based on specific requirements. The operators know what the process activity is designed to produce, whether it is a bar of soap or a toaster, and exactly what standards and specifications they are working to. Standards, specifications and working instructions will be documented, and are available where they are needed and in an appropriate form, such as diagrams, flowcharts or samples, as well as written documents.

Manufacturers must conform to what has been agreed with the customer, to industry standards such as those operating in the concrete industry, to such product standards as BS 497 for manhole covers or to legislation such as the EC Directive on Medical Devices. Because requirements are clearly documented, conformance or otherwise is relatively easy to identify. Where there are degrees of tolerance, these will be within mathematically calculated limits and no further. For example, the jar of coffee that the customer buys will contain the minimum amount stated; it might contain just a little more, but the producer's requirements for profit dictate that if the jars are too full they will be outside the tolerated limits and will not conform to overall requirements.

Services

Requirements within the service sector are based on the organization's understanding of customer expectations and requirements. It is expected that products and services meet a minimum level as a basic requirement, which may or may not be documented. It is understood, for example, that food sold at a restaurant will be edible and that the staff will not be rude. Yet it would be unusual for these requirements to be explicitly stated, although the restaurant may advertise delicious food and friendly service.

Customer expectations with regard to a basic service are merely a baseline in an organization dedicated to quality service. Unlike the majority of manufacturing organizations, company requirements may be in excess of the minimum standard needed for customer satisfaction. The motor accessories company Kwik Fit states its aims as '100% customer ~~satisfaction~~ delight', advertising that they aim to exceed mere satisfaction. Supermarket chain Asda have initiated an 'ABCD award' for

CONCEPT: Conformance to requirements

company employees whose actions are 'Above and Beyond the Call of Duty'—for example, the employee who took two customers and their shopping home when they had missed their bus.

Libraries and information services

Whilst libraries may not have the same guidelines to work to as the process operator in a manufacturing plant, there are nevertheless a number of standards and requirements to be met. As in industry, there are certain guidelines and criteria to be adhered to, such as classification schemes and cataloguing rules to which library stock is 'processed'. Library processing is invariably carried out in line with set instructions as to the position of labels or the maximum number of characters in the classification number.

Service standards may be documented in customer charters or service level agreements and provide a means of assessing whether agreed requirements are being met. For example, the service level document of Leeds Metropolitan University aims to despatch interlibrary loan requests within three working days of approval. Records of performance are kept, collected and analyzed on an annual basis. As in other services, where minimum levels of service are expected, it is the 'extras' which raise customer expectations to delight. The following is just one example. The information a user requested was not available at a small branch library but was likely to be available at the central reference library; the branch librarian telephoned the central department to confirm that the material was available, asked for it to be kept for the user and provided directions and a map to find the way there.

It is more difficult to assess whether behaviour and attitudes conform to requirements. The requirements themselves may be less clearcut, although some guidelines are available. In 1983 the Library Association issued a Code of Professional Practice for librarians. The University of Liverpool has a set of guidelines for staff working on the enquiry desk and the University of Central Lancashire has a procedure for dealing with unruly borrowers.

CONCEPT: Zero defects

Manufacturing

The goal of zero defects has been emphasized by the quality 'gurus' and is a particular theme of Philip Crosby. Where safety is a factor the absence of defects is, of course, crucial: it is of little comfort to fighter pilots to know that only 5 per cent of ejector seats are defective—they want to know that the product will perform exactly to requirements. Consequently, the manufacturer will invest heavily to produce a product which is expensive but which will perform perfectly. In contrast, it is not worth heavy investment to produce boxes of matches of perfect size and shape which are all guaranteed to strike every time. The result would be unacceptably costly to the manufacturer, whilst the customer is willing to accept a small number of matches which do not work. Despite this, the *goal* should be zero defects, for every time a match fails to ignite there is the possibility of losing a lifetime customer.

Services

Zero defects in a service context means that the service provided exactly meets customer expectations and requirements. McDonalds' mission statement declares that the goal is 100 per cent customer satisfaction, and in practice this can only be achieved if the products are *always* delivered to specification. A single failure is one failure too many.

Libraries and information services

In LIS the idea of zero defects might be interpreted as users being able to borrow the books they require at the time they require, or the information supplied being accurate 100 per cent of the time, or the service being delivered in a courteous and friendly manner every time. Beyond the customer interface, zero defects implies finding that the book on the shelf is the one described in the catalogue. It implies that the acquisitions department always checks off exactly the right item against orders and invoices. Zero defects in a library service means that the service will meet the standards which have been promised. Customer charters are a method of publicizing the service promised to users. The Westminster Libraries charter, for example, offers a wide range of books and other

CONCEPT: Zero defects

materials to serve the interests and reading needs of the local community. Information provided will be accurate, readily available and speedily supplied. As customers would expect, the service will be delivered by polite, knowledgeable, and helpful trained staff. As a means of ensuring that services being provided conform closely to the standards set, the same authority carries out regular inspection and audits. Again, the goal is to achieve zero defects.

CONCEPT: Nonconformance control

Manufacturing

Nonconformance occurs when a product is identified as not being in accordance with specified requirements—the reasons for using nonconformance control techniques are to ensure that defective items do not reach customers and to reduce operating costs. Even in a well designed system there may be occasions when the product does not exactly conform to specification. The quality managed company will have a procedure available for dealing with nonconformances so that action can be taken swiftly if needed.

In the factory environment, defective products are identified in a number of ways: they may be marked with coloured paint (usually red), or labelled and placed in a quarantine area marked off with hazard warning tape. It may be possible to repair or rework such items, or alternatively they may have to be considered as scrap: both add to manufacturing costs. Whatever action is taken, there is a financial consideration—as a result of late schedules, reduced output, or discarding faulty material. This has to be balanced against possible product failure and customer dissatisfaction. In addition, the decision whether to stop production or to carry on may need to be taken urgently.

Services

In the services sector the 'product' cannot be scrapped or reworked as easily as in the factory. The customer is frequently present, so nonconformance control in this context is to an extent a damage limitation

CONCEPT: Nonconformance control

exercise. There is a need to be seen to take the problem seriously and to take action. This may take the form of an apology for what has happened and it may be possible to replace a defective item in a retail outlet. In the case of Marks & Spencer, action on unsatisfactory items has become a selling point for the company which has a generous returns policy if items are unsuitable for any reason.

Damage to service quality is difficult to repair. The service organization may not even have the opportunity to make amends as the customer may not complain but simply not return and thus be lost to the company. The way that the complaint is handled has a bearing upon the customer's perception of the organization. In one example from the hotel business, when the telephone, television and shower did not work the customer was moved to a superior grade room where all the equipment did work, an action which might have been seen as correcting the problem. However, since no apology was offered by staff and the porter who was supposed to move the luggage did not materialize, the action can at best be seen as partially successful.

Effective action on problems draws on a range of quality management elements: the responsibilities and commitment of management and staff; a management system for dealing with complaints; analysis and review of problems to prevent recurrence and learn from mistakes; capable and well trained staff with the authority to make decisions and take action; and so on. Staff at McDonalds, for example, are trained to handle any complaints, apologizing immediately for the problem even though it may not have been their fault. They are also given the authority to correct the problem wherever possible, replacing a wrongly supplied item for example, without having to ask permission from senior colleagues first.

Preventative action can reduce the need for nonconformance control, even if it cannot be totally eliminated. In the case of Marks & Spencer, if the customer cannot find the correct size of garment on the racks, staff are not allowed to use the phrase 'if it's not on the shelf, we don't have it'. Instead, documented procedures state that they check the stockroom and if one is not available they should offer to obtain it from another store. To prevent the need for all this, however, staff monitor the stock at the end of each working day, tidying the racks and checking that there is a suitable range of items available for sale.

CONCEPT: Nonconformance control

Libraries and information services

The identification of 'nonconformances' in libraries is frequently a fairly easy matter: the borrower who has overdue books; the user who complains that the wrong interlibrary loan items have been obtained; the book that the catalogue identifies as 'in the library' but which is not on the shelf. Likewise there are immediate actions which can be taken: fine the borrower; pacify the angry user; spend time searching for the missing book. Mechanisms for dealing with problems are normally in place in library services. Customer care training, for example, is the most commonly used form of quality management activity in libraries, according to Porter (1992). However, it needs to be more than just the 'charm school' approach ('being nice to the borrowers', according to one interviewee), but rather a way of training staff to handle difficult users with confidence and to apologize for the situation having occurred whilst remaining in control.

Virtually all public and academic libraries visited during the project had a customer complaints mechanism. This was publicized to the user in a number of ways—mentioned in the library charter, information in library guides, displayed comments books, or just a pile of forms in the library. Quality management principles dictate that comments are not just recorded but action is taken, with the results notified to the dissatisfied user, and investigation initiated into underlying causes.

CONCEPT: Corrective action

Manufacturing

The intention of corrective action is to enable the cause of the problem to be eliminated so that it does not occur again. It is also a means to quality improvement as investigations into root causes can identify ways of improving operations and services. Corrective action incurs expenditure, but so does continued nonconformance. Analysis of nonconformances may suggest the need for increased preventative techniques, the cost of which must be balanced by the risk of incurring costs resulting from product failure: scrap, rework or repair; appraisal arising from

CONCEPT: Corrective action

increased checking of possibly defective items; returns and refunds; lost sales; lost goodwill; and lost opportunities.

Companies with a formal quality management system in line with ISO 9000 requirements will have a procedure on corrective action which will enable faults to be logged and the cause traced back. A fault in an assembled mechanical part may, for example, have occurred at the point where it was put together, whilst the component parts were being stored or transported, or before the part arrived at the factory gate. The problem may have been due to mechanical or human error, which may in turn have happened because of lack of equipment maintenance or staff training. Design, method or the process itself may be at fault; or in the case of a bought-in part, the wrong part may have been supplied either because of a mistake by the supplier or as a result of an error in the order sent out. Long-term corrective actions are intended to solve problems once and for all: by planning or design changes, process improvements, improved documentation, systematic sampling, improved training, and so on.

Services

As in the manufacturing sector, there is a need to identify and record nonconformance although there may not be a tangible item which can be compared to a documented specification. Nevertheless, a mechanism for the reporting of faults and complaints and the investigation into causes will be in place in a well managed company. In the case of Marks & Spencer, for example, the recording of difficulties and queries in the store is used to ascertain the nature of problems and as an aid to prevention.

By recording and investigating nonconformances, an analysis is produced which will confirm deteriorating or improving trends, whether problems are with the overall system, equipment or supplies, or in the delivery of the service itself. Data from corrective action are a source of information for selecting quality improvement projects and determining effectiveness as well as monitoring performance. The aim of a quality managed service industry is the delivery of a *consistently* good service. Research by Zeithaml *et al.* (1990) shows that customers consider reliability to be the single most important dimension when judging service quality.

CONCEPT: Corrective action

Libraries and information services

As in other organizations, there is a need in LIS to ensure that there is a mechanism that will trap recurring problems so that *long-term* preventative action can be taken. In the case of a mistake such as a wrongly-supplied interlibrary loan item, the problem can be corrected simply by obtaining the one that was wanted. This may well have been an isolated incident but if records reveal that such problems happen with unacceptable frequency then there is a likelihood of an underlying fault which needs investigation. Corrective action procedures ensure that this happens. The University of Central Lancashire Library has a formal procedure for dealing with problems that have been identified at internal audit which not only demands action on the incident recorded but also acts as a trigger for identifying the cause and taking preventative action. The request for corrective action cannot be 'closed out', or considered completed until action has been taken and monitored to ensure that it is satisfactory.

CONCEPT: Continuous assessment and improvement

Manufacturing

One of the elements that lifts quality management into Total Quality Management is the principle of improvement. In a competitive environment, improvement in performance is necessary for business survival and takes a number of forms: improved cycle times for production and delivery to help the customer receive the product more quickly; the development of new products to meet identified and anticipated needs; and expansion into new markets to make products available to a greater number of people. The process model of the organization turns into a loop here, which becomes an upward spiral in the quality managed company.

CONCEPT: Continuous assessment and improvement

Services

Improvement of the quality of services supplied is the aim of continuous assessment and improvement—to build a better burger, open more stores, reduce waiting times in queues, offer new services—the service equivalents of the ideas in use in manufacturing, since service industries are also aiming for survival and increased market share. In the public sector, efforts may be made to innovate so as to release staff for more direct customer contact. For example, British Rail introduced the 'Open Station' system and withdrew its ticket barriers. Some staff were then redeployed onto platforms to help passengers, while others checked tickets on trains but were also able to offer advice.

Libraries and information services

Reviews of performance and surveys of users and non-users, together with input from different levels of staff, can provide the basis for more efficient ways of working, higher standards, and the development of new services. Unlike in commercial companies, money for service improvements cannot be raised by increasing charges. An initiative at Sainsbury's to open more checkouts and reduce queues can be funded by increasing prices marginally. The same option is not available to the library manager (although rethinking staffing priorities might provide scope for such innovation). A commitment to quality is laudable but in the current economic climate must be tempered by the availability of resources. There are obvious implications for the quality of library services. The goal of increasing profits in the commercial sector has its parallel in the drive for value for money and increased efficiency. A library installing a self-issue system will be unable to show an increase in profits but will be able to show better value for money by releasing issue desk staff to more customer support activities, for example by providing more staff at enquiry points, so that the staff there have time to accompany users to the shelves to search out information.

Performance measurement and quality

Performance indicators need to be linked to organizational goals and to the processes involved in meeting them. There is a tension in many libraries between collecting performance data, which are readily available but tell very little about the quality of the service, and collecting data on the outcomes of the service. Burningham (1992) has identified a range of reasons for the use of performance indicators including accountability, control and development. Goodall (1988) points out that different types of libraries have different types of users and that measures of performance must be appropriate to the organization. On the other hand, performance indicators, like standards, may be decided at a local level or set by outside bodies. Government initiatives such as the Citizen's Charter have encouraged the use of published indicators of performance. Sumsion (1993) links the Citizen's Charter with performance indicators for public libraries and documents the performance indicators set by the Audit Commission for 1993/94. Critics of externally-set performance targets include Harris (1991), who prefers locally derived measures to published, 'off the shelf' measures.

There has been little completely new thinking on measurement since the rush of studies produced during the 1970s and 1980s (for example: De Prospo *et al.* (1973) on performance measurement for public libraries; SCONUL/COPOL statistics on costs and measurement of usage). However, there are now signs of new activity in this field: see, for example, 'The Effective Academic Library' (HEFCE, 1995).

Performance measurement can relate not only to service performance but also to staff performance, and may thus imply a criticism of professional skills. However, poor performance or making mistakes in any aspect of the service entails a cost to the organization. The recent introduction of National Vocational Qualifications (NVQs) in the library and information services sector and the publication of the NVQ Standards suggest that we are now closer to demonstrating 'competence' across the whole range of institutions. This may mean that the differences between public, academic and special library services may be less significant when measuring their performance. A number of European Commission funded projects are currently attempting to bring together the full range of published performance indicators into a system which will both make it easier for managers to select appropriate measures and indicators and also offer some harmonization and cohesion.[4] Winkworth (1993) suggests that we should concentrate on the key elements as identified by users and staff. The Library Association (1995) has produced a score-based set of indicators for school libraries which awards scores against a list of desirable service criteria. What appears to matter most in quality management thinking is the way performance measures are selected and used.

Performance data can indicate use (for example, head counts show usage of a reference library) but do not give any idea whether or not users' needs were satisfied. The data tell us nothing about the users' experience and whether they are likely to return, yet that experience will affect their expectations of any future visits.

User satisfaction is not always reliable as an indicator of service quality as users may be unrealistically demanding (with a 'wish list' of more books, more books, more books, regardless of the bookfund available) or, alternatively, too easily satisfied, not wishing to offend or with low expectations. Davies and Kirkpatrick (1994) state that few librarians have the time, the resources or the inclination to collect users' opinions. Some libraries have used satisfaction surveys of library users, together with surveys of non-users, whilst others rely on the number of complaints as a sort of reverse index: the latter would not be regarded as adequate within most quality management systems.

The purpose of measuring quality is to ascertain whether quality concepts have been applied effectively and whether requirements have been met. The temptation in defining what measures will be used is to choose indicators and standards which are easily available, or those which are superficial and have only a marginal effect on the overall quality of the service. It is important to consider the quality of the service as a whole. For example, it is of little use to concentrate on the operation of one department or particular service if this would give an unbalanced picture. Neither is it sufficient to simply measure results; in a true

---

4. The EQLIPSE, DECIMAL, DECIDE and MINSTEL projects are funded under the European Commission Libraries Programme.

'quality' environment results are used as a basis for planning for improvement.

The evaluation of service quality can be difficult. Measures of effectiveness may be defined as hard or soft, tangible or intangible. Valuable research has been carried out into determinants of service quality by Zeithaml *et al.* (1990), who suggest that user perceptions of 'quality' are often intangible and propose a model for assessing quality. Intangibles are, however, harder to measure than statistical data and are not necessarily dependent on resources alone (although it is always vital to get the *basics* right). It is often the intangible elements which users mean when they talk about 'quality'—how friendly and efficient staff seem to be, for example. This is an area which might benefit from further research.

A combination of measures and techniques are needed to give a complete picture of the quality of library services. These include:

- charters, codes of practice, contracts, service standards;

- performance indicators, statistics;

- surveys, work with focus groups;

- unobtrusive testing, the 'mystery shopper' approach, use of checklists;

- commitment and involvement of all levels of staff;

- third party accreditation and awards.

Each library and information service needs to examine its own requirements in the light of the needs of its own actual and potential customers, and devise or adopt a portfolio of appropriate measures. Overlaid on this set of measures will be the performance measures and indicators required by external bodies. The two may overlap, but they should not be confused.

Conclusions

Most library services already self-audit the quality of their services. This leads to the question of who is best qualified to assess 'quality': library staff, library users, the parent organization, or an independent assessor or assessment service? In recent years most services in the public sector have been subjected to a barrage of external quality audits. Academic institutions and their libraries are assessed by the HEFCs and HEQC, schools and school libraries by OFSTED (the Office for Standards in Education), public libraries and local authorities by the Audit Commission (and by a number of commercial consultancies, such as Coopers & Lybrand), health and medical libraries by the new NHS trusts. In the private sector, whose marketplace philosophy public services seek to emulate, such controls, checks and audits would be both impossible and unworkable. The market decides by either buying or not buying. Companies are left to make their own decisions and judgements about how they will internally audit the quality of their operations. It could be argued that it was the absence of adequate quality assurance and quality monitoring which left public services so vulnerable to external audits. Or, that the range of performance indicators and measures gave an inadequate picture for others to judge quality. Whatever the underlying cause of so much external monitoring and auditing, it has edged public services, including libraries, towards a more customer-driven, customer-focused approach to both developing and delivering a 'quality' service. We have much to thank our manufacturers for. In this report we have tried to make the debt more explicit, but also to show how and where the sectors must agree to differ. The end result is a complement of concepts and techniques to benefit all customers, all suppliers and providers, and all purchasers.

References and evaluative bibliography

A study of the literature reveals a vast amount of published information on quality management. Attempting to identify useful material can be difficult because of the sheer volume and because manufacturing bias and jargon make many of the texts difficult to understand. There is only a small amount of introductory material aimed specifically at library and information staff.

Abbott, C. (1990) What does good look like? The adoption of performance indicators at Aston University Library and Information Service. *British Journal of Academic Librarianship*, 5(2), 74-97.
Using performance indicators to improve service quality through the development of enhanced management tools. Describes background and approach, and evaluates some of the resultant changes. The use of performance indicators is seen as part of a broader process of organizational change. Examples of use show staff involvement at all levels in target setting and monitoring—enabling ownership of both problem and resolution. Encouraging staff to seek solutions to problems seen as an enabling process which increases commitment and job satisfaction. Place of quality measurement in overall picture: 'The measurement of quality may lead to beneficial organizational changes, but cannot of itself improve quality' (p.93).

Abbott, C. (1994) *Performance measurement in library and information services*. London: Aslib.
Performance measures are defined as management tools, designed to assist library managers to determine how well the service is performing with the aim of improvement. Reasons for using measures include accountability to both parent institution and customers, link with service level agreements, quality management and quality assurance activities. Neither performance indicators nor quality assurance will guarantee quality; rather they are complementary management tools.

Atkinson, P.E. (1990) *Creating culture change: the key to successful total quality management*. Bedford: IFS Publications.
TQM must be management-driven but is everyone's responsibility and must be company wide. TQM is an umbrella over a number of approaches and techniques. Quality improvement is a never-ending process. Not always a question of resources: '....quality is about attitude. Spending money does not promote quality ... quality is something which is engineered through effective human relations' (p7). TQM phi-

losophy outlined: Systems / Leadership and commitment / Training and participation / Commitment to change through people.

Bank, J. (1992) *The essence of total quality management.* Hemel Hempstead: Prentice Hall.
Reference work on TQM covering an analysis of concepts and the teachings of the quality 'gurus' as well as tools and techniques aimed at a readership of managers and MBA students. TQM is defined as an approach to business which looks critically at the products and services a company produces in relationship to the processes it takes to create them.

Bendell, T., Boulter, L. and Kelly, J. (1994) *Implementing quality in the public sector.* London: Pitman.
Basic principals of TQM combined with background information on the reasons for the 'quality revolution' in public services, suggestions on how to implement TQM techniques and a number of case studies drawn from the police service, health service and local government. Whilst concentrating on the UK, the authors have also included the move towards TQM in the USA and detailed information on the American Awards.

Bicheno, J. (1994) *The quality 50.* Buckingham: PICSIE Books.
Amazing little book (only 90 pages) covering 'gurus', tools and techniques, and systems for quality. No index, no introduction, very cheap, but excellent brief guide to the essentials of quality management.

British Standards Institution (1987) *British Standard 4778: Part 1: Quality vocabulary.* London: BSI.
Identical to ISO 8402: 1986, this standard gives definitions of the terms used in quality management although the terms used are very formal. For example, 'quality' is defined as 'the totality of features and characteristics of a product or service that bear on its ability to satisfy stated or implied needs'.

British Standards Institution (1991) *British Standard 5750: Part 8: Guide to quality management and quality system elements for services.* London: BSI.
Identical to ISO 9004-1, this document specifically interprets quality management system principles for service personnel. It aims to help organizations to 'manage the quality aspects of their service activities in a more effective manner'. The customer is presented as the focal point of the three key aspects of a quality system and customer satisfaction will only be assured when there is interaction of all the elements.

British Standards Institution (1992a) *British Standard 7750: Environmental management.* London: BSI.
This standard shares common management system principles with BS EN ISO 9000. It covers requirements including environmental policy, systems, audits and reviews as a basis for environmental management.

British Standards Institution (1992b) *British Standard 7850: Part 1: Guide to management principles; Part 2: Guide to quality improvement methods.* London: BSI.
There are no ISO or EN equivalents to this standard, neither is it possible to achieve certification. The application of TQM involves investment in time and people, putting into place processes and systems including quality systems, quality improvement and analysis, and diagnosis tools.

British Standards Institution (1994a) *BS EN ISO 9001-9003: Quality systems.* London: BSI.
This set of standards provides a model for quality management systems. Formerly known as BS 5750: Parts 1 to 3 (identical to ISO 9001-9003). BS EN ISO 9001 has 20 clauses covering key company activities. BS EN ISO 9002 is virtually identical, but does not include design, while BS EN ISO 9003 covers only final inspection and test. The standard was revised in 1994 to clarify the terminology and requirements but is currently under further review with substantial revisions indicated.

British Standards Institution (1994b) *BS EN ISO 9004-1: 1994 Quality management and quality system elements: guidelines.* London: BSI.
This is a generic guide to understanding the ISO 9000 series of standards. The standards are not intended to produce uniformity of quality systems as the needs of organizations vary. This part of the standard describes what elements systems should encompass, not how a specific organization should implement a quality management system. The guidelines include meeting customer and organizational needs and expectations.

Brockman, J. (1991) Quality assurance and the management of information services. *Journal of Information Science*, 17(2), 127-35.
Report from seminar—covers a range of approaches and applications, from the definitions and theory of quality assurance, to specific applications of quality assurance. Clive Weeks (then Information Service manager at ICI) defines quality as 'satisfying agreed and defined customer need every time'.

Brockman, J. and Gilchrist, A. (1995) Information management and the pursuit of corporate excellence. *FID News Bulletin*, 45(5), 160-6.

Brophy, P. (1986) *Management information and decision support systems in libraries.* Aldershot: Gower.
General management concepts and techniques have only recently been accepted within the library profession. Management information impinges differently on different 'levels' of management who need to be able to plan on an informed basis, bringing information from a wide variety of sources to bear on decision making.

Brophy, P. (1989) Performance measurement in academic libraries: a polytechnic perspective. *British Journal of Academic Librarianship*, 4(2), 99-110.
Provides a view on the key issues of performance measurement, including the need to ensure relevance of the measures used to the objectives of the service in question.

Brophy, P. (1991) The mission of the academic library. *British Journal of Academic Librarianship*, 6(3), 135-147.
The development of mission statements has become commonplace in UK academic institutions in recent years. Similarly, academic libraries have given increased emphasis to the articulation of a statement of mission. Explores the concept of 'mission' in the context of the academic library based on a study of academic library mission statements carried out in 1990-91.

Brophy, P. and Coulling, K.C. (1996) *Quality management for information and library managers*. London: Gower.
Outlines the history of quality management, with particular reference to its relevance to libraries, and then explains quality assurance and Total Quality Management in the same terms. The LIS quality management literature is summarized and suggestions made for successful implementation.

Buckland, M. (1988) *Library services in theory and context*. 2nd edn. Oxford: Pergamon Press.
Provides a theoretical and conceptual framework for libraries.

Burningham, D. (1992) An overview of the use of performance indicators in local government. In *Handbook of public service management*, ed. C. Pollitt and S. Harrison. Oxford: Blackwell.
Authors identify a number of trends which have influenced the increased use of performance indicators: new styles of corporate management, increased competition, performance related pay, role of the 'enabling authority'. Reasons for use of performance indicators can be : accountability, control or developmental. Offers a 'characteristics' model for service industries—why do people use a service and are the resulting needs met? Cites Hounslow Leisure Services' 'Yardsticks of Performance' as example of use.

Calvert, P.J. (1994) Library effectiveness: the search for a social context. *Journal of Librarianship and Information Science*, 26(1), March, 15-21.
Article based on study in New Zealand. Measures of effectiveness must be based on a wide range of opinions and not just the profession's membership. Identifies three groups of stakeholders (in public libraries): staff, users, fund holders. States that it is 'not performance which should be measured but effectiveness' (p.24).

Caplen, R.H. (1988) *A practical approach to quality control.* 5th edn. London: Business Books.
Very technical but authoritative book with an unequivocal manufacturing approach; nevertheless a good basic textbook on quality control techniques. Not for the uninformed, but useful for those with a grounding in the basics.

Carter, S. (1978) Library of the year: Dorset's scheme for encouragement of service. *Service Point,* 15 April.
In 1971 Dorset established a scheme for an award as recognition of service. The criteria used included staff efficiency, enthusiasm and sense of service, and the quality and suitability of the book stock.

Centre for the Evaluation of Public Policy and Practice (1992) *Considering quality: an analytical guide to the literature on quality and standards in the public services.* Brunel University.
More than a bibliography. Discusses the main issues with regard to quality and standards: e.g., what quality is, developments in different sectors and services. Examines three different definitions of quality but comes back to user needs. Relationship of '3Es' to quality—Economy / Efficiency / Effectiveness.

Circle of State Librarians (1992) *Developing quality in libraries: culture and measurement for information services,* ed. L. Foreman. London: HMSO.
Collection of papers covering a range of approaches: customer service; BS 5750; TQM; Customer-driven service. Lynne Brindley stresses the importance of customer perceptions and defines quality in form of formula: quality = performance - expectation. What is needed for a quality library service = top management commitment, teamwork, systems and tools - customer—driven with the Customer at the centre.

Cronin, J.J. and Taylor, S.A. (1992) Measuring service quality: a re-examination and extension. *Journal of Marketing,* 56, July, 55-68.
Authors contest the findings of Zeithaml *et al.* (1990), suggesting that their SERVQUAL model of service quality is inadequate and the 'Gap' model for measuring quality is supported by 'little if any theoretical evidence'. Offer SERVPERF model as alternative. The argument is, however, rather dense and takes insufficient account of the empirical evidence offered by Zeithaml *et al.*

Crosby, P. (1979) *Quality is free.* New York: McGraw-Hill.
Concept of zero defects. Estimates that services waste 30 per cent of revenue on avoidable error. Emphasis on prevention. Offers four 'absolutes' of quality: definition of quality seen as conformance to requirements, not as 'goodness or elegance'; the system for causing quality is prevention, not appraisal; performance standard must be zero defects, not 'that's close enough'; the measurement of quality is the price of nonconformance, not indices.

Curtis, M., Jennings, B., Wheeler, S. and White, L. (1993) Quality assurance in Kent. *Public Library Journal*, 8(1), Jan/Feb 1-4.
Implementation of a quality assurance system as part of a move towards TQM. Kent established a Quality Team who produced a documented system of standards with the assistance of library staff throughout the county.

Dale, B. (ed.) (1994) *Managing quality*. 2nd edn. Hemel Hempstead: Prentice Hall.
Broad coverage of the topic of quality including the work of the quality 'gurus', systems, and tools and techniques. The intended readership comprises managers, consultants, academics and both undergraduate and postgraduate students.

Dale, B. and Oakland, J.S. (1991) *Quality improvement through standards*. Cheltenham: Stanley Thornes.
Based on British Standards related to quality—except where best practice differs from standards (e.g. Statistical Process Control (SPC)). Authors have tried to relate text to non-manufacturing industries. Designed as a reference tool, giving the relationship to published standards and their application.

Davies, A. and Kirkpatrick, I. (1994) To measure service: ask the library user. *Library Association Record*, 96(2), February, 88-89.
A survey to measure service quality rather than user satisfaction was carried out at the University of Wales Cardiff College in 1992. User opinion complements other measures such as stock accessibility and availability, statistics, performance measurement and the efficiency of administrative systems and procedures. The survey revealed that what counts for most in the eyes of the users is the human side of a library service.

Dawes, S. (1990) *The impact of BS 5750 on library/information practice and provision in a professional environment*. Unpublished conference paper.
Describes implementation of BS 5750 at the Building Design Patnership and the central role played by Information Centre in the process. Describes the benefits: improvement of centres, user confidence in service reliability.

Dawson, A. (1992) Quality first: the Taywood Information Centre and BS 5750. *Aslib Information*, 20(3), 112-113.
Describes implementation and how it involved all staff in procedure writing. Resulting benefits described: improved working practice and record keeping. Concludes that an active quality system is above all a management tool which helps identify weaknesses and ensure corrective action. Process requires effort and commitment.

Deming, W. (1988) *Out of the crisis*. Cambridge: Cambridge University Press.
Statistical approach: stresses importance of SPC and Supplier Quality Assurance (Vendor Rating). Encourages employee participation in decision making and claims that poor management is responsible for 94 per cent of quality problems.

Ellis, D. and Norton, B. (1993) *Implementing BS 5750/ISO 9000 in libraries.* London: Aslib.

A very practical guide to using the quality management system standard written, unlike the vast majority of literature on the standard, for library and information services staff, and assuming little or no previous knowledge of the subject. The authors stress that ISO 9000 is the framework for a quality system which can be adapted for a library environment and used as a means of quality improvement.

Feigenbaum, A.V. (1991) *Total quality control.* (3rd edn.) New York: McGraw-Hill.

Definition of quality: 'Quality is what the customer says it is'. Feigenbaum approach to quality is a systematic or total approach, involving all functions, with quality built in at an early stage. Importance of human relations is stressed. Four main points: set quality standard; appraise conformance to standards; act when standards are exceeded; plan for improvements in standards.

Gillman, P. (1992) Snares and delusions: the mismanagement of quality. In *Total Quality Management: the information business, key issues '92.* HERTIS Information and Research. Hatfield: University of Hertfordshire Press.

Gives examples of the misuse of BS 5750 where the system established was either unwieldy or too rigid and warns of the dangers of setting up a rigid, prescriptive system. BS 5750 is seen as too complex for many businesses.

Goodall, D. (1988) Performance measurement: a historical perspective. *Journal of Librarianship,* 20(2), April, 128-143.

Great Britain (1994) *Citizen's Charter: second report: 1994.* London: HMSO.

Summary of 'Principles of Public Services' and progress so far. Covers the aims of the Citizen's Charter and its application to specific public services, reports on progress so far, and sets agenda for the future. Government initiative with aim of raising standard of public service to make them more responsive to user needs and wishes.

Green, A. (1990) What do we mean by user needs? *British Journal of Academic Librarianship,* 5(2), 65-78.

Examines user needs and distinguishes from 'wants'. Users may not translate wants into demands for a number of reasons: reticence; ignorance; lack of confidence. Who should be responsible for defining user needs—usually 'expert', professional librarian, but may not be best person (cites 'experts' who designed tower blocks of 1960s). Offers criteria for assessing user needs: normative, felt, attributed—these can be used for evaluation.

Harris, M. (1991) The user survey in performance measurement. *British Journal of Academic Librarianship,* 6(1).

Performance indicators were derived from the goals of the library at the University of Western Australia and the use of measures was explored for these indicators. Measures can be 'off the shelf' from the published range of performance measures, but the library tacitly adopts implied goals. It is more logical to decide specific institutional goals and use these as a basis for performance measures.

Harvey, L. and Green, D. (1993) Defining quality. *Assessment and Evaluation in Higher Education*, 18(1).
Considers the difficulties of defining what is meant by quality, and different perspectives on it (stakeholder views), within the context of higher education.

Head, M. and Marcella, R. (1993) A testing question: the quality of reference services in Scottish Public Libraries. *Library Review*, 42(6), 7-13.
Reports on unobtrusive testing, looking at: access—ease of location, authority of person answering query; customer care—how welcoming or otherwise; and reliability—the success of the enquiry and what sources were used.

HEFCE (1993) *Joint Funding Councils' Libraries Review Group: report*. (The Follett Report). Bristol: Higher Education Funding Council for England.

HEFCE (1995) *The effective academic library. A framework for evaluating the performance of UK academic libraries.* Joint Funding Councils' *ad hoc* group on performance indicators for libraries. A consultative report to the HEFCE, SHEFC, HEFCW and DENI. Bristol: Higher Education Funding Council for England.

HERTIS Information and Research (1992) *Total Quality Management: the information business, key issues '92.* Hatfield: University of Hertfordshire Press.
Summary of TQM in the information world—definitions/benefits and drawbacks/current practice, though mainly private and academic.

Van House, N.A., Weil, B.T. and McClure, C. (1990) *Measuring academic library performance*. Chicago: American Library Association.
Practical manual of measures specific to academic libraries which aim to evaluate the effectiveness of library activity. The measures are user oriented (which corresponds to the customer-centred approach of TQM) and their use is documented in detail. The volume also contains an extensive bibliography.

Ishikawa, K. (1985) *What is total quality? The Japanese way.* London: Prentice-Hall.
Pioneer of Quality Circles—this 'guru' stressed the importance of staff involvement throughout the organization, with all staff trained in the proper use of quality tools and techniques. Grassroots workers should understand and practice quality.

Jackson, P. and Jackson, D. (1993) *Implementing quality through BS 5750*. London: Kogan Page.
Practical guide aimed at small-medium size businesses but useful for library and information services considering a quality management system based on the standard. The work covers the real and perceived benefits (how to gain) and the drawbacks (how to avoid). The authors use detailed examples from case studies to illustrate what quality is, whether BS 5750 is right for the organization and how to introduce the standard.

James, K. (1989) Encounter analysis: front-line conversations and their role in improving customer service. *Local Government Studies*, May/June, 11-24.
Suggests ways of opening up of the closed organization where 'professionals' make key decisions on service provision, to change to customer and frontline staff involvement. Suggested tactics for improving customer service include service days, opinion polls, managers working for short periods on reception desk, slogans and campaigns to improve image, access improvements, consultation. Describes in particular the use of encounter analysis to learn from problems, emphasizing the involvement of all stakeholders and the avoidance of what the author calls the 'charm school' approach to customer care.

Johannsen, C. (1992) The use of quality control principles and methods in library and information science theory and practice, *Libri* 42(4), Oct-Dec, 283-93.
Overview of the commonalities between established library practice and quality management from a European perspective.

Juran, J. (1988) *Juran on planning for quality*. New York: Free Press.
Describes the quality trilogy essential for effective quality management: quality planning, quality control and quality improvement. Quality planning must concentrate on the needs of the customer to establish specific goals and the best ways of reaching them. Whilst sceptical of the use of quality circles in the West, he says that the majority of quality problems are the fault of poor management.

Jurow, S. and Barnard, S.B. (1993) *Integrating TQM in a library setting*. Howarth Press.
Collection of articles from practitioners using TQM in libraries. Defines TQM as a 'system of continuous improvement employing participative management and centred on the needs of customers'. Some USA bias but general enough to be a useful collection of ideas on the planning and implementation of quality management tools, techniques and systems. No mention of relevant standards, e.g. ISO 9000 or BS 7850, and their possible application to TQM, although the use of the Baldrige Award criteria is covered.

Lascelles, D.M. and Dale, B.G. (1993) *The road to quality*. Bedford: IFS Ltd.
Introduces quality concepts, with examples, and describes TQM in terms of a long-term commitment.

Lester, D.E. (1994) *The impact of quality management on the information sector. A study of case histories.* Luxembourg: EUSIDIC.
Report of the 1993/1994 investigation into the status of quality management in the information sector drawing on a number of case studies. Some background awareness of quality management was found which had been gleaned in a number of ways, including reading, seminars, information programmes and by accident. The survey also revealed a desire to apply sound management techniques including quality management to library and information services.

Library Association (1993) *LA/COFHE guidelines: managing after incorporation: quality matters.* London: Library Association.
Issued to assist college librarians manage their role in the transformation of colleges to corporate (independent) status. Being able to demonstrate a quality service is seen as ever more important in this context, and these guidelines offer advice.

Library Association (1995) *Library power rating for secondary schools.* London: Library Association.
A checklist for parents to complete in order to assess the quality of school library services.

Line, M. (1993) Managing change and changing managers. In *Change in libraries and information services*, ed. by L. Foreman. Circle of State Librarians. London: HMSO.
Change identified as a sign of the times, from the relatively trivial to the fundamental and dramatic, with a number of pressures for change. The library of the future will be oriented to users. As a result services will be designed around users and will be judged by outputs rather than inputs, with a need for efficient operations and procedures.

Lock, D. (ed.) (1990) *Gower handbook of quality management.* Aldershot: Gower.
Comprehensive work covering both general topics on the concept of quality, described as 'the latest buzzword?', and very practical and detailed information on the use of quality tools and techniques such as SPC and Pareto analysis. Whilst the work concentrates on engineering and manufacture, coverage of most topics is fairly broad.

Marshall, C. (1991) Culture change: no science but considerable art. Comino Lecture, 13 June 1990. *RSA Journal*, January, 895.
Reflections on the experience of a senior corporate manager (Sir Colin Marshall was Chief Executive of British Airways) on how a company can undergo a culture change in becoming more responsive to its customers and at the same time more successful in a highly competitive industry.

Morgan, C. and Murgatroyd, S. (1994) *Total quality management in the public sector: an international perspective.* Buckingham: Open University Press.
The authors comment that there is 'no single agreed formulation of TQM' (probably an accurate observation!). Looks at the ways that key TQM ideas and concepts are

relevant to the public sector and can be applied on three levels: corporate, strategies and operational. Answers a number of frequently voiced criticisms, including the argument that the manufacturing origins of TQM prevent its application to the service environment.

New Library World (1994), 95(1113).
Whole issue on theme of 'strategies for service quality'; provides a useful collection describing a number of approaches to customer care and quality improvement by a range of companies in the service sector.

Oakland, J. (1994) *Total Quality Management*. 2nd edn. Oxford: Butterworth Heinemann.
Classic textbook on TQM which discusses a number of basic concepts: quality chains, process management, the importance of commitment and leadership, planning and design (including design in the service sector). The work also covers the practical application of quality management principles, presented for a readership of both directors/managers and students of quality management. Unlike some writers, Oakland does not see ISO 9000 as incompatible with the TQM approach.

O'Neil, R.M. (1994) *Total quality management in libraries: a sourcebook*. Englewood: Libraries Unlimited.
Selection of articles, although most have appeared elsewhere, on a broad range of topics exploring the application of TQM to libraries. The second part of the book comprises extensive bibliographies organized under three headings: general background reading, those recommended for the use of library staff involved in quality initiatives and items suggested for library stock. Sources cited include journals and electronic sources.

Peters, T. and Waterman, R.H. (1982) *In search of excellence; lessons from America's best-run companies*. New York: Harper & Row.
The authors use examples of companies with outstanding customer care or service to illustrate approaches to excellence. The companies cited are all North American—McDonalds, Hewlett Packard and Delta Airlines, for example—but are chosen to show the importance of the customer and emphasis on employee involvement.

Pluse, J. (1994) People: your most valuable investment. *Library Association Record*, 96(2), February.

Porter, L. (1992) *Quality initiatives in British library and information services*. British Library R&D Report 6105. London: The British Library.
Survey of public and academic libraries carried out as part of a research project which concludes that most of the libraries responding were involved in quality assurance although there was little agreement on terminology and meaning. The author recommends a coordinated approach to quality and the study gives a number of examples of good practice and a useful contact list.

De Prospo, E.R., Altman, E., and Beasley, K.E. (1973) *Performance measures for public libraries*. Chicago: American Library Association.
Aimed to 'find new ways of describing library service in statistical terms and creating a better profile of library operation than has been possible in the past'. Of mainly historical interest now.

Richard, S. (1992) Library use of performance indicators. *Library Review*, 41(6), 22-36.
Not a 'how-to' manual but a good summary of the purposes and uses of performance indicators, including suggested indicators which are relevant to libraries.

Rosander, A.C. (1991) *Deming's 14 points applied to services*. New York: Dekker
Although this work is not aimed at library and information workers and is noticeably North American in the use of examples and terminology, it contains some important points. The importance of training is emphasized for frontline staff who have a key role in determining the quality of service to the customer. Unlike manufacturing industry, the service industry customer buys a 'sample of one' which determines perceptions of service quality.

Stebbing, L. (1990) *Quality management in the service industry*. London: Ellis Horwood.
This is a practical introductory guide to the application of quality management techniques which covers both the reasons for implementing quality management in services and the practical ways this can be done.

Sumsion, J. (1993) *Practical performance indicators—1992. Documenting the Citizen's Charter consultation for UK public libraries with examples of PIs and surveys in use*. Loughborough: LISU.
Whilst the ideal may be to construct a research programme and performance indicators from a logical analysis of need, in practice useful intellectual shortcuts can be found by copying and modifying practices already developed elsewhere. A MORI survey for the Audit Commission carried out in 1991 shows that the public rate helpfulness of staff and the variety of books held as the two main criteria for user satisfaction.

Tann, J. (1993) Dimensions of quality in a library setting. In *Quality management: towards BS 5750*. Proceedings of a seminar held in Stamford, Lincolnshire, UK, on 21 April 1993, ed. M. Ashcroft and D. Barton. Stamford, Lincs.: CPI.
A series of papers looking at the implementation of BS 5750 (ISO 9000) from a library perspective.

Taylor, M.H. and Wilson, T. (1990) *Quality assurance in libraries: the health care sector: a collection of studies*. Ottawa: Canadian Library Association.
A collection of 10 papers on a range of quality issues including standards and performance indicators. Quality is seen as an elusive concept but there are a number of practical guidelines and ideas.

Tenner, A.R. and De Toro, I.J. (1992) *Total Quality Management: three steps to continuous improvement*. Reading, Mass.: Addison-Wesley.
An overview of TQM, which lays stress on the need to see it as a journey on which an organization embarks, rather than a technique that is suddenly implemented. The single objective should be 'continuous improvement'.

Webb, I. (1991) *Quest for quality*. London: The Industrial Society.
There are two distinct halves to this book. The first part is concerned with general quality topics—definitions of quality, techniques, etc. The second part covers half a dozen case studies from both the manufacturing and service sectors, including Marks & Spencer and the National Trust.

Webb, S.P. (1995) *Pursuing quality in special libraries: a study of current activities and developments in the United Kingdom*. British Library R&D Report 6214. London: The British Library.
A report on the use of quality management by special libraries in the UK, based on a survey of over 100 organizations, including government departments, commercial and industrial firms and membership associations. Quality management activity is shown to be on the increase, and to have produced clear benefits.

Wedlake, L.J. (1993) An approach to quality assurance and a guide to the implementation of BS 5750. *Aslib Proceedings*, 45(1), January, 23-30.
This article illustrates the place of a quality management system within the philosophy of quality assurance, with particular reference to BS 5750 (ISO 9000).

Winkworth, I. (1993) Performance indicators and quality assurance. *Aslib Information*, 21(6), June, 250-251.
This short article defines how performance indicators fit into the quality assurance framework and what to consider when choosing indicators. There is a difficulty in selecting indicators which will satisfy different stakeholders within the organization: 'customer', manager, staff, funding authority.

Zeithaml, V.A., Parasuraman, A. and Berry, L.L. (1990) *Delivering quality service: balancing customer perceptions and expectations*. New York: Free Press.
Key work arising from research into service quality. Describes the development of the SERVQUAL model for measuring customer-centred performance based on ten dimensions of service quality reduced to five: tangibles, reliability, responsiveness, empathy, access. The authors also identify the gaps in perceptions and expectations

of management and customer and suggest ways to close the gaps and improve service quality.

Acknowledgements

We are grateful to the many colleagues, both in the library and information service profession and in other services and industries, who gave their time to assist us in developing the model presented in this Report. Particular thanks are due to the staff of the Centre for Research in Library & Information Management at the University of Central Lancashire, and to the University Library's staff, for their helpfulness and support.

QUALITY MANAGEMENT AND PUBLIC LIBRARY SERVICES—THE RIGHT APPROACH?

Eileen Milner
Margaret Kinnell
Bob Usherwood

Introduction

This is the final report of the Quality Management and Public Libraries project, which was funded by the British Library Research and Innovation Centre (then the British Library Research and Development Department) from September 1994 to July 1995. The project was jointly managed by the Department of Information Studies at Sheffield University and the Department of Information and Library Studies at Loughborough University. The research was directed by Dr Bob Usherwood and Professor Margaret Kinnell Evans, with Eileen Milner as the project researcher.

The 'quality' context for public libraries: a review of the literature and rationale

Quality, it is important to note at the outset, is not a recent concern in public libraries. From the mid-nineteenth century, when the Select Committee on Public Libraries (1849) reported, there has been much debate, both within and beyond the profession, on how public libraries might be organized to deliver services of quality and value to the communities they exist to serve. The works of Kenyon (1927) and McColvin (1942) were instrumental in laying the foundations for the public library services that have developed in the UK since the Second World War. Changes in local government, an issue that remains important in the 1990s, have had considerable impact on public library services, with emphasis until 1992 being upon the creation of larger and more 'efficient' authorities (Wilson and Game, 1994). (See also the Background Section to this volume for discussion of this topic.)

The concept of 'quality' in public libraries can be understood through analysis of the available literature and by reference to the development and use of standards of service and performance indicators. In England and Wales a momentum for establishing national standards of provision evolved from the work of the Roberts Committee and the influence of the Bourdillon Report (Roberts, 1959; Bourdillon, 1962). The legislation enacted by the Public Libraries and Museums Act (Great Britain, 1964) provided a framework in England and Wales for the provision of public library services. This remains, despite considerable social, economic and technological change, as the major specific piece of legislation for this sector.

A recognition of the need for library services to adopt a focus on the communities that they exist to serve is evident in much of the developmental work carried out in public libraries during the 1960s and 1970s. The work of Orr (1973) is especially important in this exploration of the quality context in public libraries, for it was he who argued that all those involved in the management of libraries should ask themselves two questions:

- How good is this library?

- How much good does this library do?

Importantly, in his analysis Orr identifies the first question as relating to the *quality* of service, particularly in respect of the way in which measurable inputs impact upon service provision. Crucially, the second question he relates to the *value* created within a community by its library service. A review of the literature suggests that this separation of quality from value was evident in this sector until the 1980s. Quality is seen to refer to measurement and assessment of performance against specified criteria. Value is derived from the actual and perceived impact on end-users of a service.

The Office of Arts and Libraries (1990) provided valuable input into the development of a methodology for objective setting and performance assessment, which has been important in providing some credible linkage between quality and value. Investigations undertaken in Scotland by the Convention of Scottish Local Authorities (COSLA) (1985), and in Wales by the Welsh Office (1984), have also served to inform the emerging debate on a more holistic approach to the adoption of quality, with a particular focus resting on the importance of monitoring and reviewing performance within the context of the expressed needs and desires of end-users of the service.

In the 1990s 'Keys to Success', a manual designed by King Research Ltd. (1990) to assist public librarians in becoming familiar with and adept in the use of performance indicators, informed by wider international practice, states explicitly what the authors feel the value of the use of performance indicators is to the development of a modern public library service:

> This is a challenging time for public libraries and their staff, but also a time of great opportunity. Challenging because of budgetary restrictions and the rapid pace of change. An opportunity because new techniques and technologies make us able to reach a wider community through new and enhanced services... Performance assessment will help you plan, communicate, sort out problems before they arise, make decisions, monitor progress and justify resource allocation.

The 'challenges' identified have had, and continue to have, a considerable impact on the way in which public libraries have developed their services and the way in which they are managed. Assessment of organizational performance, closely aligned with a review of management practices and processes, is the point at which public library management practice in the 1990s begins to converge with that found in a wide range of other organizations across both the private and public sectors. In proposing to conduct research into the practice and potential of quality management in public libraries, the team sought to contribute to the greater understanding of the causes of and the opportunities and disadvantages resulting from this convergence.

The momentum for change in the public library sector has been considerable throughout the 1980s and 1990s. Change, competition, value for money and public accountability factors underpinning the public sector philosophy espoused by Conservative governments from 1979 onwards, have all impacted upon the operation of public libraries. Education and health services too, significantly, in charting the development of change in the public sector, were exposed to the introduction of the 'market' approach to service provision, prior to its implementation in other sectors. These trends and changes have already been outlined in the Background section in this volume.

The Local Government Act, 1988, set out principles which are now familiar to all those employed within local authority organizations, focusing in particular on introducing competition through the means of contracting out and competitive tendering for services (Great Britain, 1988). The public library dimension is, at the time of writing, being explored in the KPMG/Capital Planning Information investigation of possible alternative methods of public library provision other than the predominantly direct provision by local authority managed services that currently exists.

The systematic approach to data gathering within public library services pioneered by the Chartered Institute of Public Finance (CIPFA) has been developed more fully along performance management criteria by the Audit Commission (Sumsion, 1993). In addition there have been a number of local initiatives including those in Surrey, Essex and Wiltshire (Ashcroft and Wilson, 1991). However, as a means of assessing the actual 'quality' of service that they are intended to report upon, they do appear to build upon the work of Orr (1973) previously discussed, where quality is a measurement divorced from the tangible and intangible values associated with the delivery and associated benefits of the service provided. The drawbacks associated with the use of performance indicators were highlighted in the Comedia (1993) report into the future of public libraries:

> The role of the library in community development and enrichment is a vital issue, but one which is not easily amenable to current concerns with 'performance indicators'. Such techniques can easily measure book issues, turnover of book stock and other statistics, but in no way can measure the quality of the relationship between a library, its users and the geographical area it serves.(p.35)

The publication of the Citizen's Charter in 1991 is important in any consideration of the context in which quality and related issues have developed in importance in this sector (Great Britain, 1991). Wilson and Game (1994) point to the considerable influence that this document has had upon public sector organizations as a whole. An increasingly important challenge facing public libraries arises from the reductions in funding facing almost all services in the 1990s. As the demands and pressures to implement change and deliver continuous improvement continue to grow, senior managers face the dilemma of achieving more with reduced financial resources. 'Quality' in this context is a focus for much discussion within the public library sector (Milner, 1995).

Within the public library sector quality management, including its important subset of performance measurement, has therefore been the subject of much consideration and review over a period of many decades. However, there is a momentum for change and improvement in this sector the context for which has undoubtedly developed over time, but which in the 1990s, due to the influence of political imperatives and the potential of new technologies such as that presented by the Internet, has become more urgent.

Research objectives

The project had a number of significant objectives and research goals. These were formulated with the intention of ensuring a systematic and informed investigation of the existing pattern of take up and practice of quality management philosophy, tools and techniques in this sector. The research team, drawing upon their own previous studies of management issues in public libraries (Kinnell Evans, 1991; Usherwood, 1981), felt it would be significant to investigate issues of quality that impacted on organizational structures, policy development and implementation, and end-users of services. To establish the degree and type of convergence of approach and practice that had taken place, it was also considered essential to compare the experience found in public libraries against that in other organizations in the public sector and beyond that in manufacturing, commerce and service sector businesses. The intention of extending the research in this direction was to ensure that appropriate comparison across sectors was facilitated and that the 'rhetoric' of quality found in the enormous body of literature that exists on the subject could be compared with the 'reality' of organizational application.

Addressing the questions posed by Sanderson ('what is meant by quality?') and Donnelly ('what do you as public library managers want from quality?') provided a further focus for the work of the research team (Sanderson, 1992; Donnelly, 1995). Ownership and definition of quality were felt to be important considerations in a study of a sector where there are a number of significant stakeholders, including Elected Members, Customers or Users, Employees and the Local Authority. Investigating perceptions of what 'quality' is and what various stakeholders feel constitutes a quality library service were established, at the outset of the project, as being key research objectives.

The objectives and research goals of the project may be summarized as follows:

- To define quality management in a public library context, taking account of the important difference in perceptions that may exist between various stakeholders.

- To ascertain the approach, scope and methodology employed in practising quality management in the public library sector.

- Through extensive literature searching and data collection to chart a path through the 'quality management maze' (Foster and Whittle, 1989).

- To investigate quality management in terms of the three inter-linked areas of organizational issues, end-user issues and policy issues.

- Through case study investigations to study the practice of quality management in a number of public library services and addition-ally in organizations drawn from a range of other sectors, to identify 'best practice' and barriers to implementation.

- To disseminate the research findings widely to the profession in order to support and facilitate appropriate developments in the management of public libraries.

Defining quality management

Many definitions of the word 'quality' and the term 'quality manage-ment' exist. Some of these have already been discussed in the Back-ground Section in this volume. The research team, in identifying the wide range that exists, sought through investigation of the available literature and consultation with practitioners in the public library sector, to identify the extent to which any one formal definition or composite of many definitions might be particularly appropriate to this sector. The difficulty associated with seeking any such meaningful definition lies in the problematic nature of pinning down such a nebulous term into a precise and appropriate description of the complex and sometimes diverse philosophy and methodology underpinning it.

As has already been suggested above, the question of who amongst a variety of stakeholders in an organization is responsible for defining what quality is, and how that impacts upon the development of a quality oriented service, is recognized as being an important issue. Whether it is possible or desirable in a public library context to adopt the 'definition' put forward by British Airways, a highly successful business at the forefront of the practice of quality management in the UK, is open to question: 'quality is what the customer says it is' (BA, 1995).

For public sector organizations the number of stakeholders present and the degree to which end-users have realistic and informed expecta-tions of quality of service, is a major consideration in the development of definitions and appropriate methodologies. An indication of the problematic nature of allowing end-users to determine what constitutes quality of service is highlighted in two publications. In the *Review of Public Library Service in England and Wales* much research evidence is offered to support the view that during a decade of reductions in funding, when many senior managers have felt there has been a consequent diminution of service quality, users have felt it has improved (Aslib, 1995). Similarly, in the secondary education sector, there is evidence to suggest that decisions relating to the choice of secondary school made by parents and their children took little account of factors beyond external examination results (Phoenix Research Ltd., 1993).

The contrast exhibited in the definition and expectations of end-users or customers and that of professional managers and other stakeholders such as Elected Members, illustrates the complexity of working towards any definition of quality in the public sector. Indeed it is appropriate to ask whose 'quality' is most important and is consensus attainable when a wide range of perceptions must be considered?

The work of Stebbing (1990) and Morgan and Murgatroyd (1994) both offer useful perspectives on the way in which features unique to public sector organizations can be identified within a quality management context. Referring to these works it is possible to identify public libraries as being providers of services, many of which can be classified as intangible, inasmuch as the interaction involved cannot be meaningfully counted, measured or planned for in advance of delivery to ensure consistent quality of service delivery. Additionally, public libraries serve people with very heterogeneous needs; for example, within the population of those who borrow fiction books there will be a wide variety of demands and expectations. A further distinct feature of a library service when defining quality is its inseparability, by which is meant, argue Morgan and Murgatroyd (1994):

> ...that the production and consumption of services are not separate as they are in manufacturing. As a consequence... quality is not engineered into the product at the manufacturing plant and then delivered intact to the consumer. Rather quality occurs during the delivery of the service, usually during the interaction between the client and the key contact person from the service provider.(p.10)

In this scenario, then, quality is dependent on the interaction between the organization, through most usually a frontline member of staff, and the end-user. Such a description does offer a useful perspective in a consideration of why user satisfaction with public library services should have improved during a period of considerable financial constraint; it may in fact be alerting practitioners to the high value that end-users put upon the 'quality' of interaction with frontline employees, rather than access to the resources of the library. Most users, of course, will be in a better position to judge the quality of this interaction than that of, say, the bookstock as a whole.

'Fitness for purpose' is found to be a key component of many definitions, as discussed earlier in the Background Section, and is particularly closely aligned with the development and use of formal quality standards. Total Quality Management (TQM) is yet a further dimension in the overall philosophy of quality management. Oakland (1994b) identifies TQM as being based upon four key components: management commitment;, having a documented quality control system; Statistical Process Control; and teamwork. He identifies thirteen vital 'Steps to TQM':

- Understanding Quality
- Commitment to Quality
- Policy on Quality
- Organization for Quality
- Management of the costs of Quality
- Planning for Quality
- Design for Quality
- System for Quality
- Capability for Quality
- Control for Quality
- Teamwork for Quality
- Training for Quality
- Implementation of TQM

Performance management and quality assurance are both areas that initial analysis of the research literature and data would suggest underpin the philosophy of quality management. Informing decision making through the systematic collection and review of data relating to performance and reliability emerged as a key driver in almost all of the definitions of quality investigated by the research team. For the public library sector a useful context to the issue of measurement and assurance was offered in the Wiltshire County Council Library and Museum Service publication, 'Performing for People' (Pybus, 1994):

> The term 'performance indicators' can so easily be damaged by its misuse when referring to pure statistics. The Citizen's Charter initiative and the performance indicators required by the Audit Commission from public libraries are not performance indicators, they are statistical statements. They also have little practical value as they cannot be used in any effective way to monitor the effectiveness of the service, nor do they really inform the local managers either at officer or member level of performance successes or failures.(p.2)

The same document continues by explaining why this particular element of quality management, used to its full potential, could be such an effective tool for public library managers:

> As we move into a more commercial and competitive environment, management's needs are likely to change. Not only will we need to monitor services to maintain quality and quantity, but we are likely to need to ensure that we know what we are recording and what targets we are setting.

In charting a path through the many definitions and components that comprise what is referred to as quality management, the diversity and contrast of approach is therefore striking.

In conducting a review of available definitions and components of quality management, the project team sought, at all times, to relate each dimension identified to the particular characteristics that distinguish a public library service from the primarily commercial sector organizations which have provided, in the main, the test bed for the development of the majority of definitions and concepts associated with this philosophy. Conscious that any final 'definition' should be informed by the wide ranging data collection and analysis outlined in the research objectives (see above), the team did not formulate a precise definition at the outset of the project. What was considered helpful, however, was to establish what was perceived to be the relationship between quality assurance and performance measurement and the overarching philosophy of quality management. The underpinning role of assurance and measurement in the quality management equation was identified in a wide variety of publications, reflecting practice in both public and private sectors, was recognized and incorporated into the research framework at this relatively early stage and is represented in Figure 1.

Figure 1: The role of assurance and measurement in quality management

**Quality Assurance—
the 'Bedrock' of Quality Management**

Research methodology

A review of the many definitions of quality management had highlighted the potential difficulty of establishing authoritatively what constituted current and potential best practice for the public library sector. In order that the research objectives could be properly addressed it was decided to draw upon a wide range of data and perspectives. In doing so it was the intention of the team to establish with some clarity the current practice of quality management in this sector and to facilitate comparison with chosen benchmarks in a range of other organizations. Throughout the duration of the project the team sought through consultation with practitioners and publications in the academic and professional press to promote an awareness of and interest in the research and its objectives.

The methodology used a number of distinct components, as described below.

Consultation

In order to ensure that the research objectives were formulated in such a way that they addressed the major issues of concern to practitioners in the public library sector, it was considered essential to consult widely. Professional groups and practitioners made a substantial contribution during this stage of the work.

A literature review

In order that any definition formulated by the project team was tested against the body of literature on the subject, it was important to undertake an extensive review of the literature. Identification and access to the many thousands of publications that directly and indirectly form the ever growing body of literature in this area was helped considerably through the team having access to the Institute of Management's Management Information Centre. A considered examination of the publications available which were felt to have some value for public libraries was published by the research team shortly after the commencement of the project so that practitioners could benefit from this stage of work (Milner *et al.*, 1994). It was also thought that this, at least in part, would fulfil the need to develop and sustain the interest and cooperation of public library managers for the public library debate.

A survey

A survey of all public library authorities in the UK was carried out in the Autumn of 1994, by means of a postal questionnaire, designed with the help of John Sumsion, then Director of Loughborough University's Library and Information Statistics Unit (LISU). A number of public library practitioners also 'piloted' the questionnaire and provided valuable feedback to the team on its design and content. The questionnaire was sent to heads of public library services for completion. The overall response rate was 85 per cent. Returned questionnaires were analyzed using the SPSS/X package with variables of size of authority in terms of population served, type of authority and country within the UK being considered. Table 1 shows the variation in response rate in the UK, together with the adoption rate identified by respondents of a formal system of quality management.

Table 1: Questionnaire distribution and response rate

Authority	Distributed	% Returns Received	Yes: Formal Policy % Responses	Policy in Preparation % Responses	No Policy % Responses
English Counties	39	87%	21%	18%	48%
English Metropolitan	36	94%	17%	11%	66%
London Boroughs	33	75%	22%	12%	41%
Scotland	41	85%	7%	17%	61%
Wales	13	77%	23%	8%	46%
N. Ireland	5	80%	40%	20%	20%

The questionnaire (reproduced in Appendix A) considered the following issues:

- Elements of quality management being practised;

- Who was responsible for managing quality;

- What systems were in place to facilitate quality management;

- The advantages and disadvantages perceived to come from the adoption of quality management;

- What was perceived to constitute a 'quality' public library service.

Responses to Questions 15 and 16 dealing with perceptions of the benefits and disadvantages of quality management were analyzed separately so that the diverse views could be fully recorded and incorporated into the research data.

Parasuraman's SERVQUAL model was used to establish a credible view of what senior practitioners felt the most important attributes of a 'quality' public library service were (Parasuraman *et al.*, date). Question 10 gave respondents a list of statements which related to a number of important potential determinants of service quality. These included:

- Reliability of service;

- Responsiveness to customer needs;
- Competence of those delivering the service;
- The quality of the interaction between employee and customer;
- The way in which customers are informed and consulted;
- The physical appearance of and access to buildings and facilities.

Those responding were asked to make a judgement for each statement offered, indicating how essential they felt it was in creating an 'excellent' library service. At the end of this question, respondents were given the opportunity to identify the five aspects of service which they thought most needed improvement in their own authority.

SERVQUAL was developed for use in the retail sector and has been adapted for research in a number of service sector organizations. However, throughout its ten-year history there has been a debate amongst theorists as to whether the preferential approach to quality that it suggests is appropriate for the service sector, rather than the more objective approach put forward by the majority of theorists on the subject. Webster (1994) offers a particularly good analysis of the strengths and weaknesses of the model. Its primary importance to this project was that it gave a clear picture of what public library managers felt were the most and least essential ingredients of a quality oriented service. However, in using it as a tool to explore the preferences of managers, rather than users/customers, we were breaking new ground with the SERVQUAL model. Most research to date has concentrated on establishing the essential features of a service from the viewpoint of the customer. It is likely that the work undertaken here will be much further developed by the BLRIC funded research project directed by George Philip at Queens University in Belfast (already mentioned in the Introduction to this volume), with an investigation into the applicability of the SERVQUAL model for the whole of the library and information sector.

Case studies

A number of detailed case study investigations were undertaken to identify best practice in a range of sectors. In total, twenty-four organizations took part in this stage of the research; all of them were guaranteed anonymity in research publications, although short profiles of each can be found in Appendix D. Of those cooperating, twelve were public library authorities in England or Wales; the remaining twelve were drawn from the commercial, industrial and not-for-profit sectors. Case study authorities in the public library sector were selected on a number of criteria:

- That the authority had completed a questionnaire and indicated a willingness to participate in the next stage of the research (78 per cent of respondents to the questionnaire did in fact volunteer).

- That the twelve authorities selected would reflect the range of local government organizations in England and Wales (Counties, Metropolitan authorities and London Boroughs).

- The authorities were chosen to reflect a range of experience of and commitment to quality management as indicated by the questionnaire responses.

Case study visits to individual authorities normally involved interviews with:

- A senior manager;
- A 'middle' manager;
- A library assistant;
- An Elected Member.

A schedule of questions was prepared for each of these groups, to establish current levels of adoption of quality management and personal perceptions as to the degree of success and confidence felt in current practices. The project did encounter some difficulty in gaining access to Elected Members (7 of the 12 responding authorities were able to facilitate interviews). The main reason given for this was that when approached Members had felt they would not be able to add anything to the contributions made by the members of staff interviewed.

Non-library case studies

The twelve non-library organizations were selected by using a different methodology. The literature search had indicated that the practice of quality management in the UK could not be analyzed successfully by simply breaking comparisons down in terms of 'private' and 'public' sector. A diverse range of approach was identified within a wide variety of sectors. Drawing on the evidence of the practice of quality management found in the literature and wishing to ensure that a wide range of approaches and organizational structures were incorporated, it was considered desirable to conduct case study investigations in the following sectors:

- The retail sector;
- The manufacturing sector;
- The privatized utilities;
- The National Health Service;
- The library supply industry;
- The financial services sector;
- Local government organizations with no public library responsibility;
- Service industries, including transport, hospitality and private healthcare.

Case studies in the non-library sector involved a structured interview with a senior manager responsible for quality and whatever other learning and investigative opportunities the organization felt able to offer the project team. All of the organizations offered an insight into their own best practice and also the areas where failures had occurred. Many organizations also offered the team the opportunity to join in staff training sessions and to meet other personnel involved with the implementation of initiatives.

Quality Management Workshop

In order to test previous findings and obtain further data a project workshop was held. Over forty senior public library managers took part, along with the research team, and representatives from the BLRIC, the Library Association, the CBI and a number of the non-library organizations which were supporting the research. Attendance at the workshop was by invitation with delegates selected on the basis of questionnaire responses; a wish to reflect a variety of adoption patterns was considered important. Additionally, a number of delegates were drawn from the case studies conducted in the public library sector. The programme for the workshop is reproduced in Appendix C. The workshop gave rise to stimulating debate and the opportunity for delegates to challenge the interim findings of the research team which were based upon analysis of questionnaire responses and case study data. The discussions conducted in each of the workshop groupings were documented and incorporated in the research data (Milner *et al.*, 1995b).

Generation and testing of hypotheses

Hypotheses emerging from the consultation process, literature searching and responses to the questionnaire were formulated prior to undertaking case study visits and holding the Quality Management Workshop. These were:

- Quality management, defined in a wide variety of ways, was having a limited degree of impact on the management and operation of public library services;

- Change factors within local government and the public library sector were making a focus on 'quality' ever more important;

- Quality management might offer those adopting it positive improvements and benefits.

Reformulation of hypotheses

Analysis of the available literature and responses to the project questionnaire gave the team the foundations to establish hypotheses that would later be challenged and tested against the experience of practitioners. The programme of case study visits added a rich dimension of organizational understanding and the personal perceptions of a range of stakeholders to the data. Further to this, the project workshop served to provide a forum to challenge the original hypotheses and to develop the final conclusions and recommendations. The perceptual information gathered was especially useful in developing and enriching the considerable body of other data gathered and generated by the team, which included a range of documents relating to quality generated by a number of individual library authorities.

Conclusions and recommendations

Having developed a methodology designed to achieve the objectives set out above, the team sought to draw the various strands together to reach conclusions based upon the analysis and consideration of all the available data. It was felt to be important at this stage to arrive at a definition of quality management that reflected both the scope and potential of the philosophy for practitioners. The extent to which quality management represented a means by which change and improvement could be achieved in the public library sector was also an important consideration at the final stage of data analysis. The process of consultation undertaken with public library managers had identified a desire on their part that the project make specific recommendations. These should be appropriate and attainable strategies for developing, adapting and practising quality management within their operating constraints.

Figure 2 gives an outline of the research design and the way in which the different elements were combined. The design highlights the importance of both qualitative and quantitative research methods to the work of the project.

Figure 2: Outline of the research design

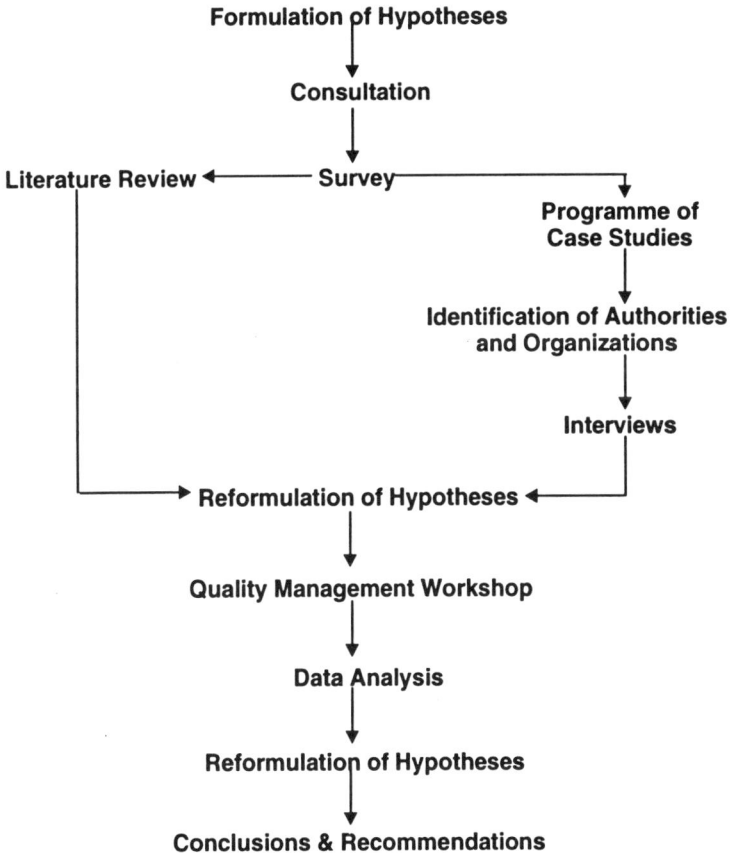

Where are we now? Quality management in UK public libraries

Introduction

In our outline of the methodology we indicated that consultation and data collection through both questionnaire and case study visits would form the basis of our analysis. Given that 85 per cent of all UK public library authorities responded to the questionnaire (reproduced in Appendix A), and that the twelve case studies selected in this sector were representative of a cross-section of experiences of quality management, these data provide a snapshot of the extent to which quality management has been adopted.

Policy issues

The questionnaire began by asking respondents to specify whether their library service had a written policy on 'quality' and also whether the local authority of which they were part had one. As Figure 3 illustrates, there is some degree of correlation between the take up patterns for the local authorities and public library services. The percentage of local authorities having an existing policy or being in the process of developing one was some 37 per cent, whilst in public libraries the figure was 33 per cent. Analysis of the type of library authorities having or preparing a written policy showed that in the English counties the percentage was some 39 per cent, in the London Boroughs 34 per cent, Metropolitan authorities 28 per cent, Scottish authorities 24 per cent, Wales 31 per cent and Northern Ireland 40 per cent. Of those authorities responding to our questionnaire, five public library services, comprising three English counties, one Metropolitan and one Welsh public library service, indicated that they had a policy in place, whilst their local authority either did not, or was in the process of preparing one. Case study visits to two of the twelve authorities cooperating with the project highlighted in-

Figure 3: Who has a policy on quality management?

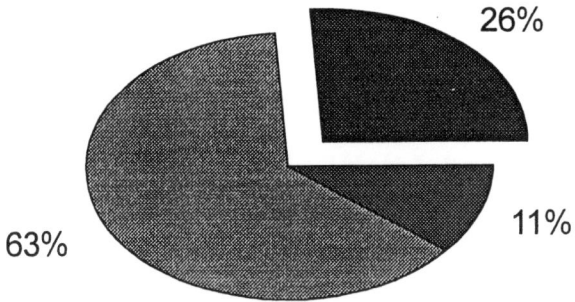

26%

11%

63%

LOCAL AUTHORITIES

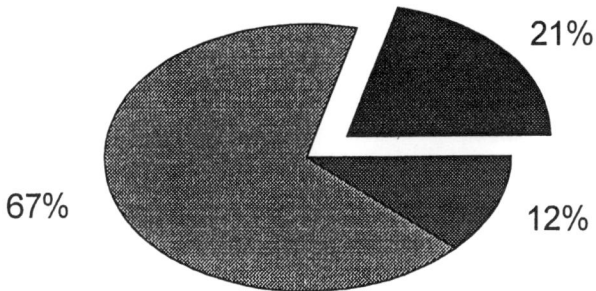

21%

12%

67%

PUBLIC LIBRARY SERVICES

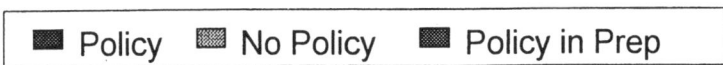

■ Policy ▨ No Policy ■ Policy in Prep

stances where developments within the library service had acted as a catalyst to authority-wide adoption of quality management. In one, where the Director had been in post for a decade and had been promoting the adoption of quality management throughout this period, the view expressed was that:

> The County Council as a whole really only pays lip service to quality; libraries are perceived very much to be a lead department...Long before the Government came out with charters, we put together our own series of standards, involving all levels of staff and from this we developed our mission and objectives.

In three other services senior library managers were members of policy and strategy groups charged with the responsibility of developing quality management on an authority-wide basis.

Question 3 asked respondents to specify whether they had, or were in the process of setting up, a formal quality programme. A large majority of authorities, some 62 per cent of those who responded, indicated that they did not have a programme in place. Of those who indicated that they did, their adoption pattern is shown in Table 2.

Table 2: Breakdown of library authorities having or preparing a formal quality programme

Authority	Yes: Programme	In preparation
English Counties	21%	23%
English Metropolitan	14%	17%
London Boroughs	19%	18%
Scotland	9%	11%
Wales	12%	6%
Northern Ireland	20%	20%

Where a written policy on quality and/or programme existed, the research team wanted to establish who had been involved in its original formulation. Question 5 on the project questionnaire listed six potential contributors to the development of a formal policy on quality. Of those authorities that had or were developing policies, 97 per cent had involved senior management, 69 per cent middle management, 53 per cent frontline employees, 33 per cent Elected Members, 29 per cent users or customers of the service, and 7 per cent external consultants. Elected Member involvement was highest in the London Boroughs, while the use of external consultancy was cited only by respondents from the English county authorities.

In considering where the impetus for adopting quality management had originated, the case study data provided a clear picture of the variation that existed. Of the twelve case study authorities, three cited the impetus as coming from the Head of the Library Service. In two of these authorities the Head of Service had been in post for more than ten years, in the other for less than two years.

Six authorities, comprising four English counties, one London Borough and a Welsh county, identified the original interest in quality management as emanating from the Chief Executive of the authority. Invariably, in these authorities, the Chief Executive had been appointed within the last two years. One case study interviewee commented on a Chief Executive taking a 'hands on' approach:

> The push for quality management came from the new Chief Executive who was keen to promote greater customer focus and improved public relations. He personally carried out an audit of all public service points and highlighted what he saw as the very poor quality of the library service. What it actually meant was that I had to find money to buy plants and guiding. The staff were quite cynical about the whole thing—they viewed it as window dressing. He has repeated the exercise again this year and the library service was perceived to have done much better.

In the remaining three case study authorities, the role of the Elected Members was identified as having been pivotal in moving the library service towards quality management. In these authorities, where political power rested variously with Conservative, Liberal Democrat and Independent councillors, those interviewed felt that the Elected Members were bringing to the authorities their own experiences as proprietors or managers of enterprises outside the public sector. In developing policies which Officers then had to implement, there was, however, a degree of disquiet expressed by some interviewees that Members did not accept Pollit's view that 'managing public services is different' (Pollitt and Harrison, 1992).

A public library senior manager described the development of policy in the following way:

> The Elected Members at the time had a certain view of how local government should operate; largely, it involved moving us onto a more businesslike footing. They were in the driving seat, really.

An interview with another Elected Member, in an authority where a new Chief Executive had provided the focus for the development of quality management, supports the above view:

> Quality management wasn't initiated by Members, but many of us will draw upon experiences from other areas of our work. We are there to represent the electorate and to preserve and improve services for them. Members therefore like theories and policies to be set in the context of how they actually impact on people.

All of the Elected Members interviewed were concerned with the need to provide services which had relevance for the communities they served.

Formal systems

Public library managers were asked to identify which, if any, from a range of formal approaches and standards relating to quality management, their authority had implemented. The adoption of formal quality standards is one method employed by many organizations in other sectors to give a focus and direction to their implementation of quality management. Establishing the extent and nature of the take up pattern of more 'formal' approaches to quality in public libraries was considered to be important in building a comparison with the practice found in other organizations. Figure 4 illustrates that almost half of all the authorities which responded to our questionnaire had no involvement with a standard or formal model. The adoption pattern displayed by the remaining authorities did not show what a review of the literature associated with formal quality programmes suggested—namely, that British and ISO standards have dominated in a wide range of business sectors (Wilkinson *et al.*, 1993).

The British Standard 5750, now more correctly referred to as the ISO Standard, has, as our research indicated, established a reputation as a

Figure 4: Adoption rates for 'formalized' quality initiatives

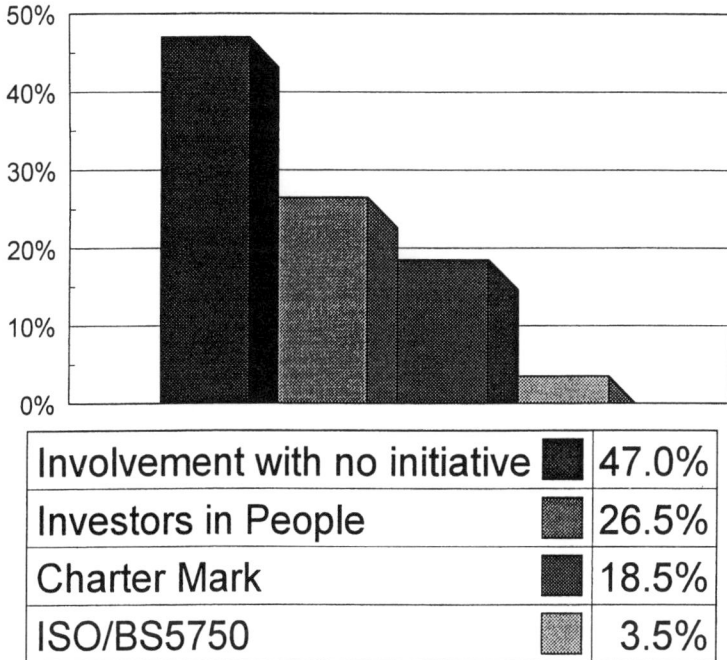

50%	

Involvement with no initiative	■	47.0%
Investors in People	■	26.5%
Charter Mark	■	18.5%
ISO/BS5750	▨	3.5%

means of improving processes, systems and overall quality of operation in many areas of business. Addressing the arguments in favour of applying the standard in the library and information sector, Brophy (1994), Johannsen (1993), and Ellis and Norton (1993) have been persuasive in their identification of the benefits associated with its adoption. However, Jackson and Ashton (1993) and Rooney (1991), who undertake a broader review of the range of sectors in which the standard might be applied, question its applicability to organizations in the public and service sectors. Their argument is that whilst it is relatively easy to assure the quality of administration and procedures, what this will actually demonstrate about the quality of service provided is negligible. Our own case study investigations did not involve any library services that were considering the adoption of BS 5750/ISO 9000. It is interesting to note, in this context, that although very little interest in this standard was revealed by either the questionnaire or case study data, the project team did receive five telephone enquiries from library managers who, having been made aware that the research was ongoing, sought the advice of team members as to whether their interest in quality management as practitioners would be enhanced by ISO 9000. There was little other evidence to suggest that this standard was likely to gain widespread interest or adoption in the public library service. A senior library manager encapsulated the view expressed by over 90 per cent of senior manager interviewees in this sector: '...adopting something as rigid as BS 5750 is far more likely to prevent change than encourage it'.

This contrasted with the relatively high adoption rate of Investors in People, which was formally established only in 1991. Originally a Department of Trade and Industry initiative, the promotion and accreditation process of the award is now administered independently in cooperation with the regionally based Training and Enterprise Councils. Its core concept lies in the connection that is made between linking human resource development (HRD) into an organization's learning and improvement cycle, with the requirement that HRD focuses not only on individuals but also on teams. Training, central to Deming's vision of quality management, is highlighted as being vital for organizational success. Both Finn (1994) and Spilsbury (1994) identify its popularity in a variety of sectors, including the public, as arising from the design of the award scheme to recognize that all investment in training and staff development must be evaluated against the organization's strategies and mission and within the constraints of resources available.

The first Investors in People award in the public library sector was made to Gloucestershire in 1995. Our research uncovered a high degree of satisfaction amongst the case study authorities working towards it. Of the total group, three library services were registered for the award, a further three were participating alongside other departments in an authority-wide initiative, and the remaining six had an interest in, but no formal links to, the award. Analysis of the distribution of authorities responding to the questionnaire that were registered or considering registering for the award revealed the greatest interest being evident in the English counties and the least in Northern Ireland and Scotland. With the cooperation of Investors UK, the managing body responsible for national administration of the award, it was possible to confirm that the regional and authority trends identified by the team were in line with their own analysis of adoption in all sectors. Amongst those not registered, there was some indication that positive feedback from colleagues in other authorities was causing them to consider the adoption of Investors in People. As one interviewee explained:

> We are not convinced of its [IiP's] value, although I must admit my view is perhaps changing. We need to look at the whole issue of buying into external badging.

The Charter Mark scheme, which 18.5 per cent of respondents had either attained or were working towards, has been operating since 1991, with the first awards made in 1992. Its stated objective is 'to recognize and reward excellence in the delivery of public services' (Great Britain, 1994). Organizations which wish to apply for the award are judged by a panel, usually comprising senior executives from large private sector organizations. There are nine explicit criteria against which submissions are judged; these are:

- Standards: the organization must set performance standards and publicize them
- Information and openness
- Courtesy and helpfulness
- Value for money
- Measurable improvements in quality of service over the last two years
- Putting things right
- Choice and consultation
- Customer satisfaction
- To deliver one innovative enhancement to services without any extra cost to the taxpayer or consumer.

The award is not made to organizations in perpetuity but must be considered every three years by a panel, who decide whether an organization is to be allowed to maintain its Charter Mark. As yet no organization has had the award withdrawn, although British Gas has been threatened with this sanction due to the large increase in the number of complaints received from customers.

Case study visits revealed that two of the library authorities had made applications for the award, one successfully, the other not. In the authority that had attained the Charter Mark considerable benefits were felt to have accrued from the actual process of making a systematic application, with the result that a formal focus on quality was explored to a greater degree than ever before. Three specific benefits were identified as resulting from the achievement of the award:

- Increased employee morale
- Opportunities for positive public relations
- Establishment of links with other award winners in the area.

In the authority that had not received the award there were no plans to resubmit documentation to the Charter Mark panel. The impetus to make an application had come from the Chief Executive in the first instance with the Head of Library Service being reluctant to devote valuable time and other resources to the award process. The feeling expressed was:

> We know that we meet and surpass all the award criteria. However, what the judges seem to be interested in is just how glossy your presentation is. I simply could not justify spending huge sums on making videos and having colour brochures printed. Our staff would resent it and I am not too sure that our customers would be impressed at our having an award but no books to fill the shelves or OPACs for them to get the best out of the service.

Formal quality systems, our data suggested, were not closely linked in the minds of practitioners in the public library sector with the attainment of a 'quality' oriented library service. A Head of Service interviewed encapsulated the prevailing opinion identified by the project team:

> Our customers don't care whether we have ISO accreditation or a Charter Mark. They are concerned with the quality of service provided for them and the skill and courtesy of the employees with whom they are in contact. That is where we concentrate our efforts.

Customer focus

Whilst the questionnaire data gave some indication of the way in which public library services regarded and sought to involve their customers or users, the main investigations in this important area were undertaken in case study visits and in discussions at the project Workshop. Discussions with employees of library services, operating at all levels, indicated that in the majority the concept of the 'customer', at least as a term in common use, was widespread. The prevailing attitude expressed by those senior managers attending the Workshop appeared to indicate that the use of the word 'customer' had grown considerably as it provided a focus for emphasizing the contract between the end-user and service provider.

However, in interviews with Elected Members it became apparent that the terminology associated with increased customer focus had generated intense political debate. Of the seven Members interviewed, the only resounding support for the use of the term in libraries came from a Conservative councillor. In one authority, an English county, the Member, whilst stressing that the service must be focused on the needs of 'users', revealed that the committee had vetoed the use of the term 'customer'; the reason given was that 'it smacks too much of buying a pound of sugar'.

Delegates to the project Workshop and employees interviewed during case studies were, however, reasonably philosophical about how end-users were described, with one senior manager reflecting the views expressed by many:

> I don't think that the people who use our library service care very much what we call them as long as they are receiving an excellent service. 'Customer' is a useful word to hang a change of public service attitude on, but it is frankly not worth the hours of debate that have been devoted to it.

The increasing centrality and importance in service planning and delivery of the needs and desires of end-users was identified in two-thirds of the case studies undertaken as representing the greatest change in the operation of library services over the past decade. Frontline and middle managers in all authorities visited expressed, albeit to varying degrees, the way in which the needs of the end-user had become the primary driver in their work. A middle manager in an English county highlighted the degree of change that had been observed:

> We would like to think that we have always provided a quality library service to our users, the difference now is that customer expectations are being taken into account. Previously things only happened if there was some degree

of professional consensus. What has happened, although it needs to be expanded even more, is that the views of users are being regarded as important. The quality of service is at long last being defined in terms of what the end-user actually wants.

Whilst no senior managers taking part in the research project suggested that they disagreed with the concept of customer focus, a number expressed the view that they felt it would be dangerous to give it too much importance in the service planning and decision making process. The reason for this was set out by a senior manager in an English county:

> If we based our decision making on what our customers tell us they want we would end up with a very imbalanced service. Of course their views are taken into account, but professional judgement has to be allowed to take priority when important decisions are under consideration.

A survey of the literature indicated that a considerable degree of divergence was apparent on the question of the degree of importance assigned to the role of the customer in influencing organizational decision making. Two different viewpoints are offered by Peters (1992) and Freemantle (1993). Peters expressed the view that good decision making must only take account of customer focus and not be dictated by it, while Freemantle stated that it must be the guiding focus of all organizations.

Adoption of the 'tools' of quality management

The combined questionnaire and case study data showed that 62 per cent of respondents in public library services perceived that they had no formal involvement with the practice of quality management. However, consultation undertaken by the team prior to other data analysis had indicated that there had been extensive adoption of various recognized 'tools' of quality in this sector. Practitioners either did not perceive these as being constituent parts of quality management, or did not wish to have them identified as such. The team therefore felt it particularly important to establish a credible view of the extent of the adoption of the practice of quality management techniques in public libraries, to explore in some detail the true pattern of adoption.

Question 6 listed eight strands of management practice which the team's extensive review of the literature indicated were important 'tools' of quality in the 1990s. Respondents were asked to identify whether they were practising or preparing to implement all or any of the eight listed: management by function; cost centres; localized decision making; flatter management structures; staff appraisal; performance indicators; management information systems; team working.

Management by function

Management by function, as opposed to senior responsibility being assigned on a geographical basis, for example by area, was identified by 19 per cent of respondents. Almost all activity in this area was revealed to be taking place in the English counties. Case study visits reflected this adoption pattern, with the Shire counties visited revealing the only significant movement towards adoption in the last five years. In the London Borough and Metropolitan authority case studies, where the geographic spread of services is less extensive than that found in the other authorities surveyed, the team identified management by function as having been in place for a considerable period of time. However, in two of these three services, respondents had not identified it on their original questionnaire response as being in place, the reason given being that this was so much part of established organizational structures that it did not fit with the 'new' concept of quality management.

Cost centres

The use of cost centres to improve organizational accountability and improve the efficiency and effectiveness of resource planning, allocation and monitoring was widespread in its adoption, particularly in England and Wales. In total, 59 per cent of respondents had assigned cost centres and a further 10 per cent were preparing to do so. Case study visits revealed that eight of the twelve authorities had cost centres in place; in two of these the original impetus had come from the directive of the Finance Director of the authority as a whole. The management of resources in this way was identified by one middle manager in an English county as:

> ...giving some teeth to the notion of having more decision making at local level. Cost centres actually mean that we can manage and monitor expenditure meaningfully at a local level.

An alternative view came from a Head of Service who, although an advocate of the adoption of quality management, felt that the use of individual cost centres was 'just a meaningless accounting technique that isn't likely to deliver any real quality improvements'.

Localized decision making

The extent to which localized decision making had been adopted was of considerable interest, especially when compared to the adoption rate identified for cost centres. It also gave some perspective on the extent to which the concept of employee empowerment was accepted and practised in this sector. The questionnaire identified 46 per cent of authorities as having already moved to a more decentralized approach to decision making, with a further 45 per cent preparing to do so. Of those authorities which had already moved in this direction the greatest level of take up was evident in the London Boroughs and English counties. Those authorities preparing to adopt this approach were spread throughout the authorities and regions surveyed, with Scotland and Northern Ireland featuring to a higher degree than they had done in other elements of this question.

Case study interviews added a rich and valuable perspective to the examination of this component of quality management. Interviews with the three members of staff and one Elected Member highlighted the fact that whilst the questionnaire data might indicate that much of the public library sector would acknowledge the move towards localized decision making as a 'good thing', the reality of practice occasionally appeared to be very different. In two authorities, one London Borough and one English county, Elected Members declared themselves to have a high degree of preference for maintaining as much decision making and control as possible at the centre, with one stating that:

> We do not expect our senior managers to delegate planning and important day to day decisions to more junior staff. It just doesn't serve the best interests of the public to have decisions being made by staff who don't have the 'whole' picture of the service and its needs.

Delegates to the Quality Management Workshop identified the importance, in delegating decision making to a local level, of providing employees with clear guidelines as to the scope of permitted decision making and, within that, supporting staff and encouraging a 'no blame' culture when decisions were not successful. In practice, many middle managers and frontline staff interviewed, whilst acknowledging that their service had 'signed up' to the use of localized decision making, felt that the way in which it had been implemented and operated marred its success. A middle manager cited the following example drawn from personal experience:

> We were told by the senior management team to encourage frontline staff to take decisions on the spot in matters of dispute over minor fines and other areas of difficulty with customers. In theory that sounds fine, but I was uncomfortable with the fact that no training, apart from the limited amount that I could provide in 'on the job' situations, was provided. Unfortunately, two of the first decisions resulting from this policy resulted in difficulties and customer complaints and it has to be said that those staff involved were not supported in any way by the senior managers who got involved. Needless to say, my staff are quite wary and to some degree cynical about the whole business.

The criteria for success identified at the Workshop appeared to have a degree of resonance for current practice, particularly in the extent to which many of those interviewed felt that much of the potential to achieve organizational improvement through the adoption of localized decision making was being dissipated through inadequate training and senior management support. Both Lovell (1994) and Pasmore (1994), in their considerations of the use of localized decision making structures in a wide range of sectors, identify the adoption of successful implementation strategies as being crucial to the success of quality management.

Flatter management structures

The introduction of flatter management structures has been identified by Stebbing (1990) as one of the major areas of the implementation of quality management in the service and public sectors. Questionnaire data provided evidence that 49 per cent of responding authorities had already implemented this and 4 per cent were working towards it. Case study and Workshop analysis of this question identified two key imperatives which were driving the adoption of management structures: there were fewer 'senior' managers, and the role of those who had previously been perceived to be operating at 'middle' manager level had increased in importance. The increasing importance of middle managers in this sector contrasts with the view put forward by Peters (1992) that their role would diminish in the 1990s.

The financial imperative to reduce the operating costs of public library services in times of considerable public sector financial constraint had meant that many senior managers, often those with many years of experience, had been offered the option to take early retirement with their posts disappearing after they had left. Nine of the case studies undertaken revealed instances where the senior management team had been reduced in size with responsibilities being reallocated to existing members or delegated away from the centre. In two English counties, management teams were identified as reducing in size over a five-year period, from a membership of six to three in one instance and two in another. Those remaining senior managers identified the commensurate increase in workload as being considerable. Middle and frontline staff perceived this 'stretching' of their senior staff as being detrimental to service quality, with one middle manager saying that:

> Of course they must accept that responsibility is very much part of the territory they enter when they take on these posts, but the workload that our senior team are carrying means that they find it very hard to take a clear view of anything and follow through on their decision making. The opportunity for consultation with employees is marginalized by pressure of time and at the end of the day I can't see how we can move forward until there is some clarity and thoughtful application on their part. At the moment there is muddle and panic.

The adoption of a decentralized approach to service provision, with more autonomy being exercised by individual or groups of libraries, and the move in some authorities to the adoption of a client and contractor split in service provision, were also identified as having brought about a flattening in management structures. Case study interviews encountered two authorities where a client and contractor split had contributed to the considerable reduction in the number of senior managers employed. Both middle and frontline staff felt that there was some lack of guiding vision in the service. Contracts and specifications were not felt to substitute entirely for the support and sense of direction that was felt to have existed under previous management structures. Middle managers, in particular, expressed their dissatisfaction that, whilst their responsibilities had increased considerably, rarely had salaries or gradings reflected this.

Staff appraisal

Questionnaire data revealed that systems of staff appraisal were operated by 40 per cent of responding authorities with 21 per cent preparing to implement one. The pattern of existing and proposed adoption of appraisal schemes is revealed in Table 3. Investigation of this issue undertaken in both case studies and in Workshop debate revealed that a majority of appraisal schemes, when they existed, involved 'professional' staff only. This mirrored the findings of the research conducted by Fletcher (1993). However, in authorities where schemes were identified as being prepared for implementation there was a positive emphasis upon involving all staff. Seven of the senior managers interviewed indicated that they were not appraised themselves, their authorities as a whole having no commitment to the concept.

Table 3: The adoption of staff appraisal schemes

Authority	Yes: Scheme	Scheme in preparation
English Counties	52%	31%
English Metropolitan	42%	24%
London Boroughs	43%	24%
Scotland	39%	23%
Wales	44%	24%
Northern Ireland	20%	0%

Performance indicators

The area of performance indicators was one where a high degree of adoption was expected due to the Audit Commission (1989) requirement that public library services collect and report a range of performance data, together with the interest expressed in the published work of practitioners and academics such as Abbott (1990) and Bloor (1991). Analysis of the questionnaire returns revealed that 86 per cent of responding authorities cited their existing use of them and that a further 7 per cent were preparing to do so. The only authorities that did not identify performance indicators as operating in their services were those who responded from Northern Ireland. Case study investigations revealed three authorities where performance measurement was being developed to an extent well beyond the scope of that set out by the Audit Commission, and that it was recognized as making a major contribution to service development and management decision making. One Head of Service revealed the rationale behind the investment in developing a sophisticated service monitoring and management information system as follows:

> It grew from our recognition as managers that successful private sector organizations don't, on the whole, base their decision making on vague perceptions and personal bias—for them information is king ... By systematically measuring and reviewing many aspects of our performance we can actually prove, when it matters—to the Elected Members for example—that we have a sound operational reason for seeking growth or arguing against reductions.

Management information systems

Responses indicated that 39 per cent of library services felt that they had a management information system in place, whilst a further 15 per cent were developing one. Most activity in this area was evident in the English counties and London Boroughs. Case study data revealed considerable interest in developing more sophisticated methods of identifying and gathering data to improve organizational effectiveness and decision making. The potential offered by the use of information already held, or with the potential to be gathered through the use of library automation packages was highlighted by several interviewees, with the view being expressed that valuable data were being under utilized in the strategic planning process of their services.

Team working

The questionnaire data identified 61 per cent of responding authorities as participating in the use of teams. However, reflection on questionnaire responses led the team to conclude that the questionnaire design could have provided more meaningful data, if we had specified that we were most interested in discovering the degree to which cross functional team working was taking place. The literature and consultation in other sectors had revealed this to be one of the major areas of development in quality management in the 1990s (Seddon, 1992; Clark, 1992a). Case study and Workshop data did, however, help to add some clarity as to the precise type of team working that was being practised. These revealed that there was a high degree of interest in, and some evidence of, cross functional team working in nine of the case study authorities. Delegates to the project Workshop reinforced the case study findings that the majority of cross functional team working remained restricted to the professional grades of staff. However, examples were identified where a whole-staff approach to the setting up of teams to examine areas of interest and concern to the service, such as information technology and public relations, was in place. A member of frontline staff in one of the authorities where this approach had been adopted expressed the positive view that:

> Teams are one of the main ways in which senior managers demonstrate that we can all make a valuable contribution to the way that the service is going. Not all of us actually want the hassle and responsibility that volunteering for membership brings but we do appreciate the fact that the opportunity is there if we want it.

Measurement and feedback

Gaining an understanding of the way in which public libraries used measurement tools as a means of monitoring and improving service performance was important to the work of the project, as measurement of performance is central to the philosophy of quality improvement. The performance indicators, primarily those set out by the Audit Commission, were identified by 88 per cent of responding authorities as being a means by which they measured and assessed their organizational performance. In four of the case study authorities visited, additional performance criteria had been put in place. These included measurements against predetermined targets of criteria, such as queuing times for the return and issue of materials and the time lapse between a telephone first ringing and being answered. A range of approaches was evident in the use of these additional performance measures, with three of the four authorities who used them identifying the 'customer' in the building as being more 'important', in terms of prioritizing staff time, than the telephone user. Discussion of this issue during Workshop sessions highlighted a general consensus that managers felt that it was, generally, better to direct employees always to deal with the library user in the building before the telephone enquirer. There was some limited evidence in both case study visits and at the Workshop that strategies for using improved telecommunications technology were being considered to divert telephone calls away from frontline service points to centrally located operators who could deal with renewals and general enquiries.

Customer complaints systems have been a public service requirement since the advent of the Citizen's Charter and therefore all responding authorities could be assumed to have access to relevant data in this area. However, only 65 per cent indicated that information on complaints was used as a measurement of service quality. Delegates to the Workshop considered that the adoption of corporate schemes of complaint actually inhibited their widespread promotion in the library service. Poor design of formal schemes and the emphasis placed upon complaint, rather than the opportunity for comment and compliment, were identified as the primary causes of failure, reflecting the findings of Martin's work in this area (1994). This was confirmed in case study interviews with employees at all levels in the organization, with frontline staff, in particular, noting that much valuable information in the form of customer comments and 'moans' was being lost because a rigid complaints scheme was not something that most library users would wish to use. Five of the case study authorities had attempted to address the perceived shortcomings of their corporate scheme by putting comments books in branch libraries, with the local manager responding in the same book to comments, complaints and suggestions made. In one English county the value of customer information and opinion picked up at the frontline was recognized by staff being encouraged to fill in brief comments forms themselves, thus providing management with data which they perceived to be of value to the service.

The seven Elected Members interviewed expressed the view that they would like to see much more information based upon complaints, comments and compliments. They all identified themselves as only really being aware of complaints where they were contacted directly by a member of the public or where a senior manager had sought to involve them. All agreed that a better reporting structure for these data would be valuable in informing their own knowledge of the service and the decision making process. One member suggested that an annual trend analysis should be compiled and tabled for discussion at committee level. No evidence was found to suggest that this had taken place or was planned in any of the authorities visited. However, a number of library authorities are known to report the number of complaints and compliments received on a regular basis to their library committee.

Value for money was identified by 35 per cent of respondents, drawn almost exclusively from the English counties and London Boroughs, as being a measurement of service quality that they employed. In case study visits the issue of achieving 'value' with scarce financial resources was identified by many senior managers as being a primary focus of their work. The use of tendering documents for the provision of services and the negotiation of enhanced levels of service with suppliers were cited as being the two main areas where the measurement and assessment of value for money were most readily facilitated. Two authorities, one English county and a London Borough, did refer to the employment of 'shelf filling' staff on rates below those offered to library assistants, as having provided evidence for Elected Members of increased efficiency in service delivery being achieved without any consequent increase in staff costs. In both these cases trades unions had not objected to this alteration in the traditional composition of public library service staffing.

Measures of customer satisfaction through surveys was identified by 25 per cent of respondents as being a methodology employed in their service. There was no evidence of activity in Northern Ireland and only one authority each in Scotland and Wales reported the use of customer satisfaction measures. The greatest use of these measures appeared to be in the English counties, a pattern reflected in case study visits. In one English county a customer survey was used every eighteen months to assist in defining service aims and plans. The success of this approach was recognized regionally with the Head of Service permitting other authorities access to the original questionnaire document. They could then make local amendments for their own use. In another English county a large scale customer survey with some 10,000 responses was causing problems of data analysis due to the sheer scale of the undertaking.

Case study visits and data gathered at the project Workshop also gave an interesting perspective on the degree to which professional staff allow information obtained from end-users to determine service development. With a number of notable exceptions, where customer opinion and perception data are systematically built into the library service planning process, it appeared that information, even when gathered, was not being fully incorporated into the decision making process. A senior library manager outlined the situation:

> We have to be seen to be collecting information from users; it is good public relations, if nothing else, and gives people the chance to have a moan which they seem to appreciate. However, at the end of the day what they tell us can only ever be a very small part of our decision making equation. The majority of our users simply don't have a whole service perspective. If we listened to them we would be awash with romances and westerns and little else. Professional judgement has to be the main contributor to achieving a balanced service ...

This raises again the difficulty in public libraries of balancing different perspectives of the determinants of a 'quality' library service. The use made of end-user input in public libraries, our data suggest, is different from that cited earlier in this report as the British Airways criterion for assessing quality of service, where 'Quality is what the customer says it is' (BA, 1995). This highlights a key difference between a service in the business sector and one in the public domain.

Respondents were given the opportunity to list any other measures of service quality that were employed. Five authorities (two English counties, one Metropolitan authority, a Welsh county and a Scottish service) responded that they sought to benchmark their own performance against that of neighbouring library services. Case study investigations and Workshop discussions gave an impression of much interest being expressed in developing existing informal networks and contact groups into something which could mirror the benchmarking exercises recognized as successful in other sectors (Karlof and Ostblom, 1993; Liebfried and McNair, 1992). The Public Libraries Quality Forum prioritized work in this area during 1995 and there is a pilot study of benchmarking involving a number of authorities including Westminster City Libraries, the London Borough of Brent and Kent Arts and Libraries. The work of the BLRIC project, *Best practice benchmarking in the library and information sector*, reported in this volume, is also likely to contribute to the development of interest and expertise.

Leadership and the management of quality

In arriving at an understanding of the way in which quality management operates in public libraries, it was important to investigate who, if anyone, was responsible for managing and developing its implementation. The responses to Question 8 are represented in Figure 5, which illustrates that over half of all responding authorities did not have an individual or team in place. This is not altogether surprising, given the proportion of services which indicated that they did not have any formal approach to quality management.

Figure 5: Who is 'managing' quality?

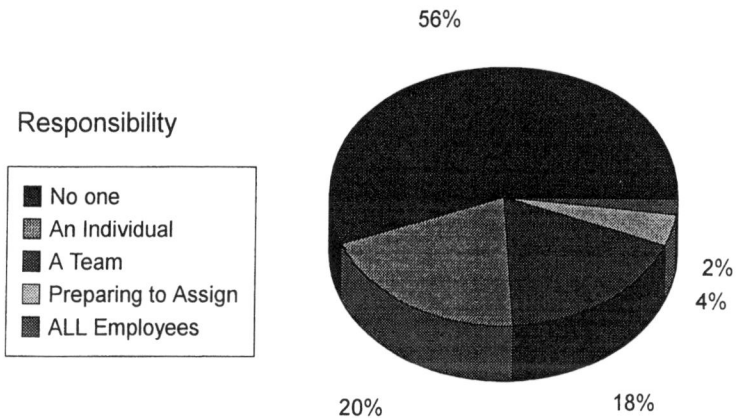

56%

Responsibility

| ■ No one |
| ▨ An Individual |
| ■ A Team |
| ▨ Preparing to Assign |
| ■ ALL Employees |

2%
4%

20%   18%

When responsibility rested with an individual this person was invariably identified as being a member of the senior team of managers, with over half being the Head of the Library Service. Case study data reflected the pre-eminence of senior management in having responsibility in this area. Where quality management had not yet been implemented, but there was some desire that it should be pursued, the Head of Service was the senior manager most closely identified with developing a strategy in this area.

Where teams were identified in the questionnaire as having authority-wide responsibility for quality related issues, follow up investigations revealed them to have a senior manager amongst their membership. The rationale behind the high degree of involvement of senior managers was explained by one delegate to the project Workshop:

> For quality management to be taken seriously it needs a senior manager to be closely identified with it and to champion its progress at all levels. Getting fellow senior colleagues on board can be the biggest challenge, so it helps if you are even more senior than them!

The management and leadership of quality were closely linked in the minds of respondents. However, the perception of the leadership skills felt to be necessary to achieve service improvement and the 'reality' identified by those at middle and frontline levels revealed, in many cases, a worrying mismatch. Interviewees were prepared to acknowledge that senior managers were often operating under such a burden of responsibility and pressure to meet deadlines that:

> They don't have enough time to inform themselves of the implications of their decision making. (middle manager)

and

> It is difficult, the function of senior management is becoming less and less clear and they are too distant, it is at odds with the way we have been going. Some staff regard the senior managers as living on a different planet. (frontline employee)

The second comment identifies the dilemma posed for senior managers by decentralized decision making. In three authorities visited, where significant shifts away from the centre had taken place, senior managers felt that, unless they themselves actually wrote service directives on quality issues, local managers were unlikely to adopt aspects of quality management.

Delegates to the project Workshop developed a useful checklist of features which they felt senior managers should possess. These were:

- Charisma
- Consistency

- Excellent communication skills
- 'Vision'
- Strategic management skills
- Immense stamina

The features identified as essential by practitioners show a strong correlation with those identified by Horton (1992) and Harari (1991) in their investigations of leadership.

In case study visits and in Workshop discussion groups there was support for recruiting additional expertise in the area of quality management to support the work of senior managers. However, most felt that the financial constraints that appeared to be preventing developments in many areas of public library activity militated against this. Purchasing external consultancy in the areas of management training, market research and external communications was a way forward identified by seven of the twelve senior managers interviewed.

Middle managers showed greatest resistance to the introduction of the tools and techniques of quality management. Reasons for this cited by senior managers ranged from the increased workload experienced by middle managers in increasingly devolved structures and the sense in which they felt their positions particularly threatened by moves to adopt a more open and participative style of management. Senior managers also mentioned the very low levels of staffing turnover at this level as presenting a further barrier. It was felt that recruiting even small numbers of new managers would help to alleviate resistance to change.

Employee recruitment

All senior managers involved in case study interviews were asked whether they considered the adoption of quality management had had, or would have, any impact on the profile of candidates selected for appointment. Low levels of staff turnover and the restrictions placed upon replacing staff were cited in ten of the authorities visited as being important factors in any consideration of service development. However, whilst it was generally held that there might be some requirement for knowledge of quality related issues at middle and senior level, in general the type of person recruited had largely remained unaltered by any of the changes that public libraries had experienced. One senior manager encapsulated a view held by many colleagues:

> Basically we still look for the same things—nice people
> who enjoy dealing with others.

A different perspective was put by another senior manager who stated
that:

> I am sick to death of all this business about library staff
> being 'nice people'—that is such a meaningless descrip-
> tion. Certainly I want to see commitment to the service at
> all levels plus appropriate skills to improve the way that
> we operate.

Employee training and development

Question 9 on the project questionnaire asked responding authorities to
identify who, if any, within the library service, received specific training
on quality related matters. Analysis of the responses received are represented in Figure 6, with almost two-thirds of authorities indicating that
no specific training was available. Case study data and the input from
the project Workshop revealed a widely held commitment to the importance of training, but with delivery being severely constrained by lack of
financial resources available to fund learning and developmental opportunities for employees—issues also raised by Morgan and Murgatroyd
(1994). The questionnaire did not ask respondents to specify their
training budget but case study investigations revealed that two of the
twelve authorities visited had an annual budget for all employees of less
than £1,000. A greater allocation of funding was evident in the English
counties visited than in any other type of authority. Two Heads of Service
commented that this had resulted from the Chief Executive of their
respective authorities having asked all senior managers to prioritize staff
training in their budgets.

The training identified as being in place was primarily that commonly
labelled 'customer care', with most activity in this area being evident in
the London Boroughs and English counties. Case study interviews with
middle managers and frontline staff revealed a degree of scepticism
about the benefits arising from the programmes offered, with several
interviewees echoing the comments of this member of frontline staff:

> We all found it extremely patronizing being told by senior
> managers just how we should answer the telephone and
> speak to the customers.

Figure 6: Quality management and training

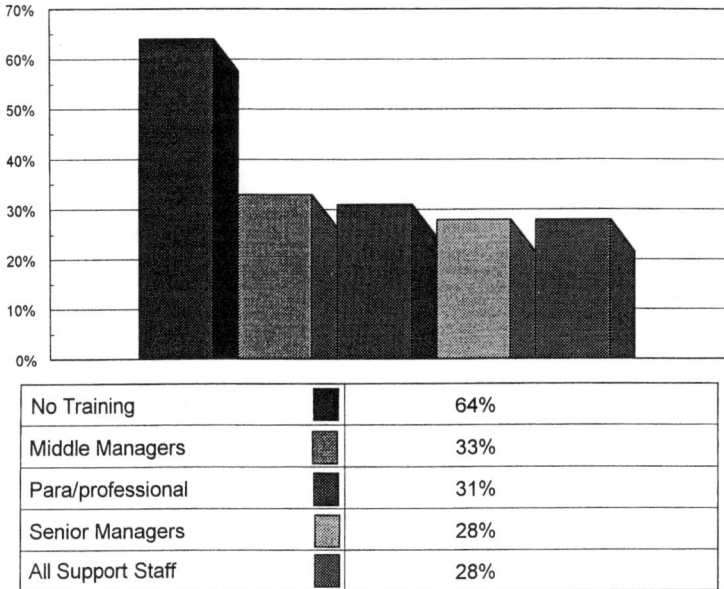

No Training	■	64%
Middle Managers	▨	33%
Para/professional	■	31%
Senior Managers	▢	28%
All Support Staff	■	28%

This view was challenged by a senior manager who explained its validity in the following terms:

> We took the view that coming on one of these courses should be treated just like a medical check up. Going on the course didn't mean that there was necessarily anything wrong with the way people were currently operating; it was a reinforcing exercise and a celebration of good practice. The greatest benefits really came from getting people together who wouldn't normally interface; the informal discussions on training days probably did more good than the actual training itself...

Delegates to the project Workshop were clear in their view that the training and learning that took place 'on the job' were extremely valuable in promoting the adoption of specific tools and approaches to quality management. Not only was this considered to be more cost effective, but many senior managers also felt that it afforded opportunities to learn in situations that actually related to the work and circumstances an individual was likely to experience. Frontline and middle managers did, however, identify the fact that opportunities for training in the workplace were severely limited due to pressure of work.

The adoption of systems of employee appraisal, discussed earlier, was also cited by case study interviewees and Workshop delegates as forming a valuable part of the training and development process. However, there were problems associated with resourcing appraisal for all staff, with one senior manager outlining the dilemma faced:

> We fully acknowledge that appraisal is a 'good thing'; the problem is that if we attempt to involve all staff the associated costs would wipe out our entire training budget and then need some more. Unfortunately everything has to be assessed on the grounds of whether it can be afforded—whole staff appraisal, unfortunately, cannot.

The seven Elected Members interviewed all indicated a desire for staff training sessions to be opened up to some degree to allow for limited participation by members. All felt that having the opportunity to learn alongside the employees of the service for which they had overall responsibility would improve communications and understanding between the two groups. Delegates to the project Workshop were, however, in the main, firm in the view that such involvement would be unproductive; it was felt that Members had an insufficient knowledge base to allow them to participate fully.

The research team sought to establish what methods and sources senior managers used to keep themselves abreast with developments in quality management. Seven of the managers revealed that training had completely disappeared from their lives due to pressures of work and inadequate funding. Two managers, in an English and Welsh county respectively, described the use they made of SDI services provided by their own staff, which they felt were vital in enabling them to keep up to date in their own and other sectors. Journals considered important were *Library Management* and *Public Library Journal*, with *Management Today* also being identified.

Informal networks, primarily based upon regional proximity, were felt to provide valuable forums for the exchange of ideas and information. The Public Libraries Quality Forum was also felt to be making a valuable contribution to the development of knowledge and practical support in the implementation of quality management. The work of the British Quality Foundation and the Chartered Institute of Marketing were also cited by senior managers in an English county and a Metropolitan authority as having been beneficial in providing information on the approach to public sector quality issues.

The essential features of a public library service

In the previous Chapter the impetus for, and rationale behind, the use of the SERVQUAL model was outlined. Respondents to Question 10 of the questionnaire were presented with fifteen statements, to each of which they were asked to assign a score of between 5 and 1, with 5 indicating that the content of the statement was absolutely essential to a 'quality' library service. At the end of the question, those completing it were then asked to review their own responses and list the five features which they considered most required improvement in their own service. A full analysis of the responses received can be found in Appendix B.

The three most essential features of a library service identified by respondents were:

- Employees will be consistently courteous to clients
- Employees will always be willing to help clients
- A good book stock will always be available to clients

Those identified as 'least essential' were:

- Libraries will make their clients aware of the standards of service they can expect
- Materials associated with the service (e.g. guides and Charters) will be visually appealing
- Libraries will consult their clients about changes in policy

These findings were debated during the project Workshop. Delegates recognized that, with 'quality' of service being so closely linked to the knowledge and interpersonal skills of frontline employees, training and development were key ingredients in achieving improvement. The lack of priority apparently assigned to communications with end-users 'dismayed' several of those present, who felt that the profession as a whole should have been, to quote one delegate, 'alive to the fact that it is the needs and perceptions of the customer that will decide what the public library of the future exists to deliver'.

Analysis of the features which respondents revealed as requiring most improvement in their own service showed that the following were given highest priority:

- All employees involved in contact with clients will have the knowledge to answer questions or to make appropriate referrals
- Libraries will have opening hours convenient to the majority of their clients
- Clients benefit from clear guiding to find their way about and make use of the library
- A good book stock will always be available to clients
- Libraries will consult their clients about changes in policy

One authority, it should be noted, felt no need for improvement.

Internal communications

Questions 11 and 12 asked respondents to consider internal and external communications. By far the largest majority, some 89 per cent, cited staff meetings as being a means of ensuring that effective internal communications took place. Despite this, in case study visits all those interviewed drew attention to the limitations associated with this approach, primarily in relation to the lack of adequate time available to ensure that such meetings facilitated any form of upwards communication. Training courses, as previously highlighted, were also considered to offer valuable opportunities for communication by 67 per cent of respondents. A frontline employee felt that:

> Just by being around staff we don't see often, if at all; you find out things and can ask questions that in your own branch would never come to the fore. It is really refreshing to have the chance to feed your own ideas and observations into the system and apart from these very rare training opportunities it just wouldn't happen at all.

Managers 'walking the floor' was cited by 60 per cent of questionnaire respondents as being utilized in their authority to encourage better communications. The services responding from Scotland and Northern Ireland indicated a particularly high emphasis being place upon this method. Case studies revealed that senior managers felt that their time was being increasingly swallowed up by meetings and increased responsibilities which prevented them from getting out to meet staff. In one English county the Head of Service uniquely identified the fact that one day per fortnight was set aside for travelling to service points. Although this was regarded as placing a degree of pressure on other commitments, the paybacks were recognized by a member of the frontline staff in the authority:

> There is no element of 'royal' visit—because we see the Head of Service reasonably regularly we have all grown comfortable in communicating our ideas and observations. Some of our customers even recognize our Head of Service because a point is always made of saying 'hello' to them and asking what they think of the library service. It may seem like a small thing but it really does help to improve our morale.

Case study interviews identified middle managers and frontline staff in eleven of the twelve library services visited as being critical of the degree to which upward communication from employees was solicited and acted upon. The positive comment above was very much in the minority of those recorded, with a particularly scathing analysis being offered by a middle manager:

> There aren't any strategies in place to encourage the staff to communicate their ideas upwards. In fact it has to be said that our senior managers value the input of the frontline staff so little, that they virtually treat them like aliens from another planet who couldn't possibly make any contribution to the service they are part of.

The potential offered by adopting a formal mechanism to encourage employees to contribute their ideas and observations to service development was initially explored in Question 12 on the questionnaire. This asked respondents to identify whether a suggestions scheme for employees existed in their service. First analysis of returns suggested that as many as 37 per cent of library services had or were preparing to implement a scheme. However, as this figure was considerably higher than the initial consultation process had suggested, further investigations were undertaken. These revealed that many of those who had responded that they had a scheme actually meant that they felt that employees could feed ideas upwards informally if they desired. The reality was that only 5 per cent had or were preparing a formal scheme. In one of the case study authorities, an English county, a scheme was found to have been in place for some ten years but without any significant activity or promotion for much of that time. Some of the literature proposed formal suggestion schemes as a potential strategy for enabling library services to overcome the difficulties of achieving successful upwards communication (Income Data Services, 1991). A review of the underlying rationale behind employee involvement and a suggested methodology for successful implementation was undertaken as one outcome of this study (Milner *et al.*, 1995a).

External communications

In external communications the two most important strands identified were the complaints schemes, considered important by 70 per cent of respondents, and the interface with frontline staff, cited by 61 per cent. The constraints on financial resources meant that several senior managers interviewed regretted that they were unable to invest in attractive advertising and information handouts for existing and potential users. There was some evidence from both the case study and Workshop data that several library services were exploiting close links with local media to achieve publicity for aspects of their services.

The public library service as the natural link in local authorities for disseminating information was a matter considered in case study interviews. In only one, an English county, was there a formal strategy and plan for developing better communication with all residents under the umbrella of the library service. In another English county a senior manager reported that the Chief Executive had set in motion a communications and information strategy team for the whole authority, on which the library service had been neither consulted nor represented. This contrasts with the positive experience identified in authorities such as Leicestershire and Hertfordshire where Library and Information Plans (LIPs) are providing a basis for the development of a coordinated approach to information provision. The importance and opportunities for libraries in adopting a coordinating role in authority-wide external communications was highlighted in the Audit Commission's 'Talkback' report on the efficacy of local authority communications (1995).

The cost of quality

The team felt it important to pursue the issue of costs that could be assigned to the implementation of quality management. Investigations in this area were undertaken in interviews with senior managers in the twelve case studies and in the project Workshop. Senior managers in nine of the twelve authorities cited 'costs' as a barrier to implementation, or to the development of the tools of quality already in place. In no authority was the cost of quality failure analyzed and set against the 'investment' costs in aspects such as employee training, which might be considered to prevent quality failures.

Only three of the twelve case study authorities had undertaken any breakdown of costs. These were related to inputs, which included time for meetings, software for statistical analysis and monitoring of performance indicators. Nonconformance had not been calculated as a cost by any of the services that were studied. The debate at the project Workshop on the need for a methodology to be developed to assist public librarians to assign and understand the costs of nonconformance indicated that this alone may represent a key area in decisions as regards the adoption of quality management in this sector. Elected Members highlighted a general lack of comprehension of the possibility that a commitment of financial resources could actually be seen as an investment with potential paybacks worth, in terms of service improvement, many times the original cost:

> We just aren't organized in local government to plan and cost in this way ... our eyes would water at the thought of investing money in quality management.

Quality management, good or bad for public libraries?

The team considered it important to discover the differing perceptions surrounding the benefits and drawbacks associated with the implementation of quality management.

In terms of benefits the amalgamated data identified the placing of the customer or library user at the centre of the planning process as having produced the greatest perceived improvements. Similarly, the systematic gathering and use of data to inform decision making processes was also felt to have resulted in improvements. To a lesser, but still significant, extent an increase in employee involvement was cited by many senior managers as having been successfully implemented, although actual case study data did not always reflect this as being the 'reality' perceived by middle managers and frontline staff.

The drawbacks recognized by practitioners could largely be assigned to three main categories:

- The amount of time devoted to meetings, team working and documentation was perceived to slow down the decision making process.
- The costs of quality were prohibitive during times of financial constraint.
- Employees were suffering from initiative fatigue and cynicism.

Some delegates to the project Workshop, in considering the balance between benefits and drawbacks associated with the adoption of quality management, expressed the view that further work was required to develop a model that would be suitable for the public library sector.

Quality management: learning from other sectors

Introduction

In this Chapter we move from the public library sector to consider the data gathered by the research team concerning the practice of quality management in a wide range of organizations, as set out earlier in the section on methodology. Conscious that the twelve case studies selected, whilst indicative of a range of sectors and experience of quality management, formed a limited sample, the team also made reference to the work of Wilkinson *et al.* (1993).

It is the aim of this Chapter to consider quality management within a broader context whilst relating it to the experience delineated in the previous one. The research team sought not just to identify best practice but to learn from the experiences of practitioners in other sectors. Extensive analysis of data led the team to focus on the critical success factors and barriers to implementing quality management identified in the investigations. The opportunity to learn from the experience of other organizations is one that Landry (1995) argues forcefully that public librarians should be seeking:

> Public libraries still talk too much to themselves and reinforce a self-contained world rather than talking to the outside.

Moving beyond this 'self-contained' view is the objective of this Chapter.

Policy issues

Each of the twelve case studies undertaken involved organizations where a formal approach to quality management had been identified. In none of the case studies was this policy found to have been in place for more than six years, with the motor vehicle manufacturer, airline and hotel group dating their first initiatives to 1989. In three other case studies—a private healthcare organization, a National Health Service hospital trust and a district council—the initial implementation could be traced to 1994. In the privatized utility visited, quality management, although introduced into sectors of the business in 1992, was felt to have 'died a death' as a result of the difficulties caused by reorganizing the business into smaller operating units and a resultant large scale programme of redundancies. However, even though the experience of quality management had not been positive, the Chief Executive is due to relaunch the programme with customer focus and employee empowerment as the twin objectives for 1995–1999. The findings of the research team, with regard to the length of time that organizations had been active in the area of quality management, are broadly in line with the take up pattern identified nationally by Wilkinson *et al.* (1993) and illustrated in Figure 7.

Figure 7: Has your organization introduced a formal quality management campaign?

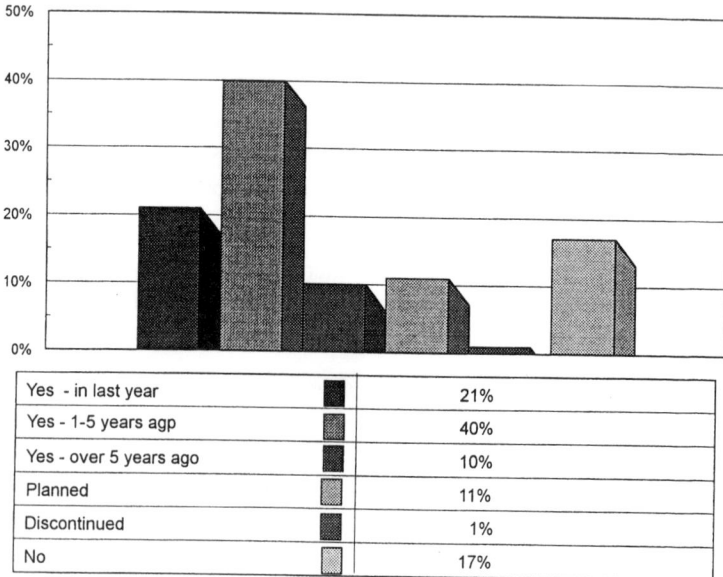

Yes - in last year	■	21%
Yes - 1-5 years agp	▨	40%
Yes - over 5 years ago	■	10%
Planned	▢	11%
Discontinued	■	1%
No	▨	17%

Just as in the public library sector, the data suggested there were a variety of sources from which the original impetus for the adoption of quality management arose. Competitor analysis provided the impetus for the motor vehicle manufacturer, with their Director of Quality and Strategy outlining the rationale as follows:

> We were patently a failing business when I arrived in 1988. There was a sense that we were simply marking time before the inevitable happened. We saw what our competitors, particularly in Japan, had done and the success that they were enjoying. Quality management has been the engine of change in our business. We are six years down the line, into our second five year planning cycle, and a highly profitable and successful business which people are proud to work for. But it hasn't been easy ...

Political influences were recognized as being influential in the NHS hospital trust, the district council and, indirectly, in a further case study, the law firm investigated. In the first two, the central government agenda for change in publicly provided services had provided the initial catalyst for change. However, the interest of local councillors was also considered to have been important in the district council, where the Deputy Chief Executive reflected:

> Local Government Review made all of our councillors wake up to the fact that 'quality' is an important issue. Our deliberations over the future of local government in this area certainly caused them to ask a great many questions about standards of service, performance monitoring and the views of the 'customers', a term which they had never used before.

In the law firm, the ISO 9000 standard had provided the initial focus for implementing quality management. This had not arisen from any particular desire to move in this direction but rather stemmed from proposals, since abandoned, that the Government would only license law firms having this standard to handle Legal Aid work.

Quality management was also cited as providing a framework for controlling and giving a structure to fast growing businesses. In one case study, an international freight handler, where the turnover had grown by over 100 per cent in every year since 1992, and the average age of the staff employed was 25, external consultants had been employed by the

Directors to provide a strategy for achieving structured and positive growth. The resultant programme put in place in 1993 involved the production of procedures held on computer, covering every aspect of operations, and an investment in staff training, particularly in the area of team working.

Impetus for the adoption of quality management was also identified as stemming from the interest and commitment of one or more senior managers. This was certainly evident in the case studies conducted in the airline and financial services industries, where particular individuals were identified as having 'championed' quality management and its adoption. A senior manager interviewed during the case study visit to the airline felt that it had been the charismatic leadership style exemplified by their Chief Executive that had made the adoption of quality management so successful:

> We wouldn't be in business today if it wasn't for the fact that we totally changed our way of working. The customer, once just a nuisance, became the focus of all our efforts. That revolution in thinking can be attributed to the efforts and commitment of only one or two individuals.

Formal systems

In the previous Chapter we considered the relatively small degree of interest exhibited by public libraries in working towards accreditation of a range of formal standards, such as ISO 9000. The results of the research conducted by Wilkinson *et al.* (1993) across all sectors, illustrated in Figure 8, indicate by way of contrast that half of the organizations surveyed had achieved a formal quality standard, with a further 25 per cent aiming for one. The non library case study investigations undertaken by this project team revealed, however, a markedly higher degree of adoption of a range of standards. The reasons for this may have much to do with the fact that when the research referred to was conducted, in 1991 and 1992, awards such as Investors in People were very much in their infancy. Table 4 charts the adoption rate found by the team for three standards and awards: BS 5750/ISO 9000; Investors in People; and the British Quality Award (discussed in detail later in this report).

Figure 8: Has your organization achieved a recognized quality stand-ard/certificate?

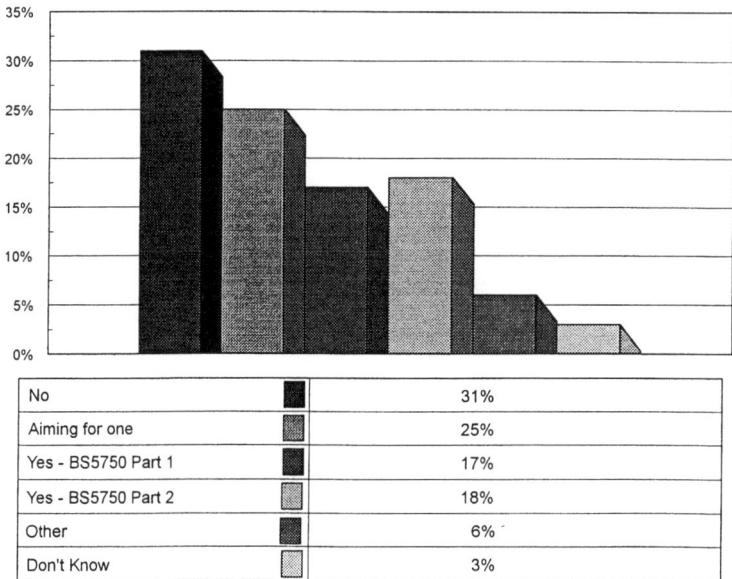

No	■	31%
Aiming for one	▨	25%
Yes - BS5750 Part 1	■	17%
Yes - BS5750 Part 2	▦	18%
Other	■	6%
Don't Know	▨	3%

Although all of the non library organizations visited by the team were participating in at least one of the formal schemes recognizing quality of practice, there was a considerable degree of variation in the amount of importance that various organizations appeared to assign to gaining them. The vehicle manufacturer studied, the only organization in the case studies to achieve all three, regarded them as 'incidentals':

> We have never set out to organize ourselves to win awards.
> They came to us because we were working in such a way
> that our business practice exceeds the requirements of all
> the formal standards and awards.

This view of awards and standards as 'incidentals' was echoed in the team's investigations of the airline, retailer and hotel group.

Table 4: The adoption of formal quality standards and awards

	IiP	BS 5750/ ISO 9000	British Quality Award
Airline	Awarded	Awarded	Registered
District council	Registered	No	No
Financial services	Awarded	No	No
Freight forwarder	Registered	Awarded	Registered
Hospital trust	Registered	No	No
Hotel group	Awarded	No	No
Law firm	Registered	Awarded	No
Library supplier	Registered	Awarded	No
Private healthcare	Registered	No	No
Privatized utility	Registered	Yes	Registered
Retailer	Awarded	No	Registered
Vehicle manufacturer	Awarded	Awarded	Awarded

The law firm and library supplier had directed much organizational effort into the achievement of a specific award, in both cases ISO 9000, and here the award criteria were felt to be influencing the development of processes and systems of work. These businesses, like the freight handler visited, suggested that the adoption of formal standards had served as the catalyst for organizational change and improvement.

Performance measurement and feedback

The case study organizations from outside the public library sector all placed emphasis on setting and measuring performance criteria and eliciting systematic feedback from a range of sources. Visits to the hospital trust and district council suggested that such a movement was a relatively recent phenomenon, with the Head of Human Relations in the NHS Trust outlining the rationale behind their year old system:

> We are obliged to gather certain data, much of which is designed to give an accurate picture of workload and the allocation of resources. However, as a management team we were aware that these data really only give a sketch of what is really happening and we didn't feel that we were actually collecting the correct data to set about improving services. We also found that data were being gathered

which were never actually used for anything, so we rationalized what we are doing, explained to the staff why some procedures have changed and it seems to be paying dividends We actually feel that we are informed now. We are now moving on to consult more extensively and regularly with our patients, GP fundholders and other organizations with which we have relationships, and that information will help even more.

Performance measurement was cited by ten of the twelve organizations visited as having been important long before any formal interest in quality management was evident. However, many of those interviewed felt that measurement of performance and feedback from customers and other groups had become much more integrated into the actual operation of their organization since the introduction of quality management tools and techniques. A Quality Manager in one of the privatized utilities outlined her perception of this more holistic approach:

As a business we have always been awash with information, data, statistics, surveys. We had them all, the only trouble was they were rarely looked at by anyone who was involved in decision making at a senior level. That has been turned on its head; we are far more focused on the kinds of information which are critical to us, and decision making and service planning always take account of the trends identified.

Developments in information technology were considered by eight of the twelve managers interviewed to have had great impact upon the gathering of relevant data. Computerized systems of recording indicators of performance, including complaints from customers and certificated illness of staff, were cited in the airline, hotel and vehicle manufacturing sectors as having benefited organizational planning and performance.

Eliciting feedback from customers, suppliers and other stakeholders in an organization was identified as being a priority in all of the non library case studies. The personnel and other resources committed to this activity, and the range of approaches used, varied considerably across the different sectors studied. In the hotel group and airline extensive use was made of customer surveys, with both businesses operating a 'frequent user' scheme, the substantial memberships of which provided a rich database from which regular survey work was undertaken. Both organizations also employed specified personnel to handle customer complaints, a practice which was also evident in the freight handling, private healthcare, retail and vehicle manufacturing organizations visited.

Ten of the organizations visited also used external companies to carry out market research on their behalf. The methods used included postal questionnaires, telephone research and the use of focus groups. Research was most usually found to be directed at specific segments of the total market for the organization's product or service. Examples of this included investigations of the colour and trim preferences of female drivers in the age group 25–45, carried out by the vehicle manufacturer, and the meal types and times of single people in the age group 18–30, conducted by the major retailer visited.

The use of benchmarking as a tool to assess and improve organizational performance through comparison with the systems and procedures found in other organizations was evident in five of the case studies undertaken. In all instances, informal contacts were felt to have provided the original impetus for benchmarking to take place. Analysis of the project data revealed that certain large commercial sector businesses appeared to be particularly active in promoting and facilitating opportunities for colleagues from other sectors to learn from them. For example, the airline offered interested parties a one day 'benchmarking experience' where their own organizational experience was examined and discussed. Managers there expressed the view that:

> Through sharing what we have achieved we are also giving ourselves valuable learning opportunities. Everybody who comes to us, from whatever sector, is feeding in ideas to our own organizational development. For us, benchmarking is definitely a two way process.

Benchmarking within a highly competitive sector, that of motor vehicle manufacturing, was revealed to be important to the developmental work carried out by the case study company in this area. Benchmarking of specific activities, such as those related to vehicle safety and security, were described as being conducted throughout Europe and taking in all major manufacturers. The potential of benchmarking, even in highly competitive sectors, was identified in the work of Bernhardt (1993) and Liebfried and McNair (1992).

Where the project identified no actual practice of benchmarking, individual respondents expressed an interest in exploring the possibilities of moving forward in this way. In four instances the project team were able to provide organizations with contacts in other organizations who were identified as being particularly supportive of this work.

Analysis of the organizational importance of 'waste' was the final strand in the performance measurement and feedback loop identified as being dominant in the non library case studies. Analyzing the way in which work is carried out within an organization has moved on considerably from the days of the 'time and motion' study. In eight of the non library case studies the project identified a clear focus on how value may be added to the end service, in the eyes of the customer, through eliminating waste and adding value whenever possible to the core activities of the organization. In the financial services sector case study, the team were given access to the findings of an organization-wide analysis of the way in which the people and processes within it worked. The conclusions arrived at in this business were that only 35 per cent of total activities concentrated on necessary or value added work. Of the remainder, 30 per cent of business activity comprised reworking processes that had not been 'right first time'; a further 25 per cent arose from an investment in unnecessary activities and processes that did not contribute to the business; and 10 per cent was the estimated amount of time wasted by individuals. Considerable productivity gains in this organization arose from concentrating on the elimination of the need for reworking and unnecessary work, such as the writing of reports that no one needed or read. In local government, while some reduction might be achieved, it should be remembered that reports to committee are an integral part of the local democratic process.

Customer focus

The centrality of the customer in an organization's approach to quality management was evident, to varying degrees, in all of the organizations visited. The importance of the customer in establishing, through communications with the business or service, their expectations, needs and desires, was referred to as being crucial in the airline and hotel sectors. The work of Williamson (1992) also provides a particularly useful exploration of this subject in an NHS context. The benefits of discovering and focusing on the expressed preferences of the customer were pointed to by the Marketing Director of the hotel group visited:

> It is probably only in the last five years that we have begun
> to really take seriously what our customers have been
> telling us. For decades we have employed consultants who
> told us how a guest room should be designed, what leisure
> facilities they expected, all sorts of things. Since we have
> been soliciting actual customer opinions we have been
> surprised by the things that they consider to be important.
> That is where we direct our efforts now.

The private health provider visited had, only in the last year, their
Quality Manager felt, begun to view their 'members' as individuals
belonging to specific market segments, as opposed to being an amor-
phous mass. The use of the term 'member' had been adopted throughout
the organization as a result of a wide ranging survey of existing customers which indicated that they preferred the term to that of customer or
client. The result for the business was that systems and processes were
being put in place to improve the interaction with different groups of
members and new products were being designed that were more successfully targeted.

Customer focus in the hospital trust and the district council was
identified by senior managers as being an area that they were anxious to
develop. In these two organizations comparison with public libraries was
especially appropriate, as the 'customers' were seen to include a variety
of stakeholders, whose views it was important to consider alongside
those of individual end-users. The district council indicated that they had
found the work of Tam (1984) useful in clarifying their approach to the
question of stakeholders. In the hospital case study, the recording of
patient (the term 'customer' had been proposed for use by a Board
member but rejected by all those present) and relative views on the
existence of mixed sex wards was highlighted as having had a persuasive
influence on the Board of Management. A result of this was the allocation
of funding to improve the provision of single sex wards.

A final and interesting perspective on customer focus arose from the
visit of the research team to the motor vehicle manufacturer. Considerable evidence was provided of extensive consultation taking place with
dealerships and individual purchasers. However, the Director of Quality
and Strategy, uniquely amongst those interviewed, suggested that customer focus could never be wholly successful in this business:

> Of course we consult widely; it is very important to do so,
> but we do recognize that there are limitations. The greatest

problem is that human beings are usually limited by their own experiences and we find that their expectations of what they want in a new car are way too low—they only want something that is a little bit better than what they've got.

A similar view has been expressed by Stewart and Walsh (1989) with particular reference to the public sector.

Leadership and the management of quality

In each of the visits and interviews conducted in non library organizations the team sought, as they had done in their work with public libraries, to establish the management structures that were in place to facilitate the practice of quality management and the styles of leadership that were evident. The diverse range of business and service sector organizations visited meant that the approach and structures adopted varied considerably. However, a degree of consensus, particularly in the area of leadership, was apparent.

As detailed in the first Chapter of this report, all the organizations visited during this stage of the research project were selected at least in part on the basis that they were active in the area of quality management. The way in which quality was being managed, and how structures had developed and evolved in those organizations which had had a commitment for a number of years, was investigated. All but one of the organizations visited identified a senior manager, often in commercial sector companies a Director, as having overall responsibility for all aspects of quality management. In the case studies conducted with a vehicle manufacturer, law firm, freight handler and privatized utility, senior management expertise in the area of quality had been recruited externally as a result of the organization deciding that it wished to adopt quality management. The one organization that did not identify a senior manager as having responsibility in this area was the hotel group visited; after four years of implementation, when a Director of Quality was employed, they had decided that they had moved to a position where quality was so firmly embedded in the organization that it had become the responsibility of all staff. Coordination of effort and approach in this organization was assigned to individual managers who had all received considerable training in quality management tools and techniques.

Quality assurance and performance monitoring functions were identified as being the responsibility of individuals, teams or departments within the various organizations visited. The size of the organization had some, but not total, influence on the approach found. For example, in the private healthcare company visited the Quality Team, which had a training remit in addition to assurance, measurement and monitoring functions, had a full time equivalent of six staff. In the financial services organization studied, with similar numbers of staff and responsibilities, there were fifteen full time staff employed. The major difference between the two was that the financial services business had been involved with quality management for some three years during which their Quality Team had grown in size, while in the healthcare company the Team had only been established some six months prior to this study.

In the hospital trust and the district council there was no specific team in place to coordinate and develop quality management, although senior managers in both organizations did hope to be in a position to recruit external expertise in 1995. The focus for quality in both organizations was from senior managers. The Chief Executive of the Trust and Deputy Chief Executive of the Council were promoting a vision of quality through their communication with other senior managers and with middle managers.

The effect of quality management on the role of middle managers was discussed at length in several of the organizations studied. All, except those interviewed in the hospital trust, law firm and library supplier, identified middle managers as being the group most resistant to the implementation of change. Quality management, with its emphasis on involving and empowering all employees, was felt by senior managers interviewed to have created a climate of fear and resistance amongst many staff employed in supervisory positions. The airline, freight handler, hotel group and retailer all indicated that they had invested considerable financial resources in setting up training packages for staff at this level. The Director of Quality of the retail organization felt these were intended to:

> ...teach new management skills. We wanted to move from the old idea of the 'manager' towards developing the culture of the team 'coach'. That hasn't always been straightforward or comfortable. Some managers have moved to work in other areas of the business as a result; others have left us altogether because they don't like the

way we are going. The vast majority once they gain confidence really love working in this way and it has paid enormous dividends for the business.

The importance of leadership in the successful adoption of quality management was identified as being critical in all of the non library case studies. Having a senior manager who is capable of formulating and communicating an organizational 'vision' of what quality management exists to do for that business or service was repeatedly identified as having contributed most to organizational success—or failure—in the organizations visited. Charismatic and dynamic leadership was felt to be present in a diverse range of the case study organizations with evidence of its success being cited in, amongst others, the airline business and the hospital trust. The Chief Executive of the airline was described as 'absolutely focused':

> When he arrived he told all the staff that we were going to become one of the most successful businesses in the world, and six years later we are. He has maintained his enthusiasm and his realism, there has been honesty right from the beginning, especially about painful things like the need for staff reductions ... He is also very visible; although we are a huge operation there are very few staff that won't have met him—he just drops in, there is no element of royal visit.

In the hospital trust, where quality management has only recently been introduced, the Chief Executive was once more identified as being the driving force in communicating the 'vision' of where the organization is going.

The research also revealed major problems arising from ineffective leadership in relation to quality management. In the law practice, where considerable investment had been made in gaining ISO 9000 accreditation and in working towards Investors in People, the Quality and Training Managers identified the lack of top level commitment as effectively preventing quality management from being integrated into all aspects of the business:

> We have invested considerable amounts in improving our systems and processes. We would like to move forward and become much more customer focused and adept at involving all the employees. The partners who collec-

tively own the business will only look at things that have an immediate impact on fee earning and generation. As a consequence of that they don't actually believe in quality management and certainly don't promote it. We have probably gone as far as we can.

Recruitment

As in the public library case studies, interviewees were asked to identify the extent to which the adoption of quality management had any impact on their recruitment policies. The managers interviewed in the library supply, law and hospital trust sectors all felt that recruitment criteria had, largely, not been affected, with the law and hospital trust organizations stating that they were primarily concerned with recruitment based upon specific professional qualifications. However, evidence was also given to the research team that people with specific expertise in the field of quality management either had been, or were planned to be, recruited.

In the remaining organizations investigated quality management was felt to have had some impact on the drawing up of job and person specifications. Personal attributes such as communication and interpersonal skills were felt to be ever more important, even where employees would have little or no contact with end-users or customers. Confidence in interaction with others and the ability to work in teams were skills also cited as being advantageous. The importance of these skills in successfully implementing quality management was identified by Janis (1989).

Part time workers formed a significant part of the workforce in the retail and private healthcare businesses, the former having 34 per cent of part time staff in 1994, and the latter having 28 per cent of its employees working on what it called a 'key time' basis. The desire to employ more part time staff was expressed in both these organizations with the underlying rationale that such an approach allowed staffing resources to be deployed effectively at peak periods for the business. An alternative viewpoint on this matter was cited by the Quality Manager in the privatized utility where there was an expressed desire to reduce the number of employees working for less than twenty-four hours per week. The reason given for this was that most of these employees were involved in customer contact via the telephone and that, due to the fewer training opportunities the organization felt able to provide for part time staff, this group had the largest proportion of quality 'failures' associated with their work.

Employee training and development

The evolution of quality management, as outlined in the Background Section of this volume, has, over a period of some fifty years, led writers to focus on the training and development function in organizations. Wilkinson *et al.* (1993) revealed that over half of all the managers they surveyed felt there was a need for more training to be available in quality management tools and techniques, while some 35 per cent of respondents indicated that they wished training to be provided in project management skills and quality management philosophy. The present study, albeit operating on a much smaller scale, revealed that there was still felt to be inadequate training provided in the areas outlined above.

Investment in training in the non library case studies varied considerably across sectors, with the airline and motor vehicle manufacturer having an average spend of £750 per employee per annum. The hospital trust and the district council, whilst acknowledging that their training budgets had increased considerably since implementing quality management, spent no more than £50 per employee; senior managers thought this inadequate to deliver the training programmes they felt would contribute to widespread understanding of and commitment to quality issues. By comparison, the twelve case studies undertaken suggest that public libraries have only £22 per employee on average to cover training and appraisal costs, with one case study authority having a total annual training budget of only £1,000.

The commercial sector businesses visited all used, to a varying degree, external training expertise. This was particularly evident in the training directed towards senior and middle managers. Considerable investment was made in the area of team working and team dynamics, with case studies in the financial, retail, freight forwarding and motor vehicle sectors identifying it as a key component in their evolving quality management strategy. A senior manager in the freight handling company outlined his organization's commitment to team working:

> As a business we have no product other than the actual service that we offer to clients; our success or failure depends entirely on the quality and commitment of our employees. Team working to encourage communications and problem solving at a local level is the way we want to move forward. We have seen how it motivates staff in other organizations and we have also learned from them

that there are no short cuts—you have to invest in training your people.

In both the 'Review of Public Library Service in England and Wales' (Aslib, 1995) and the work of Porter (1992), the importance of developing and training staff in public libraries is similarly highlighted.

Employee development through appraisal schemes was evident in all but the library supply organization and the district council, where appraisal was only in place for senior staff. In the other organizations there was an obvious commitment to using appraisal as an improvement tool, for staff at all levels, and in all cases part time employees were involved. The frequency of appraisal varied, with the private healthcare company indicating that it took place every six months and involved the setting of short and longer term goals. More typically, appraisal was on an annual basis and in five of the businesses visited there was an element of performance award linked to salary.

Appraisal of senior managers was outlined as involving a rigorous process of reviewing personal and organizational performance and of setting and reviewing goals. Although several of those interviewed indicated that their organization was interested in adopting '360 degree' appraisal schemes for managers, the only evidence that such an approach had actually been adopted was found in the study of the privatized utility, where the Quality Manager revealed that there had been considerable initial resistance to the concept from several Directors. However, implementation of the scheme in 1994 had been achieved with some success:

> They [the Directors] were really nervous about the idea of involving all grades of staff in assessing their performance. Because at a more junior level those involved were guaranteed anonymity, the Directors thought people would just use it as an opportunity to have a moan. They have actually been pleasantly surprised by the degree of understanding that junior staff have displayed about the way we do business and the difficulties that managers face. The end result has been that employees actually feel a lot more involved and the appraisal process has actually brought about some real improvements, especially in managers' approach to communications.

The questions used with frontline and middle managers in this organization are reproduced, in part, in Figure 9.

Figure 9: Key questions in 360 degree appraisal schemes

Do your senior managers:

1. Generate original ideas?
2. Learn from their mistakes?
3. Take decisions in a timely manner?
4. Seize opportunities when they present themselves?
5. Have a vision of the future that inspires employees?
6. Foster openness and two way communication?
7. Maintain consistency between words and actions?
8. Use resources effectively?
9. Understand the main trends affecting the organization?
10. Know what the customers/users really want?
11. Demonstrate a deep seated pursuit of excellence?
12. Recruit talented people?

Employee involvement and empowerment

Empowerment, the Institute of Directors (1994) suggests, arises when all employees within an organization have the responsibility to act for the benefit of the customer. It allows employees to take action, within prescribed limits, to avert or solve problems without having to gain approval from their manager or supervisor first. In this way most customer complaints can be put right before they occur. Employee involvement arises, Foy (1994) argues, from a range of strategies intended to harness the skills, ideas and commitment of all employees towards achieving organizational improvement and excellence. In both areas there was considerable evidence of such activity in the organizations visited.

The respondent from a major hotel group identified the pragmatic approach to empowerment adopted:

> Our recruitment and training has focused very much on the skills needed for this. However, we do realize that not all our employees really wish to be empowered, somehow it sounds too difficult and daunting. The truth is that they *are* empowered but don't actually realize it. Through

> being a supportive organization our employees feel hap-
> pier at taking 'risks' to satisfy the customer. Employees
> can't really fail within the dimensions of their job which
> are clearly set out for them and nothing we do asks them
> to go beyond this.

In other organizations empowerment strategies were also identified as being in place, with a considerable investment in training for frontline staff, their managers and supervisors. In the airline and financial services sectors, middle managers, once again, were identified as the group who revealed most resistance to its adoption, and training programmes had been set up specifically to support and educate them.

Critical to the success of empowerment, it was suggested by senior managers in the retail, hotel and manufacturing case studies, and supported strongly in the work of Clutterbuck and Kernaghan (1994), was the need to engender a 'no blame' culture, where mistakes, whilst recognized, were regarded as learning opportunities rather than a cause of general dismay. Also important was felt to be the need to celebrate the success of empowerment, giving organizational visibility to incidents where the approach had brought benefits and satisfaction to the customer and the organization. This was extended still further by the hotel group visited, where the success of employee empowerment was used as the basis for a Europe-wide advertising campaign.

The hospital trust and the district council felt that it would take considerable time and training to achieve empowerment in their organizations. Although there was senior level commitment to working towards achieving the no blame culture necessary, it was felt that this would involve such a considerable shift of existing culture that credible results would take a number of years to feed through. The Head of Human Resources at the hospital trust explained:

> We know that we want to move towards having a far
> greater degree of empowerment but the culture and restric-
> tions that we work with do present a significant barrier.
> We are getting there very slowly but it involves a consid-
> erable mind shift for a great many people and that won't
> happen overnight. The key for us is that we won't give up.
> Come back in five years and I hope we will be further
> down the road.

Employee involvement, achieved through a range of approaches, was evident in nine of the case studies. Whilst it was not being actively practised in the district council and the hospital trust, strategies were under consideration to achieve a degree of implementation during 1995. The approaches identified included the use of quality circles/groups, employee suggestion schemes and team working.

Quality circles were one of the tools of involvement evident in the hotel and motor vehicle manufacturing businesses. The concept had been introduced into both organizations some six years previously, at the beginning of their adoption of quality management. In both organizations they were being used less and less. They had achieved their initial purpose of stimulating knowledge and the discussion of quality related matters. The philosophy had become embedded in the operation and culture of the two companies and other methods of involvement were now felt to be more appropriate. The Director of Quality and Strategy for the vehicle manufacturer explained:

> Quality circles helped to bring the debate about quality onto the factory floor; they provided a forum for discussing the wider issues. Now that quality isn't really a talking point, it is firmly embedded in the way that we work, we use task and problem solving teams and the suggestion scheme to make sure that everyone has the chance to input to the improvement of the business.

The use of employee suggestion schemes was evident in nine of the participating organizations. There was a considerable variation identified in the resources assigned to the development and promotion of such schemes. The privatized utility operated a company-wide scheme, which was publicized through leaflets, posters and the company newspaper, and had a total budget of £250,000. Upon first analysis this appeared to be a large sum of money, but it was explained by the scheme's administrator that:

> Every pound that we invest in the scheme has been demonstrated to deliver savings to the business of some £25—that is the reality of the power of getting your workforce involved. Our biggest award for the 'star' idea of each year is some £5,000, which is great, but our evidence suggests that whether an employee is awarded a

large sum, or simply a tie, the sense of involvement and commitment being recognized is a powerful motivator.

These views were reflected in the investigation of suggestions schemes in other organizations and in a review of the scant literature available on the subject (Smith, 1989; Dunn, 1993). In two, the freight handling and financial services businesses, there had been a move towards creating team based schemes, where awards were found to be extremely limited in size, with the organization committing itself to providing training and time to enable all staff to participate, although it was not compulsory. The schemes were felt by senior managers to be contributing both to organizational improvement and to employee morale and motivation.

Team working has already been referred to as an area where considerable interest and investment are taking place. The synergy perceived to result from drawing people together into groups and supporting them in their problem solving activities was recognized almost universally as an increasingly important tool of quality management. Team working, senior managers in the financial services and airline businesses felt, also offered a positive forum in which to facilitate the acceptance of change as a constant feature of modern businesses. The benefits were explained by the airline's Quality Manager:

> We have invested considerably in setting up and supporting teams but we recognize that one of the main benefits to have come about as a result has very little to do with problems solved or ideas generated. Teams are supportive structures and in a climate of almost constant change and pressure in the business they provide employees with a time where they can actually discuss the stress that they are experiencing. Strange as it may seem, we have identified that staff who are members of these teams have far better sickness records than those who choose not to participate.

Internal communications

Many of the senior managers interviewed expressed the opinion that internal communications was the area where they felt that they had encountered greatest difficulty in implementing quality management.

The problems were outlined by the Quality Manager of the retail organization:

> We are a large organization spread throughout the country with thousands of employees, a large proportion of whom work part time. In order to achieve consistency of approach and understanding we have used all the traditional methods—staff meetings, newsletters, even a corporate video—but investigations revealed that we were still failing. We have achieved a considerable improvement, however, by building awareness raising into our training programme. It costs more than other methods but it is effective. People understand and remember far more when you dedicate a chunk of time to communicating with them and giving the opportunity for interaction.

The experience of the retailer was similar to that found in many of the other organizations the team visited. 'Traditional' approaches to communication were felt in many instances to be inadequate to convey understanding and appreciation of the concepts involved. Training was cited by managers in all but the district council, hospital trust and library supply organizations as having been incorporated into the strands of communications used.

Monitoring and measuring the effectiveness of organizational communications was undertaken in the retail, vehicle manufacturing, hotel and airline sectors studied. Having a systematic approach to measuring the efficacy of communications at all levels was identified as providing a focus for achieving measurable improvement and more successful targeting of resources. The Director of Marketing in the hotel group explained:

> Before we started monitoring our communications we simply assumed that circulars and house journals would be read by most staff. Actually talking to staff revealed that for all sorts of reasons we were wasting 95 per cent of our efforts and budget on things that people didn't perceive to be relevant to them or which, for a variety of reasons, they didn't see regularly.

Encouraging upward communication as well as ensuring top down effectiveness was something which most of the organizations felt they addressed most successfully through their adoption of formal methods of employee involvement. These, combined with the interactive opportunities available at training courses, were identified as the primary ways in which managers felt that employees could communicate most successfully with senior staff. An indication of an evolving method of upward communication was found in the freight forwarding company where all employees had an electronic mail address and were encouraged to submit ideas and opinions to senior staff through this method. An anonymous 'gripe mail' box was also put in place for employees who wished to comment or complain in a non attributable manner.

Internal communications was an area of considerable concern for all of the senior managers interviewed, with the Director of Quality at the freight handling company expressing a concern shared by many:

> One of our greatest challenges is to arrive at a point where our communications with employees are so successful that they will displace the rumour mill!

External communications

Ten of the organizations studied were larger than any single library service in the UK. Additionally, those in the for-profit sector had considerable financial resources to facilitate their communications with existing and potential customers. Many of the methods used, including the use of external agencies to deliver advertising programmes, would, because of the costs involved, not be practicable for adoption in the public library sector. However, the potential for libraries to cooperate regionally to achieve a higher profile in their external communications, using advertising and other methods found in the for-profit sectors, has been highlighted by such activities as London Library Week and the Library Power campaign.

However, what the team did uncover was a clearly defined approach to segmenting the total actual and potential markets for a product or service, and an emphasis upon prioritizing the degree of attention that each received. The necessity of adopting this approach was explained by a senior manager in the airline business:

> Our total potential market is vast. We communicate with them as a whole only to get across the corporate idea of a quality driven organization. Beyond that we consider our customers as belonging to distinct segments and we plan

our communications with them based upon our research into their opinions and preferences.

Segmentation and prioritization were also evident in the approach to external communications adopted by the hospital trust. Patients were divided into distinct groupings with particular requirements, such as the need for explanatory materials in ethnic languages, being taken into account. Fundholding GPs were also considered to be a vital group with whom to communicate and elicit feedback and this was achieved through the use of newsletters and the holding of regular seminars attended by senior managers from the Trust.

Timescales for quality management

The research conducted by Wilkinson *et al.* (1993) revealed that 80 per cent of the managers surveyed indicated they felt the adoption of quality management to be a long term commitment. This view was evident in all of the non library case study organizations visited. The reason cited by many managers as to why they had moved beyond the short term approach to change and improvement was encapsulated in the comments of the Director of Quality in the retailer visited:

> We only moved to adopt quality management some two years ago. Although we had been practising bits and pieces of it for years, we just never gave it that label. What spurred us towards a formal, organization-wide approach was that we saw what was happening in organizations that had been using and evolving the philosophy over a period of years. They were extremely successful and they were continually moving forward. Our commitment to quality is total and it is open ended. The quality management we practice in ten years time will probably be very different from what we are doing now, but what makes it right for organizations like us is that it is constantly developing to meet new challenges.

In the hospital trust and the district council there was greater pressure to deliver short term benefits from the adoption of quality management than had been evident in the commercial sector organizations visited. Scarcity of financial resources and the need to be able to justify their expenditure in terms of tangible results evident to Councillors and

Trustees, was felt to be impeding to some extent the successful adoption of a long term planning strategy. However, senior managers in these organizations were clearly aware that for quality management to be most effective it must be allowed to develop and evolve over time and there was a commitment on their part to ensure, within certain limitations, that this was facilitated. The data gathered in the public library sector highlighted the problem that senior managers perceived there to be in making long term commitments at a time when central government continually moved the goalposts. This was felt to be a particular problem if there were resource implications.

The costs of quality management

The research revealed a variety of approaches to assigning a specific 'cost' to the adoption and practice of quality management. Those organizations that had been practising quality management for several years had obviously concentrated much effort on discovering the cost of nonconformance due to failures in quality, a finding supported by the work of Dale and Plunkett (1995). In the airline and motor vehicle manufacturing sectors, the costs prior to the implementation of quality management, were assessed as being 28 per cent and 33 per cent of total turnover respectively. The reductions in nonconformance since the adoption of quality management, and the benefits of organizational improvement gained, were regarded as demonstrating that costs associated with quality management were far less than the financial savings and organizational improvements that they delivered. Quality management was thus seen as representing an investment of resources rather than a simple expenditure.

Organizations that the team visited where quality management had been introduced within the last two years provided much evidence of activity in assigning costs to nonconformance, be it the cost of abandoned telephone calls to the private healthcare company or in the failure to deliver a parcel by the specified time in the freight forwarding company. Costs of nonconformance and of 'waste' discussed earlier comprised a great deal of the initial activity that the team observed in the adoption of quality management.

The need clearly to establish the economic and organizational benefits of adopting quality management was recognized by all organizations as important, particularly so in the hospital trust. It was undertaking such an investigation when the project team visited and was experiencing considerable difficulties in establishing the financial costs attributable to quality failures. As practitioners in the public library sector had indicated, the process of assigning a 'cost' to a quality failure that could impact upon many different stakeholders was found to be an extremely complex undertaking.

Critical success factors

The data revealed common factors across all sectors, including public libraries, which resulted in the successful adoption of quality management. The factors listed below are the result of careful analysis of the research data and are intended to provide some guidance for those who have an interest in adopting and practising quality management in the public library sector.

The critical success factors identified are listed below:

- Decide in advance what the organization hopes to gain from quality management.

- Focus on the mission, goals and objectives of the organization. How does quality management impact upon their communication and achievement?

- Establish a clear focus and leadership for the process. Senior staff should be seen to be active in their support and promotion of the process.

- Set milestones and goalposts against which service improvement can be measured.

- Communicate with and seek to involve all staff in driving the process forward.

- Celebrate success at an early stage.

- Direct training and staff development towards promoting the use of specific tools of quality management, particularly team working.

- Inform, consult with and involve at all stages of progress, as appropriate, all stakeholders in an organization: employees, customers, users, Elected Members.

- Monitor the way in which all managers adapt to change.

- Commit the service to permanent adoption of quality management to achieve continuous improvement.

Barriers to implementation and success

The data also indicated six key barriers to the successful adoption and implementation of quality management. These are:

- The short term nature of organizational decision making. If the results of decisions cannot be measured quickly there is a reluctance to invest in further development.

- 'Initiative fatigue' is prevalent in many organizations and this creates an atmosphere of cynicism.

- Managers, particularly those employed in a middle ranking position, feel threatened by the move towards greater devolution of decision making and responsibility to frontline staff.

- In a period of uncertainty with regard to security of employment, many employees will not wish to be empowered, with the element of risk taking that this implies.

- With an emphasis on consultation and team working it takes far longer to reach and implement a decision.

- Quality management is seen as a cost and therefore a potential drain on resources.

The management of quality

Introduction

Analysis of the data collected revealed that quality management, when implemented successfully, was linked with organizational awareness and the practice of related management skills and disciplines. Those areas for consideration described in this Chapter include the importance of organizational structures, change management, marketing, assigning priorities in the strategic planning process, and the effective management of the political environment.

A key objective of this project was to identify areas of best practice and to assess if quality management could be implemented successfully in public libraries. The issues set out above for discussion in this Chapter, while not components of quality management itself, were suggested by the data to be of some importance in achieving and maintaining a focus on quality management.

Organizational structures and approaches to management

The research data suggested that in all sectors, including public libraries, there was considerable evidence of a movement towards decentralized decision making, with an emphasis placed on encouraging employee involvement and empowerment. Drawing upon the data gathered in public library case studies, the discussions held during the project Workshop and the evidence revealed by the case studies in other public sector organizations, the research team uncovered evidence to support Lovell's assertion (1994) that there are two distinct approaches to management evident in the UK public sector.

The first approach to the management of local authorities is termed 'public choice' which points to the importance of the role of Elected Members in setting and monitoring an agenda for the services for which they are responsible (Lovell, 1994). Public library research data suggested that this was increasingly the case, with Elected Members in several authorities identified as adopting a far more 'hands on' approach than had been evident in the past. A senior manager in an English county described the impact that this had had:

> Up until the last two years we, as senior managers, felt that the Members were primarily concerned to let us get on with delivering the very best service for the community that we serve. The difference now is that our first priority is held to be to regard the Members as being the 'community' that we serve before all others.

The second approach recognized by the project is termed the 'managerialist', which is concerned to move away from an emphasis upon administration towards the effective management of resources to achieve results (Lovell, 1994). The adoption of a managerialist focus was evident in a small number of the public library authorities visited and was the subject of heated discussion at the project Workshop. The reason for this was that the managerialist philosophy was closely identified with private sector management practices which, as with quality management itself, many feel may not always be appropriate to the public sector (Tyerman, 1995).

Investigations of the non library sector revealed that widespread structural reorganizations were evident in some 75 per cent of the private sector businesses visited. Among the reasons given for restructuring were the need to facilitate the adoption of quality management, the improvement of efficiency and the need to increase customer focus and service through the prioritization of certain key functions. In two of the public library case studies, one a London Borough, the other an English county, the library service had been divided into two distinct areas, that of Client and Provider. This resulted in a system of management where a small group of managers set levels of service agreements for individual or groups of libraries, whose performance was then monitored and measured against the contract agreement. Comparison of this type of structure with those found in other sectors revealed, the team felt, some degree of weakness in achieving the communication of a whole service 'vision' and objectives. In essence, the importance and benefits of having a clear corporate identity were found to be diminished in library services where there had been a clear separation into such distinct business units.

Management structures were found to differ less across the sectors studied than the team had initially expected they might. The reason for the relatively high degree of consensus of approach identified was explained by a senior manager in the airline visited:

We are all organizing ourselves to achieve success along quality management lines. This means that the structures that we employ, allowing for variations in the size and demands of the business, will all be directed at achieving the same things. We are constantly learning from one another and that is probably why our structures can appear similar.

In public libraries the size of the authority as a whole and its place within the overall corporate structure, the research data suggested, were important factors in determining the management structure of the public library service. The work of Midwinter and McVicar (1994) is important in any consideration of the impact of size on the efficiency and effectiveness of public library services. The case study investigations revealed that the larger county authorities were more likely to have adopted flatter management structures and to be using cross functional team working to drive forward service development. Appearing to have even greater impact was the position of the library service within the corporate structure of the local authority. Of the twelve case studies undertaken, nine of the library services were subsumed within either larger Education or Leisure departments. The remaining three, two English counties and a Welsh county, remained as departments of Libraries and Arts in their own right. Interestingly, in the three services which were 'stand alone' departments the team identified the most complete adoption of the managerialist approach outlined above. The experience of senior managers interviewed in services where libraries had been subsumed within larger directorates indicated, the data suggested, that those within a Leisure grouping felt that they had greater autonomy to develop structures appropriate to effective and efficient provision of library services than did those operating within Education directorates. Important considerations of the structures within which public library services operate are provided by Lomer and Rogers (1983) and White (1993).

Change management

The impact of change and strategies for managing change have been responsible for an explosion in the production of related literature which rivals that of quality management itself. However, the importance of change and its impact upon organizations and those employed within them were cited so regularly during the data collection process, that the team felt a brief consideration of its significance should be included in the final report. The political imperatives for change affecting public libraries, discussed earlier in this report, represent only a part of the overall experience of past and ongoing change identified by those interviewed in public library case studies. To the political dimension must be added the developments in information technology and the diverse range of leisure and other activities competing for the people's time and attention. Additionally, changes in levels and patterns of employment have created further changes within British society.

The major difference that the team detected in comparing the data drawn from the public library sector with those gathered in a range of other organizations was the degree to which acceptance of continuous change was built into the planning processes of many of the non library organizations. In public libraries there was some evidence of a belief that stability was essentially desirable and that it would return at some point in the future. A senior manager in an English county did, however, provide an approach to change and the management of change which reflected the planned approach found in other sectors. In order to plan the specific actions and measures necessary to achieve change this library manager felt that it was important to have a clear view of the following:

- Who will actually be seen to lead the process of change?

- Who are the key people who will be managing implementation?

- Is the change required of such a size that it can be broken down into key elements?

- Clarify who is responsible for ensuring the completion of each element

- Establish milestones for completion of each stage of the process of change and monitor performance and associated costs throughout.

An understanding of the extent to which organizational change impacts upon all employees was regarded as being extremely important in five of the non library case studies undertaken. In two of these case studies, the airline and the private healthcare company, analysis of certified illnesses amongst employees attributed over 40 per cent of absences to workplace stress resulting primarily from the fear or impact of change. Although none of the library services visited had conducted such a formal review, several senior managers did express a concern that, as the momentum for change increased, more and more employees were experiencing higher levels of stress than was desirable. Further data on stress amongst middle managers in public libraries can be found in the work of Hodges (1993).

Improving organizational communication, states Livingston Booth (1985), is one of the most successful ways of overcoming the proven link between change and stress. In one English county public library service this approach was reflected in the decision of senior Elected Members to host a meeting for a large number of service employees. The Members used the occasion to set out their personal commitment to the service and to the employees within it, and also gave the opportunity for those present to question them on matters of concern. Reflecting the experience that the team found in other sectors, this type of meeting involving interactive and supportive discussion of change appears to offer opportunities to at least reduce workplace stress and increase employee morale.

Marketing

Marketing was found to be of pivotal importance in the development of management strategies in the private sector organizations visited by the research team. Similarly, in the hospital trust and the district council there was clear evidence of marketing expertise being used to segment the total 'market' and target services at specific groups identified. In the public library sector the contribution of marketing skills and expertise to service development appeared to be much less evident, with only three of the twelve services (an English and a Welsh county and a London Borough) identifying themselves as having any formal approach to marketing. The findings of this project in relation to the adoption of marketing techniques in public libraries reflect those of Kinnell and MacDougall (1994) in earlier work in this area.

The concept of market segmentation was identified as being particularly important in the organizations where there was a strong organizational commitment to achieving greater customer focus. Specialist marketing expertise, data gathered through existing interactions with customers and feedback from employees were found to be the major activities and ingredients associated with successful market segmentation. The Director of Quality and Strategy in the vehicle manufacturer visited highlighted the importance attributed to segmentation:

> Until a few years ago we regarded the market for our products as being largely comprised of a homogeneous mass. All we knew about existing and potential customers was that they appeared to want and need a means of transport. Now we know much more about the various different groups who we currently sell to and we are always assessing them to see if they are still important to us. Looking for new market segments is also a key activity.

From analysis of the research data and the extensive literature that exists in the area of marketing, the research team sought to establish some criteria which public library services might find useful in defining and testing market segments. It was felt that public library managers, in considering data that might lead them to identify a distinct segment, could find it useful to consider all or some of the following questions:

- Is the segment homogeneous? Will all members of the segment react in the same way to the marketing input they receive?

- Is the segment measurable? How big is it and exactly how does it differ from the total market of users?

- Is the segment accessible? Can it be reached by existing channels of communication and service points? If not—and if the segment is felt to justify the investment—it may require a realignment of both communications and service delivery strategy.

- Is the segment substantial? Is it of enough social importance? Or big enough to justify associated costs?

- Is the segment recognized by customers themselves? If they don't identify with the segment they will not accept the promotion or communication aimed at them.

- Is the segment one that 'competitors' are or may be active in? Does the library service wish to engage in direct competition with external suppliers?

Setting objectives and assigning priorities

A core function of management is to set objectives and assign priorities for the business or service for which they are responsible. Johnson and Scholes (1988) explore these concepts within a framework where effective resource management and customer focus are the most important components. The data demonstrated the greater complexity, in assigning service priorities, that managers of public sector services faced compared to that found in commercial sector organizations (Pfeffer and Coote, 1991; MacDonald, 1994).

The importance of planning, access to and use of management information systems and marketing information was evident in the non library case studies conducted. A senior manager in the motor vehicle manufacturer visited explained the rationale behind the planning process in his organization:

> Since implementing quality management some six years ago we have also adopted a longer term approach to planning and setting business goals and objectives. What we have is a five year framework for each section of the business which is communicated to every single employee with the intention that they can clearly understand where they fit into it. But the framework is not a rigid document. We are constantly updating it; all sorts of factors impact on the business and we have to be ready and flexible enough to respond very quickly.

The influence of parent companies, shareholders, sub contractors, employees, competitors and customers were all cited as being important considerations in determining business priorities. However, the research team found no evidence to suggest that senior managers had experienced any real difficulty in maintaining their own authority over this process. The skill of successfully communicating it to the various stakeholders was, in ten of the non library case studies, identified as presenting a greater challenge. In local government long term planning is constrained by the rapidly shifting political agendas and the fact that some 80–85 per cent of funding is provided by central government. This is a major problem for the whole of the public sector and is one that differentiates it from commercial sector organizations.

The experience of public libraries and other public sector organizations visited highlighted the degree to which senior managers felt that, particularly in the area of agreeing service priorities, the views of other stakeholders, especially the Elected Members, were becoming increasingly important. The 'public service' approach to management outlined above was perhaps responsible in part for this (Lovell, 1994). Elected Members in a number of public library services were identified as having modified the service priorities drawn up by senior managers. In two authorities this had involved a refusal to allow the closure of service points which were identified as 'unviable' by senior staff. The decision of Elected Members in one authority was described in the following terms:

> The only thing that the Members had in mind was the next election. Even though we had proved that there were far better ways to spend the resources improving other aspects of the library service, they just wouldn't listen. Eighty per cent of the Members I deal with actually have no interest in or understanding of libraries and yet they have the real power at the end of the day to prevent service improvements. Sometimes I just despair ....

Apart from the involvement of Elected Members the research team found that only half of the case study authorities identified themselves as planning and setting service objectives in any systematic way. In those services where such a systematic approach was evident, the views and perceptions of other stakeholders, including end-users, other departments within the corporate structure and employees, were found to be successfully incorporated into the process. Extending the process beyond senior managers and Elected Members, a Head of Service felt, was one way of actually ensuring that objectives and priorities were achieved:

> Elected Members are always those I face with most trepidation but going to them armed with piles of supporting evidence, including that drawn from their own constituents, is often the only way to get them to face rather than avoid the really difficult decisions.

This highlights the fact that senior librarians must often also be skilled political managers. Reductions in service funding mean that, increasingly, 'difficult decisions' are having to be made. The Review of the Public Library Service in England and Wales cites the proposed 'Planning Guidance Notes' from the Department of National Heritage as potentially offering assistance in this vital area (Aslib, 1995).

The role of the Elected Member

In his study of the role of Elected Members in public library services, Usherwood (1993) highlights the fact that many of those who find themselves allocated to a committee responsible for libraries are those who have been recently elected and who would hope, in time, to progress to higher profile areas of responsibility. Others may have some interest in libraries but devote the greater proportion of their time to other committees. For only a small minority is the library service their major focus of interest. The interviews conducted for this research revealed that local politicians varied greatly in their knowledge of and commitment to the library service for which they were responsible. A Chairperson said:

> I would say that out of the entire membership of the council there are only three of us who have any interest in or passion for the public library service. Most of those who sit on the committee only really come to life if we mention the possibility of closing a service point in their ward ... A good Head of Service could exploit that lack of interest by getting a few key Members on board with their ideas and achieve quite a lot, apart from the closures that are desperately needed!

As discussed above, many senior public library managers revealed a degree of concern about the increasing 'involvement' of Elected Members in certain areas of organizational decision making. Gyfford (1995) identifies what is perhaps the underlying difficulty:

> What may be occurring is that increasing complexity of proposals for innovations are tending to increase the gap in understanding between Member and officer.

In the authorities where change, development and improvement appeared to have been handled most successfully, managing Elected Members appeared to be a key activity for senior managers. The most active approaches and strategies appeared to generate the greatest benefits, developing a more informed and involved outlook on the part of the Members. Whilst taking committees on coach tours to several branches was identified in one case study authority as being a useful awareness raising exercise, more valuable long term results were felt to come from establishing links between individual members and the service managers operating in their areas.

The role of the Elected Member was identified by the team as being crucially important in achieving service improvements and developments. The importance of the political affiliations of Members and the likelihood of periodic change of personnel and political control are factors that public library managers have long had to address. The challenge revealed by the research data in this investigation of quality management appeared to lie in developing an awareness and understanding of approaches to service development in Members who, in some authorities, wished to exert a greater influence than ever before.

The continuing evolution of quality management: ways forward

Introduction

The Background Section of this book charted the evolution of quality management and identified the increasing impact that it appeared to be having upon public sector organizations. Extensive consideration of the literature available, and access to practitioners in a wide range of organizations and businesses, contributed a valuable perspective on this continuing evolution (Juran, 1992; Juran and Gryna, 1993; Waterman, 1994). In this chapter we will consider in particular the growing importance of an incremental approach to quality and the development and adoption of models of organizational self-assessment. Within this evolutionary context we will then move to consider the conclusions and recommendations arising from this research.

TQM becomes 'total'

Oakland (1994a) suggests an approach to quality which seeks to involve all aspects of an organization in working towards improvement. The task this presents to senior managers is immense. A case study interviewee in the airline sector revealed the approach that had evolved in his business:

> TQM was where we started really but we soon realized that the systems and procedures that were central to it, or so the theory and consultants suggested, were actually detracting from what we felt was our priority in improving the quality of the business, to actually achieve far greater customer focus. We couldn't say that our approach today is what the theorists understand as TQM; it is incre-

mental—we had our revolution at the beginning, but you can't live life in a state of constant revolution.

Achieving the initial revolution and putting quality 'on the agenda' was the major contribution made by TQM to management practice identified by Wilkinson, Redman and Snape (1993). The research data collected for the present project in commercial sector organizations supported this view. The incremental approach to quality management was one with which public sector organizations appeared to be more comfortable. The senior manager interviewed in the hospital trust visited expressed the view that:

Our perception of quality management in the mid 1990s is one which has to fit with the needs of all those whom we serve and employ. TQM would never have worked here, it is too insistent, too rigid. We have adopted a holistic approach which is about being 'total' but in a calmer, more considered and appropriate manner.

Self-assessment

The process of self-assessment, whereby organizations measure and manage their competencies in a number of identified areas, was one that the team identified as generating considerable interest and activity in the non library case study organizations. The focus for the work and development in these areas was identified as resulting from the activities of the British and European Quality Foundations, which had developed the European Business Excellence Model, illustrated on page 40, through a process of extensive consultation with senior managers in private sector enterprises throughout Europe. Each of the criteria listed in the model, which include Leadership, Customer Focus, Resource Management and Impact on Society, is assigned a weighting, each of which is reviewed annually by the European Quality Foundation to ensure that they remain appropriate to the needs of practitioners.

Peacock (1995) claims that a formal methodology of self-assessment provides:

- A factual assessment of performance
- A sound basis for the development of strategy
- A clear focus for improvement
- A motivator for people and teams

- A clear link between change and performance
- A framework for benchmarking

The adoption of self-assessment using the European Foundation Quality Model has been formally embraced by six of the non library case studies, with one being amongst the first winners of the British Quality Award which was made on the basis of external judging of the impact of the model upon the business. Many of those interviewed who were already using or were planning to adopt the use of a formalized methodology for self-assessment reflected Barnett's view (1995) that:

> To work, it needs commitment from the top, a strong interest in serving customers, a willingness to change, honesty, preparedness to repeat and review the process for continuous improvement and involvement of customers in quantifying their satisfaction.

Self-assessment was found to be gaining such widespread interest that even traditionally external inspection standards, such as ISO 9000, are planning to incorporate aspects of it into their redefined quality management standards due in 1999 (Peacock, 1995). Given such interest it seems likely that organizational self-assessment will be at the forefront of developments in quality management.

The research data revealed that only one library service, an English county, had expressed any interest in adopting self-assessment in a formal manner. However, links established between the project team and the British Quality Foundation revealed that work is in progress in the UK in a small number of public sector organizations (none of which is a library service) to assess the potential of the European Foundation for Quality Management model for use in the public sector. The British Quality Foundation anticipates making the model available for more general use in the public sector during 1995, with eligibility for the British Quality Awards being granted in 1996. In discussions with the project team the British Quality Foundation suggested that certain benefits might be achieved through the adoption of the model in the public library sector. The framework provided a planned and systematic approach and emphasized organizational learning and improvement.

The democratic approach

As quality management philosophy, tools and techniques have become more widely adopted in the public sector, there has been some debate as to what might constitute an appropriate model for the public sector. Pfeffer and Coote (1991), in their study of health and social services, put forward what they term a 'democratic' approach to quality management. As in the work of Stewart and Walsh (1989), the questions of 'who is the customer?' and 'what is their relationship to the organization?' are seen in the democratic approach as provding major areas of divergence between public and commercial sector organizations. This approach acknowledges that the main purpose of modern public services is to achieve equity—not giving everyone the same service, but ensuring that all potential users have access to a service appropriate to their needs. Pfeffer and Coote (1991) argue that if such a model were adopted public services would be more responsive to individual needs, and that the public would be more powerful both as citizens and as customers.

Conclusions

In undertaking this research the team was guided by the objectives set out earlier in this report. The formulation of conclusions and recommendations was informed by analysis of the extensive body of research data gathered and through consultation with practitioners from the public library sector and a wide range of other organizations. In making comparisons and identifying best practice across sectors it was considered essential to acknowledge the constraints, uncertainties and forces for change unique to the public library sector. These organizational issues were perceived to be key determinants of what was appropriate and attainable in the adoption of quality management in public libraries. Conclusions and recommendations were therefore formulated with a desire that they should be both credible and feasible for implementation in a sector experiencing considerable constraints.

Defining quality management

An earlier section identified a wide range of formal and informal definitions of quality management. Investigations in the public library sector revealed that, with some notable exceptions, the prevailing opinion expressed by practitioners associated it primarily with the use of performance indicators and the adoption of formal quality systems, primarily BS 5750/ISO 9000. The identification of performance measurement as a major component was not altogether surprising, given that the Audit Commission requires public libraries to submit indicators of their performance against specified criteria. The strong association made between what was understood to be meant by quality management and the use of formal systems, revealed some lack of understanding of the philosophy and tools that theorists usually assign to any definition in this area. There was also a strong body of feeling which suggested, occasionally forcefully, that management philosophies and techniques associated with the commercial sector are not always appropriate for use in public libraries.

In other organizations, in both the private and public sectors, quality management was usually defined in terms of planning, measuring, involving and communicating to achieve continuous improvement. Quality systems adopted were cited, most often, as being tools to improve organizational processes and systems which, in turn, contributed to continuous improvement. Quality management, when defined by senior managers, was also found to have a much clearer focus on the importance of the people within an organization and customers as contributors to the overall drive for continuous improvement. In those organizations where implementation had appeared to bring greatest rewards, practitioners recognized that both a definition and a strategy for the implementation of quality management were attained when consensus was achieved on the major areas of organizational activity affected by it. Considerable benefits appeared to derive from an approach that acknowledged the equal importance of objective setting, allocation and management of resources, including employees, and the need to allow sufficient time for the philosophy and tools of quality management to become embedded. This is illustrated in Figure 10.

Analysis of the research data suggests that any 'definition' of quality management appropriate to the needs of the public library sector should reflect the holistic approach that was identified as delivering greatest benefits in the organizations visited. Thus, quality management is both an underpinning philosophy and a variety of tools and techniques, which focus the organizational structure, its resources, the people within it and the views of all relevant stakeholders on attaining and continuously improving measurable organizational objectives informed by the preferences and needs of the end-user.

Figure 10: Triangle of feasibility in defining and implementing quality management

OBJECTIVES

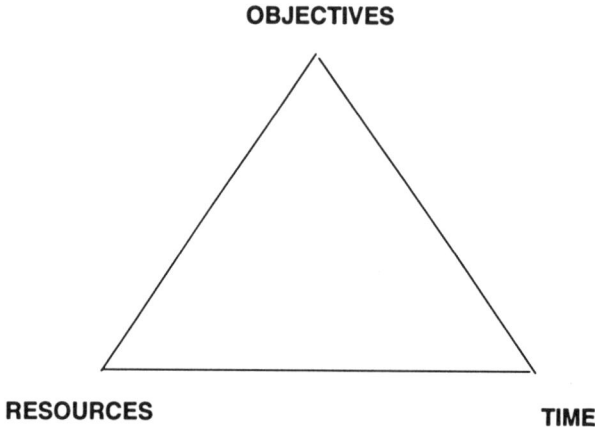

RESOURCES   **TIME**

Policy issues

In public libraries and other organizations where quality management was found to be delivering benefits a clearly formulated and effectively communicated policy on quality management was regarded as essential by senior managers. The research findings identified two-thirds of all public library services as not having any formal policy in place, even though it was found that many of these services had actually adopted specific tools of quality management. Public libraries were found to be broadly in alignment with Local Authority adoption patterns of a formal approach.

The experience of other sectors and of a small number of public library services suggested that the formulation and continuing evolution of a policy on quality management served to gain the interest and commitment of the 'stakeholders' of a business or service. Involving Elected Members in the initial preparation of policy contributed to giving them a sense of ownership and understanding of the organizational objectives sought through the adoption of quality management. Analysis of other sectors also suggested that it was important to establish from the outset that any formal commitment should be recognized as being long term and directed at the achievement of continuous improvement. Elected Members interviewed indicated that for them to support such a long term strategy and any attendant resource implications would require some of the expected benefits to be quantified explicitly in terms of the reductions in quality failures and nonconformances. Such an approach was much in evidence in the commercial sector and was cited as important in maintaining organizational momentum and senior management commitment to quality management.

The use of quality systems and, more often in the public library sector, of in house mechanisms of quality assurance provided both a structure and means of monitoring performance. However, on their own, such systems are not usually recognized as delivering the breadth of approach associated with quality management. The more holistic approach to quality, the data suggest, provides public library managers with opportunities and benefits.

Organizational issues

The successful adoption of quality management was identified in studies outside the public library sector to be dependent on the commitment and skills of senior managers. The role and importance of leadership emerged strongly from the research data as a key area of interest. The public sector organizations studied revealed the greatest levels of expressed dissatisfaction with the style of leadership displayed. In public libraries there was some feeling that decision making was undertaken without sufficient knowledge or understanding of the implications for the service. Senior managers, although much criticized for their perceived remoteness from the frontline, were also felt in certain instances to have poorly defined roles and to lack team cohesion and commitment. The Review of Public Library Service in England and Wales (Aslib, 1995) also highlights the importance of leadership and the development of senior managers in achieving improvements in public library services.

Private sector organizations provided far more examples of visible and charismatic leadership contributing to successful adoption of quality management. This perhaps reflects the fact that they were able to make far greater investment in developing leadership skills. Similarly, senior managers had clearly defined roles which appeared to be fully understood by subordinates, with most organizations being managed on a functional rather than a geographical basis.

The strategies for implementing and managing quality management were many and varied. However, across all sectors the importance of having a member of senior management seen to be in overall charge was important in successfully communicating and maintaining a momentum for change and improvement. Specific teams dealing with monitoring, measurement, inspection and improvement activities were evident in a wide variety of the organizations visited. However, where they were identified in the public library sector the emphasis was felt to fall upon measurement and inspection roles. Commercial organizations were found to have expanded their teams beyond this remit to support improvement activities, including team working and internal communications. Whilst there was some interest in the public library sector in moving in this direction and away from a purely inspection oriented approach, no service had yet implemented such a strategy.

Training was highlighted in all the sectors visited and in the extensive body of literature as being a vital element in establishing quality management within an organization. Public libraries were, however, characterized by a lack of financial resources to support and extend a planned and systematic approach to employee training and development. There was considerable evidence, in particular, of a lack of opportunities to invest in developing management and leadership skills. Private sector organizations, due to the larger budgets which they had been able to assign to this function, also made greater use of external expertise. It was felt that external consultants brought the benefits of a wider perspective to the challenges and opportunities facing organizations. Internally sourced training, whilst valuable, was largely held to offer too narrow a focus for those employed in management positions who were encouraged to explore beyond the confines of their existing structures. Public library services, in contrast, were rarely found to be able to afford such training opportunities.

Empowerment of employees was identified as creating a great deal of interest and activity in the non library organizations. Senior managers had, in many instances, prioritized working towards its attainment as an organizational objective. All those interviewed were clear that it could not be achieved without an investment in training and developing staff to have the skills and confidence to accept additional responsibility. Middle managers and supervisors were also recognized as requiring considerable support to help them to understand and be at ease with their role within an empowered organization. The cultural change required, to move to a position where empowerment was firmly embedded, was found to be significant and to have been achieved only over a considerable period of time. Supporting employees and engendering a 'no blame' approach to management were identified as being critical to success in this area. The investment of time and training, and the need to achieve a transformation of organizational culture to achieve empowerment, were issues that few public library managers had yet addressed. The increased decentralization of decision making had not, in most instances, brought about a commensurate movement towards the empowerment of frontline employees in particular.

Employee involvement strategies, the data suggested, were tools that contributed both to the achievement of some sense of empowerment and to the improvement of organizational communications. The use of formal suggestion schemes, properly constituted and promoted, appeared to be a key factor in the achievement of ongoing organizational improvement. The data drawn from the public library sector revealed considerable interest but little practice in this area, with pressures on senior management time and financial constraints being cited as reasons for this. Team working, although more in evidence in public libraries, was not being developed to the extent found in other sectors where it was being developed as a key component in an organization-wide employee involvement strategy. Public libraries did not appear, the research data suggested, to have adopted a strategic approach to the question of employee involvement, although it was apparent in the other public sector organizations studied.

The importance of internal communications was highlighted in all the sectors studied by the project team. The successful dissemination of information and the encouragement of feedback was considered problematic by senior managers in both public libraries and in other sectors. Employee involvement strategies, outlined above, were evident in many commercial sector organizations as facilitating some upwards communication. However, strategies for successful top–down communications, although employing a wide range of tools and techniques, were found to be limited in their success. The importance of internal communications during periods of change and instability was referred to by many senior managers. An active approach was adopted by many of those interviewed whereby they 'walked the talk' and facilitated exchange of information and ideas with employees. However, the data suggested some reluctance on the part of a significant proportion of senior managers to adopt this approach to communication. Many public library managers did not feel that they could prioritize the time required for visiting and communicating with frontline employees. The experience of successful organizations indicates that such an investment of time can produce considerable benefits both in terms of the enhanced efficacy of the two–way communication process and in terms of employee morale.

The issue of external communications was one where greatest divergence was found to occur between the public and private sectors. Commercial organizations were able to make considerable investments in both advertising and promotional activities. Public libraries, although increasingly producing documentation for existing users, such as customer charters, relied largely upon the reporting of activities for external coverage in local media. Public libraries do, however, appear to have an opportunity to put themselves at the centre of their local authority's external communications strategy, if the recommendations of the Audit Commission (1995) are acted upon. This active approach already found in authorities such as Bedfordshire, provides opportunities for libraries to become more professional and clearly focused in their approach to external communications.

Allowing sufficient time for initiatives to take hold and demonstrate their contribution to the attainment of organizational improvement was found to be a particular problem for all public sector organizations studied. The move towards making a long term commitment to continuous improvement was identified as a relatively recent phenomenon in the UK's private sector enterprises. Public library managers, in the main, appeared to be closely tied to the need to achieve any improvements in the short and medium term. Where a longer term approach was identified in this sector it was closely allied to the skills of the Head of Service in their interactions with Elected Members.

The customer

The concept of the customer and of the importance of customer focus, the data suggested, were found to be increasingly prevalent in the public library sector. Employees at all levels within the organization identified the end-user as having become more central to the processes and systems of the service as a whole. However, whereas in the commercial and other public sector case studies undertaken, the role of the customer and importance of successfully segmenting the total population of existing and potential users into homogenous groupings was recognized, public libraries had, in the main, not moved to adopt this approach to any significant extent. Public libraries, Donnelly (1995) recognizes, in undertaking to serve all of the population do not have the opportunity to exploit the full potential of niche marketing only to certain groups where greatest 'profit' is perceived to exist. This is crucial to organizations in the commercial sector.

Whilst there is obviously a much greater focus on the 'customer' in public libraries, irrespective of whether that is the term used or not, the data suggested that senior managers, on the whole, were reluctant to base the entire service development upon the expressed wants of existing library users. The context for this may be explained in part by the findings of the research conducted for the Review of Public Library Service in England and Wales, which identified end-user expectations of public libraries as generally not promoting any great demand for changes or realignment in existing provision (Aslib, 1995). Research in other areas suggests that by defining specific segments of the total potential group of users and developing communication strategies targeted specifically at reaching them, it may be possible to increase expectations of the level and type of service demanded (Williamson, 1992).

Quality management: the right way to manage?

The research provided a basis upon which the philosophy and tools of quality management could be assessed in terms of their appropriateness for implementation in the public library sector. While we recognize challenges, pressures for change and financial constraints much in evidence in this sector, the data suggest that appropriate quality management tools and techniques with their emphasis on continuous improvement and employee involvement, offer considerable potential for public librarians to '... promote excellence in the management of public libraries and the delivery of their services' (Aslib, 1995).

Excellence and the opportunities for achieving sustained organizational improvement were identified as being the key factors in the widespread adoption of quality management. The general reluctance on the part of senior managers in public libraries to embrace the concept more fully was revealed by the data to stem primarily from a partial understanding of quality management and an expressed reluctance to adopt techniques which may not always be appropriate in a public service organization.

The project team found that where quality management offered an approach that is flexible and did not require slavish adherence to specific rules and formulae, considerable and continuing improvements in the service could be achieved.

Recommendations

The critical success factors and barriers to implementation outlined earlier set out some of the key factors with regard to the adoption of quality management identified by the research data and these inform the recommendations which follow.

- Public libraries should place special emphasis upon training, developing and supporting the skills of leadership. Cooperative arrangements for purchasing external training might be considered either regionally or nationally. The input of the Library Association, Public Libraries Quality Forum, Federation of Local Authority Chief Librarians and relevant educational establishments, in providing guidance in the development of regional or national programmes of leadership development, could help to achieve success in this area. A similar recommendation is to be found in the Review of Public Library Service in England and Wales (Aslib, 1995).

- Public library services should consider the benefits of implementing systems of development appraisal for all employees, including part time staff. Senior managers should consider the benefits of adopting a 360 degree system of appraisal for themselves and other senior colleagues. The appraisal of senior staff should ideally be overseen by, or at least involve, senior managers from other departments within the same authority or senior library managers drawn from other authorities.

- Public library services should build upon informal links with other library services to undertake systematic and regular benchmarking exercises of specific aspects of service. Wherever possible senior managers should also develop contacts with and opportunities for learning from organizations outside their own sector.

- Cooperative training, as discussed in the work of MacDougall and Prytherch (1989), should be developed and enhanced from the basis of systems and relationships already in place.

- The research data suggested that a move towards the adoption of suggestion schemes and an increased emphasis on cross functional team working could deliver considerable benefits.

- The increased involvement of Elected Members is recommended. This could come through the provision of training opportunities and also facilitating and encouraging their communication with employees.

- Public librarians should develop a greater awareness and understanding of the potential offered by marketing, in particular the benefits associated with market segmentation as discussed in the work of Kinnell and MacDougall (1994). Customer feedback from market segments should contribute to priority setting and decision making within the service.

- The potential of library automation packages to provide regular data on the performance and market penetration achieved by the library service with regard to particular end-user groups or types of service should be more fully explored. Data generated should be regarded as an important and credible input to the decision making processes employed.

- Public libraries should become more active within their authority as a whole in the process of external communications. Opportunities to be seen as a central information provider on all council provided services are considerable, as can be seen, for example, in Bedfordshire and Leicestershire.

- Research testing appropriate methods and models should be undertaken to support public libraries in their adoption of quality management. This should include investigations of the potential offered by self-assessment and of the democratic approach to quality in the public sector.

- Research should be undertaken to explore a means by which public libraries could have access to a reliable methodology for calculating the costs of nonconformance and quality failures in their services.

As we have seen, quality management can be beneficial to the public library sector. However, it is by no means an easy option, nor does it guarantee major short term improvements. It requires the commitment

and vision of senior managers and the support of politicians. Appropri-
ately used, it can help librarians to '... find ways to break the shackles of
today's problems, so that they can address the critical issues of tomorrow
(Aslib, 1995).

References and bibliography

Abbott, C. (1990) What does good look like? *British Journal of Academic Librarianship*, 5(2), 74-97.

Adair, J. (1988) *Effective communicator.* London: The Industrial Society.

Adamson, C. (1993) Evolving complaints procedures. *Managing Service Quality*, 3(2), 439-444.

Armistead, C. (ed.) (1994) *The future of services management.* London: Kogan Page.

Ashcroft, M. (ed.) (1991) *Maximising income generation in libraries.* Stamford: Capital Planning Information.

Ashcroft, M. and Wilson, A. (eds.) (1991) *Performance indicators for public libraries: proceedings of a seminar held in Stamford, Lincolnshire, 6th November 1990.* Stamford: Capital Planning Information.

Ashcroft, M. and Wilson, A. (eds.) (1992) *Competitive tendering and libraries.* Stamford: Capital Planning Information.

Aslib (1995) *The review of public library service in England and Wales.* London: Aslib.

Asser, M. (1993) The demand for quality and the pressure for change on Oxfordshire's Department of Leisure and Arts. *Library Management*, 14(4), 13-16.

Atkinson, J. and Spilsbury, M. (1994) Evaluating the investment. *Training Tomorrow*, July, 21-22.

Audit Commission for England and Wales (1989). *Managing services effectively: performance review.* London: HMSO.

Audit Commission for England and Wales (1995). *Talkback.* London: HMSO.

Audit Commission for Local Authorities and the National Health Service in England and Wales (1993) *Putting quality on the map: measuring and appraising quality in the public service.* London: HMSO.

BA (1995) *British Airways benchmarking day.* London, April.

Barley, P. (1994) Looking for trouble. *Marketing Business,* September, 21-24.

Barnett, J. (1995) Self-improvement. *UK Quality,* March, 18.

Bates, J. (1993) *Managing value for money in the public sector.* London: Chapman & Hall.

Beaumont, A. and Libiszewski, R. (1993) A prescription for quality. *Management Services,* 37(3), 18-23.

Bennett, M. (1994) Internal affairs. *Marketing Business,* April, 24-27.

Bernhardt, D. (1993) *Perfectly legal competitor intelligence: how to get it, use it and profit from it.* London: Pitman.

Bloor, I. (1991) *Performance indicators and decision support systems for libraries.* London: British Library.

Bourdillon, H. (1962) *Standards of public library service in England and Wales.* London: HMSO.

Brockman, J. (1992) Just another management fad? The implications of TQM for library and information services. *Aslib Proceedings,* 44(7/8), July/August, 283-288.

Brophy, P. (1994) BS: a curse or blessing? *Library Association Record,* 96(6), 320-21.

Brown, R. (ed.) (1988) *Partnership schemes and joint ventures between the public and private sector.* Stamford: Capital Planning Information.

Brown, R. (ed.) (1989) *Moving to contract.* Stamford: Capital Planning Information.

Brown, T. (1993) *Understanding BS5750 and other quality systems.* Newbury: Commonsense Publishing.

Carr, C. (1994) Empowered organisations: empowering leaders. *Training and Development USA,* 48(3), 39-44.

Citizen's Charter Complaints Task Force (1993) *Effective complaints systems.* Citizen's Charter Unit.

Clark, F. (1992a) Public awareness. *Total Quality Management,* December, 373- 378.

Clark, F. (1992b) *Quality and service: a key focus for performance in the public sector.* Henley on Thames: Henley Management College.

Clark, G. and Stanley, P. (1994) Service with a smile. *Management Training UK*, 2(1), 26-31.

Clayton, C. (1993) Quality and the public services. *Public Library Journal*, 8(1), 11-12.

Clutterbuck, D. (1993) Clarify your purpose. *Managing Service Quality*, November, 5-6.

Clutterbuck, D. and Kernaghan, S. (1994) *The power of empowerment: release the hidden talents of your employees.* London: Kogan Page.

Clyne, S. (1992) Investing in your people. *Training and Development UK*, 10(11), 24-26.

Comedia (1993) *Borrowed time? The future of public libraries in the United Kingdom.* Bournes Green: Comedia, 35.

Convention of Scottish Local Authorities (1985) *Standards for the public library service in Scotland.* Report by a Working Party appointed by the Arts and Recreation Committee of the Convention of Scottish Local Authorities. Edinburgh: COSLA.

Cook, S. (1992) *Customer care.* London: Kogan Page.

Crosby, P. (1979) *Quality is free.* New York: McGraw Hill.

Curtis, M., Jennings, B., Wheeler, S. and White, L. (1993) Quality assurance in Kent. *Public Library Journal*, 8(1), Jan/Feb, 1-4.

Curzon, S. (1989) *Managing change.* London: Neal-Schuman.

Dale, B. and Plunkett, J. (1995) *Quality costing.* 2nd ed. London: Chapman and Hall.

Dobbyns, L. and Crawford-Mason, C. (1991) *Quality or else.* Boston: Houghton Mifflin.

Donnelly, R. (1995) *An overview of quality management in United Kingdom public libraries.* Presentation to BLR&DD Workshop on Quality Management. London, 24 April.

Drummond, H. (1992) *The quality movement.* London: Kogan Page.

Dunn, A. (1993) Decent suggestions. *Human Resources,* Summer, 16-20.

Eccles, T. (1993) The deceptive allure of empowerment. *Long Range Planning,* 26(6), 13-21.

Ellis, D. and Norton, B. (1993) *Implementing BS5750/ISO9000 in libraries.* London: Aslib.

Finn, R. (1994) Investors in People: counting the dividends. *Personnel Management,* May, 30-33.

Fletcher, C. (1993) *Appraisal, routes to improved performance.* London: Institute of Personnel Management.

Foster, M. and Whittle, S. (1989) The quality management maze. *Total Quality Management,* 1(3), 143-8.

Fowler, A. (1994) How to obtain an Investors in People award. *PM Plus,* 5(6), 13-21.

Foy, N. (1994) *Empowering people at work.* Aldershot: Gower.

Freeman, L. (ed.) (1991) *Developing quality in libraries.* London: HMSO.

Freemantle, D. (1993) *Incredible customer service.* London: McGraw Hill.

Fukuda, R. (1990) *CEDAC: a tool for continuous systematic improvement.* Cambridge Mass: Productivity Press.

Fulmer, W. and Godwin, J. (1994) So you want to be a superior service provider. *Business Horizons,* 37(6), 23-26.

Goodswen, M. (1993) Rewarding empowerment. *Involvement and Participation,* Summer, 8-11.

Great Britain (1964) *Public Libraries and Museums Act 1964.* London: HMSO.

Great Britain (1988) *The Local Government Act 1988.* London: HMSO.

Great Britain (1991) *The Citizen's Charter—raising the standard.* London: HMSO.

Great Britain (1994) *Citizen's Charter: Charter Mark Scheme 1994: Guide for Applicants.* London: HMSO.

Gyfford, G. (1995) *Local politics in Britain. 2nd ed.* London: Chapman and Hall.

Hammons, C. (1990) Total quality management in the public sector. *Management Decision,* 28(4), 15-19.

Handy, C. (1993) *Understanding organizations.* 4th ed. London: Penguin.

Hanman, R. (1993) *Kaizen for Europe.* Bedford: IFS.

Harari, O. (1991) The essence of leadership. *Management Review,* November, 63.

Harari, O. (1992a) Nourishing the complaint procedure. *Management Review,* February, 41-42.

Harari, O. (1992b) Thank heaven for complainers. *Management Review,* January, 59-60.

Hassall, J. and Ainley. J. (1993) Investor in People award, is it worth having? *NVQ SVQ Focus,* 1(5), 24-27.

Heller, R. (1994) Putting the total into total quality. *Management Today,* August, 56-62.

HERTIS Information and Research (1992) *Total Quality Management: the information business, key Issues '92.* Hatfield: University of Hertfordshire Press.

Hodges, J. (1993) *The effects of external factors on levels of stress among middle managers in public libraries.* PhD thesis. University of Sheffield, Department of Information Studies.

Hopson, B. and Scally, M. (1991) *Twelve steps to success through service.* London: Mercury Books.

Horton, T. (1992) Delegation and team building: no solo acts please. *Management Review,* September, 58- 61.

Imai, M. (1986) *Kaizen.* New York: Random House.

Income Data Services (1991) *Suggestion schemes study 495.* London: Income Data Services.

Industrial Society (1993) *Training trends.* London: The Industrial Society.

Institute of Directors (1994) *Customer care: a director's guide.* London: Institute of Directors and UNISYS.

Institute of Management (1994) *Raising the standard: a survey of managers' attitudes to customer care* London: Institute of Management.

Jackson, P. and Ashton, C. (1993) Investing in people. *Total Quality Management,* June, 51-54.

Janis, I. (1989) *Crucial decisions: leadership in policymaking and crisis management.* New York: Free Press.

Johanssen, C. (1992) The use of quality control principles and methods in library and information science theory and practice. *Libri,* 42(4), Oct-Dec, 283-293.

Johanssen, C. (1993) Can the ISO standards on quality management be useful to libraries, and how? Paper presented at the *Open Session on Quality and Quality Management in libraries, IFLA Conference, Barcelona, Spain, 22-27 August 1993.*

Johnson, G. and Scholes, K. (1988) *Exploring corporate strategy.* London: Prentice Hall.

Juran, J. (1992) *Juran on quality by design: the new steps for planning quality into goods and services.* New York: Free Press.

Juran, J. and Gryna, F. (1993) *Quality planning and analysis: from product development through use.* London: McGraw Hill.

Karlof, B. and Ostblom, S. (1993) *Benchmarking a signpost to excellence in quality and productivity.* Chichester: John Wiley.

Keiser, B. (1994) Quality management in libraries and information centres. *Congresboek Kwaliteitszorg in Informatiedienstverlening Rotterdam, 1st & 2nd Dec 1993.* Den Haag: NBBI, 3-20.

Kenyon, F. (1927) *Report on public libraries in England and Wales.* London: HMSO.

King Research Ltd. (1990) *Keys to success: performance indicators for public libraries.* Library and Information series no.18. London: Office of Arts and Libraries.

Kinnell, M. (1994) Quality issues for academic and industrial library and information services. *Nordinfo.* Oslo: NYTT, 3-20.

Kinnell, M. and MacDougall, J. (1994) *Meeting the marketing challenge: strategies for public libraries and leisure services.* London: Taylor Graham.

Kinnell Evans, M. (1991) *All change? Public library management strategies for the 1990s.* London: Taylor Graham.

Lancaster, F. (1993) *If you want to evaluate your library.* 2nd ed. London: The Library Association.

Landry, C. (1995) The cultural institutions of the 21st century. *The Independent,* 17 June, 17.

Lewin, K. (1935) *A dynamic theory of personality.* New York: McGraw Hill.

Lewis, B. (1991) Customer care in service organizations. *Management Decision,* 29(1), 31-34.

Library Association (1994) *A charter for public libraries.* London: The Library Association.

Liebfried, K. and McNair, C. (1992) *Benchmarking: a tool for continuous improvement.* New York: Harper Collins.

Livingston Booth, A. (1985) *Stressmanship.* London: Severn House.

Local Government Management Board (1994) *Investors in People: the local authority perspective.* Luton: LGMB.

Local government: the management agenda (1993) London: ICSA.

Lomer, M. and Rogers, S. (1983) *The public library and the local authority.* Birmingham: University of Birmingham Institute of Local Government Studies.

Lovell, R. (ed.) (1994) *Managing change in the new public sector.* Harlow: Longman.

Lucas, P. (1993) Customer consultation and its implications for service delivery. *Public Library Journal,* 8(20).

Macaulay, S. and Cook, S. (1994) Handling difficult customers. *Training Officer,* 30(2), 53-55.

MacDonald, J. (1994) *But we are different: quality for the service sector.* Didcot: Management Books 2000.

MacDougall, A. and Prytherch, L. (1989) *Cooperative training in libraries.* Aldershot: Gower.

Madder, K. (1990) Swift handling of complaints is the key to quality service. *Local Government Chronicle,* 9 November, 23.

Marchington, M. (1992) *New developments in employee involvement.* Manchester: UMIST.

Marsh, J. (1993) Economics to fight decline. *Managing Service Quality,* November, 15-20.

Martin, D. (1994) *Dealing with demanding customers.* London: Pitman.

Matthes, K. (1992) What is the big idea? Empower employees through suggestion schemes. *HR Focus,* 69(10), 17.

McColvin, L. (1942) *The public library system of Great Britain: a report on its present condition with proposals for post-war reorganization.* London: Library Association.

McConville, J. (1990) Innovation through involvement. *Total Quality Management,* October, 295-297.

McConville, J. and Wood, A. (1990) *Ideas unlimited: how to run suggestion schemes successfully.* London: The Industrial Society.

Midwinter, A. and McVicar, M. (1994) *The size and efficiency debate.* British Library R&D Report 6143. London: The Library Association.

Miller, T. (1992) IiP status, is it a wise investment? *Personnel Management,* 24(10), 63-67.

Milner, E. (1995) *Where are we now?* Presentation to the BLR&DD Workshop on Quality Management. London, 24 April.

Milner, E., Kinnell, M. and Usherwood, B. (1994) Quality management: the public library debate. *Public Library Journal,* 9(6), 151-157.

Milner, E., Kinnell, M. and Usherwood, B. (1995a) Employee suggestion schemes: a management tool for the 1990s. *Library Management,* 16(3), 3-8.

Milner, E., Kinnell Evans, M., and Usherwood, B. (1995b) Maintaining momentum down the quality street. *Library Association Record,* 97(7), 395.

Mitchell, A. (1994) The people factor. *Marketing Business*, October, 24-28.

Mitchell, V. (1993) Handling consumer complaint information: why and how. *Management Decision*, 31(3), 21-28.

Mitchell Stewart, A. (1994) *Empowering people*. London: Pitman.

Morgan, C. and Murgatroyd, S. (1994) *Total Quality Management in the public sector: an international perspective*. Buckingham: Open University Press.

Naumann, E. and Shannon, P. (1992) What is customer driven marketing? *Business Horizons*, 35(6), 44-52.

Nichols, D. (1989) Bottom-up strategies: asking the employees for advice. *Management Review*, December, 44-49.

Oakland, J. (1994a) *Cases in Total Quality Management*. Oxford: Butterworth Heinemann.

Oakland, J. (1994b) *Total Quality Management*, 2nd edn. Oxford: Butterworth Heinemann.

Office of Arts and Libraries (1990) *Setting objectives for public library services*. London: HMSO.

Orr, R. (1973) Measuring the goodness of library services: a general framework for considering quantitative measures. *Journal of Documentation*, 29(3), 313-332.

Parasuraman, A., Zeithaml, V. and Berry, L. (1988) SERVQUAL: a multiple item scale for measuring consumer perceptions of service quality. *Journal of Retailing*, 64(1), 12-40.

Pasmore, W. (1994) *Creating strategic change*. New York: John Wiley.

Peacock, R. (1995) *Organisational self-assessment*. A presentation to the Institute of Electrical Engineers, London, 9 June, 1995.

Peters, T. (1992) *Liberation management*. London: Macmillan.

Pfeffer, N. and Coote, A. (1991) *Is quality good for you?* London: Institute for Public Policy Research.

Phoenix Research Ltd. (1993) *Parental preferences in selecting a secondary school*. Hertford: Unpublished research report.

Pickard, J. (1993) The real meaning of empowerment. *Personnel Management*, 25(11).

Plunkett, L. and Fournier, R. (1991) *Participative management*. New York: John Wiley.

Plymie, J. (1990) Transforming complaints into opportunities. *Supervisory Management*, June, 11-12.

Pollitt, C. and Harrison, S. (eds.) (1992) *Handbook of public services management*. Oxford: Blackwell.

Porter, L. (1992) *Quality initiatives in British library and information services*. British Library R&D Report 6105. London: The British Library.

Private process/public advantage: the value to public library authorities of special services provided by library suppliers (1987) London: British National Bibliography Research Fund.

Pugh, D. and Hickson, D. (1989) *Writers on organizations*. London: Penguin.

Pybus, R.L. (1994) *Performing for people*. Trowbridge: Wiltshire County Council Library and Museum Service.

Randall, L. (1993) Perceptual blueprinting. *Managing Service Quality*, May, 7-12.

Redfern, M. (1990) Giving an account: performance indicators for libraries. *Library Review*, 39(5), 7-9.

Rienzo, T. (1993) Planning Deming management for service organizations. *Business Horizons*, 36(3), 19-29.

Ripley, R. and Ripley, M. (1992) Empowerment: the cornerstone of quality management in innovative organizations in the 1990s. *Management Decision*, 30(4), 20-43.

Roberts, S. (1959) *The structure of the public library service in England and Wales*. London: HMSO.

Rooney, M. (1991) Applying common sense. *Managing Service Quality*, 2(1), 13-16.

Sanderson, I. (ed.) (1992) *The management of quality in local government*. Harlow: Longman.

Sanford, K. (1989) The customer isn't always right. *Supervisory Management*, October, 29-32.

Scholtes, P. (1988) *The team handbook: how to use teams to improve quality*. Madison, Wi: Joiner Associates.

Scott, C. and Jaffe, D. (1991) *Empowerment: building a committed workforce*. London: Kogan Page.

Seddon, J. (1992) *I want you to cheat: the unreasonable guide to service and quality in organisations*. Buckingham: Vanguard Press.

Select Committee on Public Libraries (1849) *Report from the Select Committee on Public Libraries with the proceedings of the Committee and the minutes of evidence*. Education, Public Libraries, 12 June.

Shaugnessy, T. (1987) The search for quality. *Journal of Library Administration*, 8(1), 5-10.

Shore, C. (1985) What's wrong with 'off the shelf' quality management systems? *Quality Assurance*, 11(2).

Simon, H. (1993) Stein der Weisen. *Manager Magazin*, February, 134-140.

Skelcher, C. and K. Walsh. (eds.) (1992) *Customer contracts and complaints systems*. Birmingham: University of Birmingham.

Smith, P. (1989) *How to set up and run effective employee suggestion schemes*. London: Kogan Page.

Speller, S. and Ghobadian, A. (1993) Change for the public sector. *Managing Service Quality*, September, 29-34.

Spilsbury, M. (1994) *Evaluation of Investors in People in England and Wales*. Brighton: Falmer (Flamer on p.140).

Stebbing, L. (1990) *Quality management in the service sector*. London: Ellis Horwood.

Stewart, J. and Walsh, K. (1989) *The search for quality*. Luton: Local Government Training Board.

Sumsion, J. (1993) *Practical performance indicators—1992. Documenting the Citizen's Charter consultation for UK public libraries with examples of PIs and surveys in use*. Loughborough: Library and Statistics Information Unit (LISU).

Suzaki, K. (1993) *The new shop floor management: empowering people for continuous improvement.* New York: Free Press.

Tam, H. (ed.) (1984) *Marketing, competition and the public sector.* Harlow: Longman.

Tam, H. (1993) *Serving the public.* Harlow: Longman.

Tam, H. (1994) Empowerment: too big a task? *Professional Manager,* 3(2), 8-9.

Tyerman, K. (1995) *Presentation to quality management workshop.* London, 24 April.

Tylczak, L. (1990) *Effective employee participation.* London: Kogan Page.

Usherwood, B. (1981) *The visible library.* London: The Library Association.

Usherwood, B. (1989) *The public library as public knowledge.* London: The Library Association.

Usherwood, B. (1993) *Public library politics.* London: The Library Association.

Vanes, S. (1993) Do you communicate? *Library Management,* 14(2), 19.

Vine, A. (1993) Do you care for your customers? *Library Management,* 14(2), 15-18.

Wakin, E. (1991) Give employees feedback, not criticism. *Today's Office,* August, 22-23.

Walker, D. (1990) *Customer first: a strategy for service quality.* Aldershot: Gower.

Walsh, K. (1991) *Competitive tendering for local authority services.* London: HMSO.

Walsh, K. and Davis, H. (1993) *Competition and service: the impact of the Local Government Act 1988.* London: HMSO.

Walton, M. (1991) *Deming management at work.* New York: Perigree.

Warner, M. (1992) The great paradox: responsibility without empowerment. *Business Horizons,* 35(3), 55-58.

Waterman, R. (1994) *The frontiers of excellence.* London: Nicholas Brealey.

Webster, C. (1994) Measuring service quality and promoting decentering. *TQM Magazine,* 6(5), 50-55.

Welsh Office (1984) *The review of district library functions 1984.* Cardiff: Welsh Office.

White, J. (1993) *Frogs or chameleons: report to the Library Association, February 1993.* London: The Library Association.

Whitehall, T. (1992) Quality in library and information services: a review. *Library Management,* 13(5), 23-25.

Wilkinson, A., Redman, T. and Snape, E. (1993) *Quality and the manager.* Corby, Northants: Institute of Management.

Williams, M. (1993) A measure of success. *TQM Magazine,* 5(3), 47-50.

Williamson, C. (1992) *Whose standards?* Buckingham: Open University Press.

Wilson, D. and Game, C. (1994) *Local Government in the United Kingdom.* Basingstoke: Macmillan.

Acknowledgements

We should like to thank all librarians who, despite heavy professional workloads, took the trouble to return questionnaires and to discuss issues with us. Particular thanks are due to all those who participated in the case study programme and who shared their experiences and perceptions of quality management with the research team. We are especially indebted to the members of our Advisory Group for their encouragement and constructive advice in the research programme: Carl Clayton (The Library Association), Michael Curtis (Kent), Guy Daines (The Library Association), Rob Donnelly (CBI), Geoff Elgar (Lincolnshire), Isobel Thompson (BLRIC), Andrew Stevens (Westminster), Karen Tyerman (Brent) and Pearl Valentine (North Eastern Education and Library Board, Northern Ireland). The team are also greatly indebted to John Sumsion, formerly Director of the Library and Information Statistics Unit at lLoughborough University, for his advice and support throughout the project. The staff of the Institute of Management's Management Information Centre also greatly assisted the research team in their exploration of the literature available on the subject of quality management.

Appendix A

Project questionnaire

POLICY & PLANNING

1. Does your Local Authority have a written policy on quality?
   Yes ☐   No ☐   In preparation ☐

2. Does the Library Service have a written policy on quality?
   Yes ☐   No ☐   In preparation ☐

3. Do you have a formal quality programme in place?
   Yes: in place ☐   In the process of being set up ☐   No ☐

4. Which of the following initiatives is the Library Service involved with? (Please tick as appropriate)

   Total Quality Management ☐   Customer contract ☐
   Quality circles ☐   The Learning Organisation' ☐
   BS5750 ☐   Charter Mark ☐
   Investors in people ☐   None ☐

   Other (please specify)

   ....
   ....

5. Who was involved in developing the policy on quality for the Library Service? (Please tick as appropriate)

   Elected members ☐   Frontline Staff ☐
   Senior managment ☐   Clients ☐
   Middle management ☐   External consultants ☐

6. Has your Library Service implemented any of the following?

	Yes	No	In preparation
Management by function	☐	☐	☐
Cost centres	☐	☐	☐
Localised decision making	☐	☐	☐
Flatter management structure	☐	☐	☐
Performance indicators	☐	☐	☐
Staff appraisal	☐	☐	☐
Management information system	☐	☐	☐
Team working	☐	☐	☐

7. How is the quality of your service measured?

Number of complaints received	☐
Number of compliments received	☐
Through existing performance indicators	☐
Customer satisfaction surveys	☐
Success against predetermined targets	☐
Greater value for money	☐

Other (please specify):

....
....
....

PERSONNEL & TRAINING

8. Is there a specific person or team responsible for quality within the Library Service?

Yes ☐   No ☐   In preparation ☐

If **yes**, please give job or team title:

....

9. Do you have a training programme designed to enhance the knowledge and skills of staff in relation to quality within the Library Service? (Please tick as appropriate)

Training for Senior Managers ☐
Training for Middle Managers ☐
Training for Paraprofessionals ☐
Training for Library and Information Support Staff ☐
No specific training in quality is offered ☐

[We would be grateful if you could send us examples of course outlines that you may have.]

ESSENTIAL FEATURES OF QUALITY IN A PUBLIC LIBRARY SERVICE

10. In this question we would like you to consider each of the statements made and to give a response based upon your own judgement as to how essential the following features are to a quality library service. The scale used is from 5 - strongly agreeing with the statement to 1 - strongly disagreeing. If you judge a service to be desirable rather than essential you should tick a number in the middle of the range.

Tick (✓) one box in each row

	Essential				Unnecessary
	5	4	3	2	1
(a) A good book stock will always be available to clients	☐	☐	☐	☐	☐
(b) Materials associated with the service (such as library guides, Charters) will be visually appealing	☐	☐	☐	☐	☐
(c) Clients will have the right to request books and materials from other libraries for a nominal fee	☐	☐	☐	☐	☐
(d) Library stock is displayed attractively	☐	☐	☐	☐	☐
(e) Clients benefit from clear guiding to find their way about and make use of the Library	☐	☐	☐	☐	☐
(f) When the library promises to do something by a certain time, it does so	☐	☐	☐	☐	☐
(g) Employees are always willing to help clients	☐	☐	☐	☐	☐
(h) Clients always receive prompt service	☐	☐	☐	☐	☐
(i) Employees are never too busy to respond to requests from clients	☐	☐	☐	☐	☐

Tick (✓) one box in each row

	Essential			Unnecessary	
	5	4	3	2	1
(j) Employees are consistently courteous to clients	☐	☐	☐	☐	☐
(k) All employees involved in contact with clients will have the knowledge to answer questions or make appropriate referrals	☐	☐	☐	☐	☐
(l) Libraries will have opening hours convenient to the majority of their clients	☐	☐	☐	☐	☐
(m) Libraries will offer services which are relevant to their clients' needs	☐	☐	☐	☐	☐
(n) Libraries will make their clients aware of the standards of service they can expect	☐	☐	☐	☐	☐
(o) Librarians will consult their clients about changes in policy	☐	☐	☐	☐	☐

We would ask you now to review your responses to the statements in Question 10. On the basis of this review can you choose five of the statements which, in your judgement, most require improvement in your Library Service. [For example, if you believe statements a, f, g, m and n require most improvement you would simply give the letter next to each statement.]

....

COMMUNICATION

11. How are specific policies and initiatives on quality communicated to staff of the Library Service? (Please tick as appropriate)

Staff meetings	☐	Mission statement	☐
Training courses	☐	Team briefing	☐
Quality groups	☐	On the job training	☐
Appraisal scheme	☐	Bulletin/newsletters	☐
Managers 'walking the floor'	☐		
Visits and presentations by elected members	☐		

12. Does the Library Service operate a suggestions scheme for staff?

Yes ☐   No ☐   In preparation ☐

13. How is the Library Service's attitude to quality communicated to the public? (Please tick as appropriate)

Local radio and TV	☐	Suggestions scheme	☐
Handouts	☐	Interface with frontline staff	☐
Posters	☐	Local newspapers	☐
Charter document	☐	Adverts in local publications	☐
Complaints scheme	☐	Public meetings	☐

GENERAL

14. Has the Library Service developed strategies for developing quality partnerships with suppliers and other organisations (eg. suppliers, TECs, Arts Council)

    An example of this might be a guaranteed settlement of payment period for suppliers in return for guarantees on delivery speed of stock.

    Please give any examples.

    ....
    ....
    ....
    ....
    ....
    ....

15. If you have implemented quality initiatives what have been the three major impacts for good or bad?

    ....
    ....
    ....

16. What in your opinion are the three most important 'quality' features of a Public Library Service?

    ....
    ....
    ....

A number of authorities will be invited to take part in a follow-up interview. If you are willing to take part in the second stage of this project, please indicate by ticking the box. ☐

If yes, who would be the most appropriate person to contact in the first instance?

....

Name/Title of person completing questionnaire:..............................

Address: ....
                 ....
                 ....
                 ....
Tel. No.   ....
Fax No.   ....

Appendix B

Results of questionnaire responses

The project team sent a questionnaire to every public library authority in the UK, with responses invited between October and December 1994. In total, the response rate was 85%.

Policy and planning

Q1.   Does your Local Authority have a written policy on quality?

  63%   had no written policy
  26%   did have a written policy
  11%   had a policy in preparation

Q2.   Does the Library Service have a written policy on quality?

  67%   had no written policy
  21%   did have a written policy
  12%   were preparing a policy

There is an undoubted correlation between the responses to questions 1 and 2. If the Local Authority did not have a written policy on quality then it would seem to be extremely unlikely that the Library Service would. However, it is worth noting that, in our returns, five Library Services identified themselves as having a written policy whilst their Local Authority did not have a written policy, or was in the process of preparing one.

Q3.   Do you have a quality programme in place?

  62%   did *not* have a quality programme in place
  19%   of Library Services indicated that they did
  19%   were in the process of setting one up

Q4. Respondents to the questionnaire were asked to indicate which, if any, of a number of specific quality initiatives, their service was involved with.

47% of respondents indicated that their service was involved in *none* of these

26.5% adoption rate for Investors in People

18.5% adoption rate for the Charter Mark

13.5% adoption rate for Customer Contracts

10% adoption rate for Total Quality Management

10% adoption rate for Quality Circles

3.5% adoption rate for BS 5750/ISO 9000

2% adoption rate for the Learning Organization

Q5. Who was involved in developing the policy on quality for the Library Service?

49% had not yet developed a policy.

Of the remaining respondents who had a policy:

97% had involved Senior Management

69% Middle Management

53% Frontline Employees

33% Elected Members

29% Clients

7% External Consultants

Q6. In this question we sought to establish how widespread certain management practices were. This was particularly helpful when considering those responding authorities who did not feel that they were involved in quality management, in as much as it indicated what was actually being *practised* in library services.

19% had adopted *Management by Function* (rather than geographical area)

5% were preparing to implement it

59% had adopted *Cost Centres*

10% were preparing to do so

46% had implemented *Localized Decision-Making*
45% were preparing to do so

49% had *Flatter Management Structures*
4% were working towards this

40% had a system of *Staff Appraisal*
21% were preparing to implement one

86% were using *Performance Indicators*
7% were preparing to do so

39% had a *Management Information System* in place
15% were developing one

61% of those responding indicated that their service was involved in *Team Working*

Q7. We sought to establish what criteria were being used to measure the quality of the service delivered. Respondents were asked to indicate which of the criteria listed they used as a means of measurement.

88% used existing *Performance Indicators*
65% indicated that *Complaints* were used as a measurement
49% measured *Success against predetermined targets*
49% used *Compliments*
35% took account of *Greater value for money*
25% used *Customer Satisfaction Surveys*

Respondents were invited to give examples of other measures used. Examples of interest included:

» Comparison with other library services
» Number of books issued
» The perceptions of elected members

Personnel and training

Q8. We wished to establish if there was a specific person or team responsible for quality within the library service

    56%   identified *no* individual or team as being responsible for quality

    20%   reported responsibility resting with an *individual*

    19%   indicated that they had a *team* in place

    5%   were preparing to assign the responsibility

Two authorities responded that *all employees* shared the responsibility for quality issues.

Of the 44% who had, or were preparing to, assign responsibility, most individuals or groups identified were members of the senior management group.

An interesting array of individual and team titles were cited, including:

»   Quality of Service Team

»   Quality Improvement Team

»   TQM Champion

Q9. The question asked respondents to identify whether their service offered specific training on quality related matters, and if so, to whom it was offered.

    64%   offered *no specific* training in quality

    33%   had provision for *Middle Managers*

    31%   made training available for *Paraprofessionals*

    28%   indicated that training was available for *Senior Managers*

    28%   to all groups of *Support Staff*

Many respondents did, however, comment that they felt that certain quality 'issues' would naturally arise in other training courses and would be dealt with there.

Essential features of quality in a public library service

Q10. The model that was used had been adapted from 'SERVQUAL', a system of assigning priorities developed for use in the retail sector. Prior to sending out the questionnaire, the project team felt that it was likely that the majority of responses would identify a large proportion of the fifteen statements featured, as being essential. As the results shown in the table overleaf indicate, broadly speaking this has indeed happened. However, it is interesting to look at those particular statements that were not universally acknowledged to be *absolutely* essential.

Those respondents were then asked to review the fifteen statements and to use their professional judgement to select the five which most required improvement in their service. Setting aside the one service that felt it did not need to improve *any* of the features mentioned, the priorities highlighted have provided very useful data for the project.

56%	identified (k) as being a priority
49%	identified (l)
48%	identified (e)
44%	identified (a)
40%	identified (o)
33%	identified (d)
32%	identified (i)
31%	identified (b)
30%	identified (m)
21%	identified (h)
17%	identified (f)
14%	identified (j)
13%	identified (n)
6%	identified (c)
6%	identified (g)

	Essential			Unnecessary	
	5	4	3	2	1
	%	%	%	%	%
(a) A good book will always be available to clients	87.9	8	5.1	0	0
(b) Materials associated with the service (e.g. guides & Charters) will be visually appealing	28.6	47	20	2.4	2
(c) Clients will have the right to request books and materials for a nominal fee	69.3	16.4	8	3.3	3
(d) Library stock is displayed attractively	53	41	5	1	0
(e) Clients benefit from clear guiding to find their way about and make use of the Library	56	36	3	2	1
(f) When the library promises to do something by a certain time, it does so	68	27	5	0	0
(g) Employees are always willing to help clients	89	8	1.5	1.5	0
(h) Clients always receive prompt service	62	32	5	1	0
(i) Employees are never too busy to respond to requests from clients	68	26	6	0	0
(j) Employees are consistently courteous to clients	93	7	0	0	0
(k) All employees involved in contact with clients will have the knowledge to answer questions or make appropriate referrals	78	21	1	0	0
(l) Libraries will have opening hours convenient to the majority of their clients	73	24	3	0	0
(m) Libraries will offer services which are relevant to their clients' needs	71	26	3	0	0
(n) Libraries will make their clients aware of the standards of service they can expect	41	36	18	3	2
(o) Libraries will consult their clients about changes in policy	23	35	33	7	3

Communication

Q11. As communication is a vital part of the success or failure of policies initiatives, we asked library services to indicate which, of a range of methods, they employed.

89% indicated the use of *staff meetings*
67% believed that communication took place through *training courses*
66% used *on the job training*
60% of managers *'walk the floor'*
51% *bulletins and newsletters*
47% team briefing
46% used a *mission statement*
28% used an *appraisal scheme*
9% used *quality groups*
5% cited visits and presentations by *elected members*

Q12. The question of employee involvement is an important one in any study of quality management. By asking if the library service operated a suggestion scheme for staff, it was hoped to establish just how many services had *formalized* this aspect of encouraging employee involvement. What the responses, and follow-up queries, identified was that the majority of those responding positively that they operated a scheme (30%, with 7% indicating that they were preparing to do so) actually meant that their staff knew they could pass an idea upwards if they wished to do so. The reality is, that only some 5% of respondents actually had in place, or were about to implement, the mechanism for a formalized employee suggestion scheme.

Q13. The question addressed the way in which the library service's attitude and policies on quality are communicated to the public. A range of options was listed, respondents being able to select all of those appropriate to their service.

70% indicated the use of *complaints scheme*
61% *the interface with frontline staff*
54% *handouts*
54% *suggestions scheme*

44%   *local newspapers*
43%   *posters*
42%   *Charter documents*
19%   *local radio and TV*
17%   used *public meetings*
11%   placed *adverts in local publications*

General

Questions 14, 15 and 16 all relied upon gaining an open-ended response and thus do not readily lend themselves to analysis. However, it was possible to identify discernible trends coming from the responses and it is these more generalized 'headings' which will be referred to.

Q14.   Asked if any strategies had been implemented for the development of quality partnerships.

79%   identified *no* partnerships existing
15%   identified partnerships with *Library Suppliers*
6%   identified partnerships with the *TECs*
4%   identified *Business Link and City Challenge initiatives*
3%   *arts bodies*

Q15.   We asked respondents to identify the three major impacts for good or bad, that had arisen from the implementation of quality initiatives. Those who responded gave a wide range of observations based upon practical experience.

41%   identified *no* impacts for good or bad
21%   increased communication with clients
18%   identified the increased number of meetings and volume of paperwork
14%   need for a large amount of management input in order to maintain momentum for improvement
13%   the emphasis placed upon monitoring and inspecting services
11%   identified positively the greater emphasis on customer care
11%   greater empowerment of employees
6%   the use of formal Performance Indicators

6%   greater use of Management Information System
5%   attempting to empower those who had no desire for it
4%   cited the greater use of devolved management

Q16. We invited those completing the questionnaire to share with us their views on what the three most important 'quality' features of a public library service were. Although a great many features were cited, there was some degree of consensus in the responses.

62%   highlighted the importance of having skilled, courteous employees
57%   providing an appropriate range and quality of resources
32%   stated that a welcoming environment was important
17%   cited the importance of identifying and meeting client expectations and needs
14%   consistency of service delivery
11%   cited the importance of making services accessible through increased opening hours
9%   identified the need for clearly defined aims and objectives
9%   wide range of services available
2%   the need for committed management
1.5% wide range of services available

Appendix C

Programme of the Quality Management Workshop held in London on 24th April 1995

09.45–10.10	Registration
10.15–10.45	Where are we now?
	Presentation on the background of the research
	Dr. B. Usherwood, Eileen Milner,
	Professor Margaret Evans
10.50–11.20	Group discussion of Leadership
11.20–11.30	Coffee
11.30–12.00	Group discussion of Customers/Clients/Members
12.00–12.30	Group discussion of Empowerment
12.30–13.10	Group feedback
	Chairman: Rob Donnelly,
	Head of Employee Relations, CBI.
13.10–14.15	Lunch
14.15–14.45	Group discussion of Systems for Quality
14.45–15.15	Group discussion of Training for Quality
15.15–15.30	Tea
15.30–16.00	Group feedback
	Chairman: Andrew Stevens,
	Westminster City Libraries
16.00–16.20	An overview of the day
	Karen Tyerman, Brent Library Service
	Rob Donnelly, CBI
16.20–16.30	Closing questions
16.30	Workshop closes

Appendix D

Profile of case study organizations

As all the organizations who participated in this stage of the research were guaranteed anonymity in publications, the details given below are necessarily limited, in order to protect their identities.

Public library case studies

The case studies in this sector comprised 6 English Shire authorities, 2 London Boroughs, 1 Metropolitan authority and 2 Welsh counties.

Case Study A

Population served:	545,000
Annual budget (approx):	£6.2 million
Original impetus for QM:	Chief Executive, since 1991
Responsibility in library service:	Assistant Director
Elements of QM adopted:	Devolved management structures
	Performance indicators
	Cross-functional teams
	Customer Focus Groups
	Externally commissioned market research
	Increased investment in training 1994/95
	Authority-wide complaints scheme

Case Study B

Population served:	959,000
Annual budget (approx):	£8.6m
Original impetus for QM:	Chief Executive, since 1992
Responsibility in library service:	Not assigned

Elements of QM adopted:

Performance indicators
Customer care training
Devolved management structures
Inspection of service points
Employee suggestion scheme
Appraisal introduced for all staff
in 1995
Cross-functional teams
Customer questionnaires
Authority-wide complaints scheme

Case Study C

Population served: 410,000
Annual budget (approx):   £4.7 million
Original impetus for QM: Head of Library Service, since 1989
Responsibility in library service: TQM Champion
Elements adopted: Training in customer care
Complaints/comments books
Open Days
Cross-functional teams
Customer questionnaires
Registered for Investors in People
Performance indicators

Case Study D

Population served: 467,000
Annual budget (approx):   £5 million
Original impetus for QM: National and local political
environment
Responsibility in library service: Not assigned
Elements adopted: Customer care training
Marketing training
Customer questionnaires
Inspections of service points
Authority-wide complaints scheme
Employee suggestion scheme
Performance indicators

Appraisal introduced in 1995 for all
employees

Case Study E

Population served:	1.5 million
Annual budget (approx):	£13.5 million
Original impetus for QM:	Elected Members and Chief Executive since 1992
Responsibility in library service: f.t.e. 1.5 staff	Senior Manager plus Quality Team,
Elements of QM adopted:	Charter Mark winners
	Performance indicators
	Market research
	Devolved management structures
	Cross-functional team working
	Authority-wide complaints procedure
	Appraisal for all staff
	Customer questionnaires
	e-mail for staff comments

Case Study F

Population served:	117,000
Annual budget (approx):	£1.5 million
Original impetus for QM:	Head of Library Service
Responsibility in library service:	Not assigned
Elements of QM adopted:	Performance indicators
	Authority-wide complaints scheme

Case Study G

Population served:	575,000
Annual budget (approx):	£6.8 million
Original impetus for QM:	Head of Library Service
Responsibility in library service:	Head of Service and part-time Service Monitoring Assistant
Elements of QM adopted:	Flatter management structures
	Localized decision-making

Training in customer care
Customer questionnaires
Inspection of service points
Visits to service points by Head of
Service
Authority-wide complaints scheme
Comments books in service points
Performance indicators

Case Study H

Population served:	825,000
Annual budget (approx):	£7.8 million
Original impetus for QM:	Chief Executive of the authority
Responsibility in library service:	Senior Manager
Elements of QM adopted:	Authority-wide complaints scheme
	Flatter management structures
	Performance indicators
	Appraisal for professional staff

Case Study I

Population served:	190,000
Annual budget (approx):	£3 million
Original impetus for QM:	Chief Executive of the Authority
Responsibility in library service:	Not assigned
Elements of QM adopted:	Authority-wide complaints scheme
	Performance indicators

Case Study J

Population served:	185,000
Annual budget (approx):	£3.5 million
Original impetus for QM:	Elected Members
Responsibility in library service:	Senior Manager and Contract Monitoring Team f.t.e. 3
Elements of QM adopted:	Authority-wide complaints scheme
	Customer questionnaires
	Inspection of service points
	Training in customer care

Staff appraisal
Localized decision-making
Performance indicators

Case Study K

Population served:	700,000
Annual budget (approx):	£8 million
Original impetus for QM:	Head of Service
Responsibility in library service:	Not assigned
Elements of QM adopted:	Authority-wide complaints scheme
	Customer questionnaires
	Performance indicators

Non-Library Case Studies

Case Study 1

Primary area of activity:	Private healthcare
Annual turnover (approx):	£252 million
Employees:	3,800
Original impetus for QM:	Chief Executive
Responsibility for QM:	Senior Manager and Quality Team, f.t.e. 6
Elements of QM adopted:	Monitoring of complaints
	Employee appraisal
	Employee suggestion scheme
	Training in tools of QM
	Performance monitoring
	Measurement of the effectiveness of internal communications
	Registered for Investors in People

Case Study 2

Primary area of activity:	Freight handling
Annual turnover (approx):	£210 million
Employees:	1,500
Original impetus for QM:	Chief Executive

Responsibility for QM:	Director of Quality and team of f.t.e. 8
Elements of QM adopted:	ISO 9000
	Employee appraisal
	Monitoring of complaints
	Employee suggestion scheme
	Training in tools of QM incl. team working for all staff
	Performance monitoring
	Registered for Investors in People
	Extensive market research activity
	Informal benchmarking against businesses in other sectors
	Planning to adopt EFQM

Case Study 3

Primary area of activity:	Motor vehicle manufacture
Annual turnover (approx):	£3 billion
Employees:	36,000
Original impetus for QM:	Competitor analysis
Responsibility for QM:	Director of Quality and Strategy
Elements of QM adopted:	Employee appraisal
	Employee suggestion scheme
	Customer focus groups
	Market research activity
	ISO 9000
	Investors in People
	British Quality Award winner
	Performance monitoring
	Benchmarking against other businesses in the same sector and external to it
	Team working

Case Study 4

Primary area of activity:	Financial services
Annual turnover (approx):	£1 billion
Employees:	3,800

Original impetus for QM:	Directors
Responsibility for QM:	Director of Quality and f.t.e. 15
Elements of QM adopted:	Market research
	Employee appraisal
	Employee suggestion scheme
	Team working
	Training in the tools of QM
	Audit of internal communications
	Performance measurement
	Monitoring of complaints
	Audit of organizational 'waste'

Case Study 5

Primary area of activity:	Retailing
Annual turnover:	£7 billion
Employees:	87,000
Original impetus for QM:	Chief Executive
Responsibility for QM:	Director of Quality
Elements of QM adopted:	Customer complaints and comments scheme
	Employee appraisal
	Employee suggestion scheme
	Training in tools of QM
	Audit of internal communications
	Registered for Investors in People
	Performance monitoring
	Customer focus groups
	Market research

Case Study 6

Primary area of activity:	Hotel industry
Annual turnover:	£4 billion
Employees (UK only):	4,800
Original impetus for QM:	Chief Executive of parent company in USA
Responsibility for QM:	Not assigned
Elements of QM adopted:	Customer complaints and comments scheme

Employee appraisal
Employee suggestion scheme
Cross-sectoral benchmarking
Training in the tools of QM
Performance monitoring
Empowerment

Case Study 7

Primary area of activity:	UK District Council
Annual budget:	£25 million
Employees:	375
Original impetus for QM:	Deputy Chief Executive
Responsibility for QM:	Not assigned
Elements of QM adopted:	Performance indicators
	Complaints scheme

Case Study 8

Primary area of activity:	National Health Service Hospital Trust
Annual budget:	£52 million
Employees:	1,750
Original impetus for QM:	Chief Executive
Responsibility for QM:	Not assigned
Elements of QM adopted:	Performance indicators
	Complaints scheme

Case Study 9

Primary area of activity:	Privatized utility
Annual turnover:	£6 billion
Employees:	62,000
Original impetus for QM:	Chief Executive
Responsibility for QM:	Director of Quality
Elements of QM adopted:	Customer comments and complaints scheme
	Market research activity
	Employee suggestion scheme
	Team working

Training in tools of QM
Employee appraisal
360 degree appraisal for senior
managers
Performance measurement and
monitoring

Case Study 10

Primary area of activity:	Library supply
Annual turnover:	£25 million
Employees:	500
Original impetus for QM:	Senior managers
Responsibility for QM:	Not assigned
Elements of QM adopted:	ISO 9000
	Performance monitoring
	Market research

Case Study 11

Primary area of activity:	Airline
Annual turnover:	£6 billion
Employees:	28,000
Original impetus for QM:	Chief Executive
Responsibility for QM:	Director of Quality
Elements of QM adopted:	Employee appraisal
	Training in tools of QM
	Monitoring of customer complaints and comments
	Audit of internal communications
	Team working
	Employee suggestion scheme
	Cross-sectoral benchmarking

Case Study 12

Primary area of activity:	Law firm
Annual turnover:	Not disclosed
Employees:	500

Original impetus for QM: Anticipation of Government
                                     legislation
Responsibility for QM: Not assigned
Elements of QM adopted: ISO 9000
                                       Registered for Investors in People

THE DEVELOPMENT OF A SCALE TO MEASURE THE QUALITY OF AN ACADEMIC LIBRARY FROM THE PERSPECTIVE OF ITS USERS

Philip Brooks
Don Revill
Tony Shelton

Introduction

The aim of this project was to develop a scale to assess the quality of an academic library from the perspective of its users.

Academic libraries in the UK face the challenges of:

- growing and more diverse service demands;

- reduced or frozen budgets which mean that 'value for money' issues are now of paramount importance;

- increasing demands on staff and resources due to more student-centred methods in higher education;

- decreasing 'face to face' interaction between staff and users with far less live feedback on library services;

- accelerating demand for access to new information technologies incorporating a range of information services and sources;

- servicing a wide range of users.

In order to improve the quality of their service, library administrators will increasingly require detailed user evaluations of the quality of their service provision and performance (see, for example, Davies and Kirkpatrick 1994). They will need to target limited resources by adhering to policies of resource maximization based on the library users' own explicit requirements (Library and Information Services Council, 1986).

With this background, there is an obvious need to develop a valid and reliable measure for evaluating the quality of academic libraries. Indeed, over the past few years, increased competition within the retail, business and industrial sectors has led to a growth in research directed towards measurement of service quality. There was felt to be a need to differentiate on grounds other than the quality of goods on offer within these sectors. Whilst goods quality can be measured objectively, using indicators such as durability, defect rate, etc., service quality is a much more elusive construct because of its intangibility. One of the best known instruments designed to measure service quality across a variety of environments is SERVQUAL, which was developed by Parasuraman,

Zeithaml and Berry (1988). It involves the calculation of differences between perceptions and expectations on a number of issues. When factor analyzed, the standardized 22-item scale reveals five underlying factors:

- Tangibles—appearance of physical facilities, hardware, equipment, personnel.

- Reliability—the accuracy and dependability of the service.

- Responsiveness—the promptness and helpfulness of the service providers.

- Assurance—trust and confidence in the service

- Empathy—the individual attention and care the firm provides to customers.

SERVQUAL has been used to measure the quality of service in a variety of areas including banking, appliance repair and maintenance, securities brokerage, credit card companies, a dental school, a hospital and estate agencies (see Dickens, 1995). However, the instrument has been criticized on a number of grounds, including the use of difference scores as an approach to measurement and because of doubts about whether a scale to measure quality can be universally applicable (Brown *et al.*, 1993). Indeed, Carman (1990) argues that SERVQUAL needs to be customized by adding new items, or rewording existing ones, to facilitate its use with particular sectors, even though it was originally intended as a generic tool.

A number of different approaches have arisen specifically to measure the quality of libraries (Bolton and Drew, 1991; Murfin and Gugelchuk, 1987). However, recent research (Edwards and Browne, 1995; Hébert, 1994; Millson-Martula and Menon, 1995) has suggested a possible dichotomy between the quality expectations of library users and librarians' own perceptions of their users' expectations.

In the light of these possible problems, there is an obvious need for a more user-centred approach to the measurement of library quality. It would be unwise to derive an instrument solely from the subjective (and possibly biased) opinions of librarians and other experts. They, alone, should not have the final say regarding what is appropriate and important (e.g. Dalton, 1992). The imposition, on to library users, of external, authoritarian definitions cannot be justified.

The present project focused directly upon library users' own perceptions of quality by developing an instrument for measuring dimensions of quality based on the opinions, knowledge, judgements and expectations of a representative user community. In deriving items for inclusion in such an instrument, the views of users from a wide range of academic levels, backgrounds and disciplines were elicited. In addition, other factors (e.g. age, experience and cultural differences) could also influence users' expectations of quality. Clearly, the opinions of first year English Literature undergraduates may differ from those of experienced researchers in Medicine.

Some dimensions of perceived quality are likely to be idiosyncratic, whilst others will be more generally accepted. It is also possible that users will be more adept at appreciating key aspects than at defining their properties. When characteristics of quality have been defined by others, however, these might well be easily recognized as pertinent indicators.

In summary, the major advantage anticipated for this instrument rested in its underlying user-centred philosophy. Items included were not imposed by outside, 'expert' authorities. Rather, the key dimensions were identified from a statistical consideration of users' judgements of quality. The key point was to allow users themselves to be the final arbiters. In order to determine how users perceive quality, the present authors believe that users, themselves, should be asked!

The development process

The goal of the project was to develop a reliable and valid user-based evaluation instrument for use in assessing the quality of higher education libraries. The target population to be sampled was users of academic libraries in the UK. The sample of library users would include a wide spectrum of disciplines, educational levels and cultural backgrounds.

It should be recognized that this study was explicitly targeted on *current* library users. It was considered that other users would lack appropriate recent knowledge or experience of library quality. Therefore the instrument was developed directly as an end-product of analysis and refinement of the expectations and ideas of a large, representative sample of the current library user community. The sample included part-time and full-time undergraduates and postgraduates, staff and researchers.

Stage one—identification of potential discriminators of good/bad academic library quality

A number of focus groups consisting of library users were formed in order to consider two questions. These were: 'What characteristics make a bad quality academic library?'; and 'What characteristics make a good quality academic library?' These questions were presented in written form (see Appendix 1) and individuals were encouraged to write down their ideas. The questions were presented in reverse order for half of the respondents. Additional items were derived through a sift of relevant literature.

After elimination of duplicate items, this process resulted in 85 separate statements thought to characterize good or bad quality academic libraries. The item statements were compiled together into a single document, comprising a randomly ordered list. This was considered by an independent panel of 60 library users selected from a wide range of staff and students at Liverpool John Moores University.

The document requested panel members to consider each of the 85 items in turn. They were asked to indicate the extent to which each is an indicator of academic library quality. A five point scale was presented alongside each statement allowing a range of possible responses from

'1—a very poor indicator' to '5—a very good indicator'. They were required to circle a number on the rating scale for each of the item statements. A copy of the document is shown in Appendix 2.

The mean ratings for each item are shown in Appendix 3. Items which achieved a mean rating of 3.5 or more were considered by the panel to be good indicators and they were carried forward to stage two.

Stage two—the pilot instrument for measuring users' perceptions of academic library quality

The pilot instrument for measuring users' perceptions of academic library quality is shown in Appendix 4. Following a short introduction explaining the objective of the current exercise, initial questions identified the usual academic library attended by the respondents, their frequency of library usage and their status as library users.

The main body of the pilot instrument consists of 40 item statements (e.g. 'Counter waiting times are acceptable', 'Computing facilities are up-to-date') grouped under six headings which the focus groups had indicated as being of particular relevance to academic library users. The headings were: 'Environmental Issues'; 'Information Retrieval'; 'Relevance of Information'; 'Special Needs'; 'Information Technology and Electronic Equipment'; and 'Items about Library Staff'. A final item was included in an 'Overall' category.

Respondents were requested to consider each of the statements in turn, in relation to their usual academic library, and to indicate the extent to which they agreed or disagreed with it. This was to be done by circling an appropriate number on a five point rating scale which ranged from '1—Strongly Agree' to '5—Strongly Disagree'.

Each respondent was asked to respond to two open questions. The first requested identification of any issues, not raised in the questionnaire, which might be of help in improving the quality of their usual academic library. The second requested constructive feedback, or beneficial changes, which might improve the questionnaire. It was considered that additional items might still be raised which could be incorporated into a *beta* version of the questionnaire. Finally, for sampling identification purposes, the time and date of completion of the questionnaire was requested.

The pilot study was conducted in the academic libraries of the University of Bristol and Liverpool John Moores University during May 1995. Pilot instruments were distributed in the two universities by counter staff. They selected respondents, at random, from their library users in accordance with a schedule derived from the 1994 SCONUL sample counts. The schedule, shown in Appendix 5, included 300 users from each library attending morning, afternoon or evening sessions, during the week or at weekends. Respondents were asked to return completed questionnaires to the counter staff. This distribution method proved satisfactory and yielded an overall return rate of 81 per cent.

In order to sample the most reliable items from amongst the 40 presented, Cronbach's *alpha* was utilized. This is a reliability coefficient which is based on the internal consistency of the items in a test. We would expect items to be highly positively correlated with each other if they are measuring a common entity (in this case 'library quality'). An iterative procedure was adopted whereby items were eliminated if their removal would cause the overall value of the *alpha* coefficient to increase. The aim was to obtain the maximum possible value of *alpha* by selecting from the set of 40 items originally presented. The final value of Cronbach's *alpha* for the 30 items remaining after following this procedure was a highly satisfactory 0.8912 indicating that the scale is quite reliable.

A table showing the individual scale items and the value of Cronbach's *alpha* is shown in Appendix 6. The 30 items identified from this stage were passed on to stage three for inclusion in the *beta* instrument. Also, a number of suggestions were made by respondents indicating areas of concern and suggesting additional items which had been neglected in the pilot instrument. These were also to be incorporated into the *beta* instrument.

Stage three—the *beta* instrument for measuring users' perceptions of academic library quality

Stage two identified 30 items directly from the questionnaire together with additional items, from the open ended questions, which could act as useful discriminators of library quality. It was decided to incorporate these at this stage. Furthermore, the pilot study indicated that the format of the quality instrument required some minor improvements including the extension of the rating scales from five to seven points.

The *beta* instrument for measuring users' perceptions of academic library quality is shown in Appendix 7. A short introduction indicated the major objectives of the project. The section 'About You' investigated the academic background of the respondents, their usual academic library and their frequency of usage. Respondents were asked to indicate any disability that affected their use of the library, to specify any special needs required and to state whether or not these were met.

The main section of the instrument consisted of the 47 item statements (e.g. 'Up-to-date books are readily available', 'The range of items is poor') presented in a randomized order. Half of the items were presented in a positive format (e.g. 'Training in library use is satisfactory') and the other half in a negative format (e.g. 'Items are incorrectly located on the shelves'). Each item was followed by a scale allowing possible responses ranging from '1—Completely Agree' to '7—Completely Disagree'. Respondents were instructed, as in stage two, that the questionnaire concerned the academic library that they used most often and to circle the number on the scale which best indicated their level of agreement. Whilst a 'Not Applicable' response category was provided, respondents were requested to try to avoid using it. This was included to identify individual items to which respondents had difficulty responding.

As in the pilot instrument, each respondent was asked to answer two open questions. The first requested specification of issues that were not raised but which might help to improve the quality of their library. The second requested constructive feedback which might improve the questionnaire.

The *beta* instrument was delivered to six academic libraries for completion during the last week of November 1995 (one of the universities had to delay the survey for one week due to non-receipt of questionnaires because of a postal strike). The institutions taking part were the University of Coventry, the University of Hertfordshire, the University of Napier, the University of Northumbria, Robert Gordon's Institute and the University of Teesside. These particular institutions were selected since, between them, they incorporated a diverse range of single-site and multi-site library types. As previously, counter staff handed out and collected the questionnaire to a random sample of their library users in accordance with the schedule shown in Appendix 8. The overall return rate was 62 per cent.

In order to facilitate data analysis, responses to negative items were recoded into an equivalent positive format. The discriminative power of the items was assessed by calculating a 'quality score' for individual library sites. This was done by summing rating scores for each respondent, at a particular site, to the 47 items and deriving the mean rating score for that site. The discriminative index for each of the 47 items in turn was then calculated as the difference between the three library sites achieving the most positive ratings of quality and the three achieving the least positive ratings. The rank ordered discriminative power of all 47 items is shown in Appendix 9. The ten items with the lowest indices were eliminated at this stage.

The remaining 37 items were submitted to an iterative process using Cronbach's *alpha* (as in stage two), eliminating items if their removal would allow *alpha* to increase. The final value of Cronbach's *alpha* attained was 0.8683, once again a highly satisfactory level indicating a reliable scale. A table showing the individual scale items and the value of Cronbach's *alpha* is shown in Appendix 10.

The responses to the 23 items identified from this stage were submitted to a principle components analysis, with direct oblimin rotation. This procedure was used to identify the underlying structure of these most reliable and most highly discriminating items. The non-orthogonal rotation was used because it was quite possible that the underlying dimensions would be intercorrelated, rather than entirely independent of each other. The resultant structure matrix is shown in Appendix 11. The descriptive statistics which emerge show that the analysis is satisfactory in that:

- the correlation matrix does not suffer from multicollinearity or singularity (determinant > 0.00001);

- the Kaiser-Meyer-Olkin measure of sampling adequacy (KMO=0.89972) can be classed as meritorious;

- Bartlett's test of sphericity (p<.00001) indicates that the correlation matrix is not an identity matrix.

The six factors which emerged to characterize the responses reflect:

- staff characteristics—knowledge, responsiveness and helpfulness;

- relevance, range and currency of stock;

- ease of locating stock;

- borrowing characteristics and potential costs;

- potential frustrations—staff numbers, waiting times, reshelving efficiency, aisle width and security of personal items;

- physical comfort issues—lighting and cleanliness.

Stage four—the final instrument for measuring academic library quality

This project's objective was to design an instrument for the measurement of library quality from the users' perspectives. The final instrument is shown in Appendix 12.

When a test is scored from its items it is normal practice to sum items to obtain an overall test score (Rust and Golombok, 1989) and this procedure is recommended for the first 23 items in the present instrument. It is suggested that the simple summation of these item scores will give a fair estimate of the overall quality of a specific library. The 24th item ('Overall, the quality of the library meets my expectations') is included as a quick indicator of users' expectations. In summing scores for the first 23 items, it should be remembered that the scale values of negatively polarized items should be reversed. That is, scores on items in third, ninth, thirteenth, fifteenth, seventeenth, twentieth and twenty-third positions should be reversed prior to analysis (i.e. a score of 1 become 7, 2 becomes 6, 3 becomes 5, 4 remains as 4, 5 becomes 3, 6 becomes 2 and 7 becomes 1).

Concise items were utilized in the final instrument by following accepted rules for questionnaire design (Borg and Gall, 1983). These suggest:

- the use of clearly worded items;

- the use of short items which are easy to understand;

- the avoidance of confusing negative items;

- the avoidance of technical language and jargon;

- the avoidance of biased questions.

For each item, users should indicate the strength of their agreement on the 7-point Likert scale in which the differences between scale positions are considered to be equivalent and balanced. A major advantage of this approach is that the scaled responses can be analyzed with parametric statistical methods.

Survey questionnaires are often regarded with either apathy or hostility by potential respondents. However, the neat appearance and organized layout of this short instrument, in a single page document, should help to overcome any negative attitudes, thus leading to an increased number of meaningful responses.

References

Bolton, R.N., and Drew, J.H. (1991) A multi-stage model of customer's assessment: service quality and value. *Journal of Consumer Research*, 17, 375-384.

Borg, W.R. and Gall, M.D. (1983) *Educational research: an introduction* 4th ed. New York: Longman.

Brown, T.J., Churchill, G.A. and Peter, J.P. (1993) Improving the measurement of service quality. *Journal of Retailing*, 69(1), 127-139.

Carman, J.M. (1990) Customer perceptions of service quality: an assessment of the SERVQUAL dimensions. *Journal of Retailing*, 66(1) 33-55.

Dalton, G.M.E. (1992) Quantitative approach to user satisfaction in reference service evaluation. *South African Journal of Library and Information Science*, 60, 89-103.

Davies, A. and Kirkpatrick, I. (1994) To measure service: ask the library user. *Library Association Record*, 96(2), February, 88-89.

Dickens, P. (1995) *Quality and excellence in human services*. Chichester: Wiley.

Edwards, S. and Browne, M. (1995) Quality in information services: do users and librarians differ in their expectations? *Library and Information Science Research*, 17, 163-183.

Hébert, F. (1994) Service quality: an unobtrusive investigation of interlibrary loan in large public libraries in Canada. *Library and Information Science Research*, 16, 3-21.

Library and Information Services Council (1986) *The future development of libraries and information services: progress through planning and partnership*. London: HMSO.

Maxwell, R.J. (1984) Quality assessment in health. *British Medical Journal*, 12(5), 84-86.

Millson-Martula, C. and Menon, V. (1995) Customer expectations: concepts and reality for academic library services. *College and Research Libraries*, 56(1), 33-47.

Murfin, M.E. and Gugelchuk, G.M. (1987) Development of testing of a reference transaction assessment instrument. *College and Research Libraries*, 48, 314-338.

Parasuraman, A., Zeithaml, V.A. and Berry, L.L. (1988) SERVQUAL: a multiple item scale for measuring consumer perceptions of service quality. *Journal of Retailing*, 64(1), 12-40.

Rust, J. and Golombok, S. (1989) *Modern psychometrics: the science of psychological assessment*. London: Routledge.

Zeithaml, V.A., Parasuraman, A. and Berry, L.L. (1990) *Delivering quality service: balancing customer perceptions and expectations*. New York: Free Press.

Acknowledgements

We are grateful to the British Library Research and Innovation Centre for providing support for this project and in particular for the advice of Isobel Thompson.

We would also like to thank our colleagues, Martin Coffey and Alan Stockley, for their advice concerning consumer perspectives on quality issues.

We are indebted to library staff and users in the following institutions: Robert Gordon's Institute; University of Bristol; University of Coventry; University of Napier; University of Hertfordshire; Liverpool John Moores University; University of Teesside; University of Northumbria.

Appendix 1

Initial instrument to elicit discriminators of good/bad quality academic libraries

Please answer Question 1:

What characteristics make a bad quality academic library?

_____
_____
_____
_____
_____
_____
_____
_____
_____
_____

Now, please answer Question 2:

What characteristics make a good quality academic library?

_____
_____
_____
_____
_____
_____
_____
_____
_____
_____

Appendix 2

Potential discriminators of academic library quality for prioritization

Please refer to the items on the following pages and indicate, by circling the appropriate number in each case, the extent to which each is an indicator of academic library quality. The numbers represent the following values:

1 = a very poor indicator
2 = a poor indicator
3 = uncertain
4 = a good indicator
5 = a very good indicator

The size of the library budget for staff	1	2	3	4	5
The size of the library budget for materials	1	2	3	4	5
Policies of all library services being available to all users	1	2	3	4	5
The simplicity of search and retrieval	1	2	3	4	5
The level of publicity for library services	1	2	3	4	5
Non-racist or non-sexist policies	1	2	3	4	5
A policy of no censorship	1	2	3	4	5
Well-defined study spaces	1	2	3	4	5
Noise levels in the library	1	2	3	4	5
A feeling of tranquillity	1	2	3	4	5
Remote access—24 hours a day	1	2	3	4	5
The tidiness of the shelves	1	2	3	4	5
The negotiability of loan periods	1	2	3	4	5
The availability of up-to-date books and journals	1	2	3	4	5
The speed of replacement of books on to shelves	1	2	3	4	5
The range of items in the library	1	2	3	4	5
The ease of locating books and journals	1	2	3	4	5
The range of the 'opinion making' popular press	1	2	3	4	5

The number of items in the library	1	2	3	4	5
The numbers of journals from student reading lists	1	2	3	4	5
The numbers of books from student reading lists	1	2	3	4	5
The level of journal provision	1	2	3	4	5
The availability of journals which can be borrowed	1	2	3	4	5
The waiting time for reserved books	1	2	3	4	5
The supply of 'key' texts	1	2	3	4	5
The speed of the identification and replacement of lost books and journals	1	2	3	4	5
The speed of removal of out of date books	1	2	3	4	5
The condition of the books	1	2	3	4	5
The relevance of the books for your studies	1	2	3	4	5
The provision of relevant books not specifically on the precise researched topic	1	2	3	4	5
The ability to borrow books	1	2	3	4	5
The range of subject areas	1	2	3	4	5
The number of seats	1	2	3	4	5
The ease of location of journals	1	2	3	4	5
The ease of access to old journals	1	2	3	4	5
The helpfulness of the library staff	1	2	3	4	5
The level of staff training	1	2	3	4	5
The efficiency of the air conditioning	1	2	3	4	5
The level of communication with library users	1	2	3	4	5
The flexibility of the library accommodation	1	2	3	4	5
The coordination of furnishings	1	2	3	4	5
The ease of access for disabled users to the library	1	2	3	4	5
The library facilities for special needs user groups —tape recorders, etc.	1	2	3	4	5
The design of the furniture and desks	1	2	3	4	5
The adequacy of the equipment	1	2	3	4	5
The level of provision of video players	1	2	3	4	5
The level of provision of video tapes	1	2	3	4	5
The presence of irrelevant notices	1	2	3	4	5
The cleanliness of the library	1	2	3	4	5
The level of security	1	2	3	4	5
The temperature in the library	1	2	3	4	5
The illumination in the library	1	2	3	4	5
The humidity in the library	1	2	3	4	5
The layout of the library	1	2	3	4	5
The classification schemes	1	2	3	4	5

The plans of subject locations	1	2	3	4	5
The amount of space in the library	1	2	3	4	5
The simplicity of the catalogue system for locating items	1	2	3	4	5
The provision of quiet areas for private study	1	2	3	4	5
The level of provision of OHPs	1	2	3	4	5
The availability of discussion/group areas	1	2	3	4	5
The comfort of the surroundings	1	2	3	4	5
The provision of library tours	1	2	3	4	5
The clarity of the library notices	1	2	3	4	5
The provision of training for library users	1	2	3	4	5
The provision of information handouts about library facilities	1	2	3	4	5
The level of library fines	1	2	3	4	5
The speed of access to photocopiers	1	2	3	4	5
The level of reservation charges	1	2	3	4	5
The provision of slide projectors for presentations	1	2	3	4	5
The level of computing facilities	1	2	3	4	5
The speed of access to CD-ROMs	1	2	3	4	5
The number of computer breakdowns	1	2	3	4	5
Access to computer-based bibliographies	1	2	3	4	5
The provision of Internet and e-mail facilities	1	2	3	4	5
The adequacy of the computer referencing	1	2	3	4	5
The provision of an interlibrary loan system	1	2	3	4	5
The length of the opening hours	1	2	3	4	5
The range of loan periods on popular texts	1	2	3	4	5
The waiting times at counters	1	2	3	4	5
The cost of photocopying facilities	1	2	3	4	5
The ease of ordering books	1	2	3	4	5
The provision of a short loan facility	1	2	3	4	5
The ease of obtaining interlibrary loans	1	2	3	4	5
The ease of renewals	1	2	3	4	5

Appendix 3

Mean ratings of discriminators

Item	Mean	N
The size of the library budget for staff	3.30	60
The size of the library budget for materials	3.28	60
Policies of all library services being available to all users	3.22	60
The simplicity of search and retrieval	4.05	60
The level of publicity for library services	3.30	60
Non-racist or non-sexist policies	3.26	59
A policy of no censorship	3.16	59
Well-defined study spaces	3.97	60
Noise levels in the library	3.80	60
A feeling of tranquillity	3.29	59
Remote access—24 hours a day	3.26	58
The tidiness of the shelves	3.40	60
The negotiability of loan periods	3.35	60
The availability of up-to-date books and journals	4.07	60
The speed of replacement of books on to shelves	3.58	60
The range of items in the library	4.40	60
The ease of locating books and journals	4.17	60
The range of the 'opinion making' popular press	3.48	60
The number of items in the library	3.63	59
The numbers of journals from student reading lists	4.13	60
The numbers of books from student reading lists	4.05	60
The level of journal provision	3.90	60
The availability of journals which can be borrowed	3.49	59
The waiting time for reserved books	3.40	60
The supply of 'key' texts	4.02	60
The speed of the identification and replacement of lost books and journals	3.57	60
The speed of removal of out of date books	2.92	60
The condition of the books	3.55	60
The relevance of the books for your studies	4.18	60

The provision of relevant books not specifically on the precise researched topic	3.21	59
The ability to borrow books	4.27	60
The range of subject areas	4.41	59
The number of seats	3.45	58
The ease of location of journals	3.98	59
The ease of access to old journals	3.47	60
The helpfulness of the library staff	4.35	60
The level of staff training	3.87	60
The efficiency of the air conditioning	3.41	59
The level of communication with library users	3.67	60
The flexibility of the library accommodation	3.23	60
The coordination of furnishings	2.95	59
The ease of access for disabled users to the library	4.12	60
The library facilities for special needs user groups —tape recorders, etc.	4.02	59
The design of the furniture and desks	3.23	60
The adequacy of the equipment	3.90	60
The level of provision of video players	3.57	60
The level of provision of video tapes	3.45	60
The presence of irrelevant notices	2.44	59
The cleanliness of the library	3.45	60
The level of security	3.73	60
The temperature in the library	3.42	60
The illumination in the library	3.85	60
The humidity in the library	3.52	60
The layout of the library	3.08	60
The classification schemes	3.90	60
The plans of subject locations	3.90	60
The amount of space in the library	3.42	60
The simplicity of the catalogue system for locating items	4.17	60
The provision of quiet areas for private study	4.03	60
The level of provision of OHPs	2.90	60
The availability of discussion/group areas	3.33	60
The comfort of the surroundings	3.48	60
The provision of library tours	2.73	60
The clarity of the library notices	3.08	60
The provision of training for library users	3.95	60
The provision of information handouts about library facilities	3.89	60

The level of library fines	3.50	60
The speed of access to photocopiers	3.62	60
The level of reservation charges	3.57	60
The provision of slide projectors for presentations	3.15	60
The level of computing facilities	4.13	60
The speed of access to CD-ROMs	3.92	60
The number of computer breakdowns	3.38	60
Access to computer-based bibliographies	3.75	60
The provision of Internet and e-mail facilities	3.82	60
The adequacy of the computer referencing	3.90	60
The provision of an interlibrary loan system	3.92	60
The length of the opening hours	4.20	60
The range of loan periods on popular texts	3.73	60
The waiting times at counters	4.07	60
The cost of photocopying facilities	3.72	59
The ease of ordering books	3.22	60
The provision of a short loan facility	3.38	60
The ease of obtaining interlibrary loans	3.78	60
The ease of renewals	3.97	60

Appendix 4

The pilot instrument for measuring users' perceptions of academic library quality

USERS' PERSPECTIVES ON THE QUALITY OF ACADEMIC LIBRARIES

INTRODUCTION:

This questionnaire is designed to measure the quality of academic libraries from the point of view of individuals who use them. The questionnaire is still at an early stage of development and the designers wish to take account of the views of library users so that all essential aspects are incorporated into the final version. Our ultimate aim is to facilitate improvement in the quality of academic libraries. We would like to have your help in this enterprise. Please complete it, without discussion, by indicating your own views on each of the issues raised.

ABOUT YOU: (*please fill in this section to indicate your status as a library user*)

* What is the name and site of your usual academic library?
  ....

* How often do you use the library? (*please circle*)

Daily	More than once a week	About once a week	About once a month	About once a year	First visit

* Are you registered disabled? (*please circle*)   Yes   No

If Yes, indicate any special needs that you have concerning your academic library and whether, or not, they are met:

....
....

● *Please go to the appropriate subsection below:*

Undergraduate Student: *(please circle)* Year of Study   1   2   3   4   5

Full Time   Part Time Day   Part Time Evening

Title of Course *(please state)* ....

Postgraduate Student: *(please circle)* Year of Study   1   2   3   4   5

Taught Course   Research Qualification

Full Time   Part Time

Title of Course *(please state)* ....

Academic Staff: *(please circle)*   Full Time   Part Time

Academic Department *(please state)* ....

Non-Academic Staff: *(please circle)*   Full Time   Part Time

Other Library User: *(please specify status)* ....

INSTRUCTIONS

This questionnaire concerns the academic library that you use most often.

Please consider each of the statements below. Circle the number on the scale which indicates the extent to which you agree or disagree with it.

The numbers represent the following levels of agreement:

1 = Strongly   2 = Agree   3 = Uncertain   4 = Disagree   5 = Strongly
     Agree   Disagree

Environmental Issues   *Please circle the appropriate number*

The library is located appropriately	1	2	3	4	5
The library is responsive to user feedback	1	2	3	4	5
There are adequate quiet areas for private study	1	2	3	4	5
The opening hours are acceptable	1	2	3	4	5
The physical environment is comfortable	1	2	3	4	5
It is safe to leave personal items unattended	1	2	3	4	5
It is quiet enough to study	1	2	3	4	5
Texts are in an acceptable condition	1	2	3	4	5
Reservation charges are appropriate	1	2	3	4	5
Levels of fines are appropriate	1	2	3	4	5
Training in library use is satisfactory	1	2	3	4	5
Documentation on using the library is satisfactory	1	2	3	4	5

Information Retrieval

Loan periods on key items are appropriate	1	2	3	4	5
Interlibrary loans are easy to obtain	1	2	3	4	5
Books and journals are easy to locate	1	2	3	4	5
Book loan facilities are adequate	1	2	3	4	5
The range of subject areas is sufficient	1	2	3	4	5
The catalogue system is simple to use	1	2	3	4	5
Items are shelved at the correct location	1	2	3	4	5
Items are reshelved efficiently	1	2	3	4	5
Search and retrieval facilities are simple to operate	1	2	3	4	5
Counter waiting times are acceptable	1	2	3	4	5

Relevance of Information

Up-to-date books are readily available	1	2	3	4	5
Up-to-date journals are readily available	1	2	3	4	5
The range of items is good	1	2	3	4	5
The library contains sufficient books relevant to my studies	1	2	3	4	5
Journals from student reading lists are readily available	1	2	3	4	5
Books from student reading lists are readily available	1	2	3	4	5

1 = Strongly   2 = Agree   3 = Uncertain   4 = Disagree   5 = Strongly
    Agree   Disagree

Please circle the
appropriate number

Special Needs

Access to library buildings, for disabled users, is satisfactory	1 2 3 4 5
Access to the library stock, for disabled users, is satisfactory	1 2 3 4 5
Adequate library aids are provided for special needs users	1 2 3 4 5

Information Technology & Electronic Equipment

Photocopying facilities are satisfactory	1 2 3 4 5
Photocopying charges are appropriate	1 2 3 4 5
Computing facilities are up-to-date	1 2 3 4 5
Available Information Technology equipment meets my needs	1 2 3 4 5
Electronic search facilities are satisfactory	1 2 3 4 5
Availability of Audio-Visual equipment is satisfactory	1 2 3 4 5

Items About Library Staff

Library staff are helpful	1 2 3 4 5
Library staff are knowledgeable	1 2 3 4 5
There are enough library staff available	1 2 3 4 5

Overall

Overall, the quality of this library meets my expectations	1 2 3 4 5

- Are there any issues which we have failed to raise that you think would help to improve the quality of your usual academic library? Please specify:

....

....

....

- We would like some constructive feedback which you feel might improve this questionnaire. Please indicate any changes that you feel would be beneficial:

  ....

  ....

  ....

- Finally, please indicate when this questionnaire was completed:

Day: .... Date: .... Time: .... (*please circle*) am / pm

Please check that you have completed all sections and then return the questionnaire

Many thanks for your help

Appendix 5

Distribution details and return rates for the pilot instrument

University of Bristol:

	Mon	Tues	Wed	Thur	Fri	Sat	Total
open-13.00	22	23	22	23	23	17	130
13.00-17.00	26	26	26	26	25	1	130
17.00-close	9	9	9	9	4	-	40
Total	57	58	57	58	52	18	300

Returns 250. Return rate 83.3 per cent

Liverpool John Moores University:

	Mon	Tues	Wed	Thur	Fri	W/end	Total
open-13.00	20	22	20	19	22	19	122
13.00-17.00	22	26	22	20	20	20	130
17.00-close	12	12	12	12	-	-	48
Total	54	60	54	51	42	39	300

Returns 238. Return rate 79.3%

Appendix 6

Cronbach's *alpha* showing reliability for selected items from the pilot instrument

Item		Alpha if Item Deleted
EN01	—The library is located appropriately	.8902
EN02	—The library is responsive to user feedback	.8880
EN03	—There are adequate quiet areas for private study	.8902
EN04	—The opening hours are acceptable	.8912
EN0	—The physical environment is comfortable	.8888
EN06	—It is safe to leave personal items unattended	.8911
EN0	—Reservation charges are appropriate	.8885
EN10	—Levels of fines are appropriate	.8905
EN11	—Training in library use is satisfactory	.8872
EN12	—Documentation on using the library is satisfactory	.8862
IR1	—Loan periods on key items are appropriate	.8879
IR2	—Interlibrary loans are easy to obtain	.8874
IR5	—The range of subject areas is sufficient	.8846
IR6	—The catalogue system is simple to use	.8884
IR7	—Items are shelved at the correct location	.8863
IR8	—Items are reshelved efficiently	.8856
IR10	—Counter waiting times are acceptable	.8872
RI1	—Up-to-date books are readily available	.8827
RI2	—Up-to-date journals are readily available	.8858
RI3	—The range of items is good	.8838
RI4	—The library contains sufficient books relevant to my studies	.8855
SN1	—Access to library buildings, for disabled users, is satisfactory	.8907
SN3	—Adequate library aids are provided for special needs users	.8907

IT1	—Photocopying facilities are satisfactory	.8903
IT2	—Photocopying charges are appropriate	.8901
IT4	—Available Information Technology equipment meets my needs	.8882
IT5	—Electronic search facilities are satisfactory	.8873
STAFF1	—Library staff are helpful	.8873
STAFF2	—Library staff are knowledgeable	.8862
STAFF3	—There are enough library staff available	.8863

Reliability Coefficients
N of Cases   = 488.0
N of Items   = 30
Cronbach's *alpha*   = .8912

Appendix 7

The *beta* instrument for measuring users' perceptions of academic library quality

USERS' PERSPECTIVES ON THE QUALITY OF ACADEMIC LIBRARIES

INTRODUCTION:
This questionnaire is designed to measure the quality of academic libraries from the point of view of individuals who use them. The questionnaire is still being developed and the designers wish to take account of the views of library users so that all essential aspects are incorporated into the final version. Our ultimate aim is to facilitate improvement in the quality of academic libraries. We would like to have your help in this enterprise. Please complete it, without discussion, by indicating your own views on each of the issues raised.

ABOUT YOU: (*please fill in this section to indicate your status as a library user*)

- What is the name and site of your usual academic library?
  ....

- How often do you use the library? (*please circle*)

Daily	More than once a week	About once a week	About once a month	About once a year	First visit

- Do you have any disability affecting your use of the library? (*please circle*)   Yes   No

If Yes, indicate any special needs that you have concerning your academic library and whether, or not, they are met:

....
....
....

- *Please go to the appropriate subsection below:*

Undergraduate Student: *(please circle)* Year of Study 1 2 3 4 5

(please circle) Full Time Part Time Day Part Time Evening

Title of Course *(please state)* ....

Postgraduate Student: *(please circle)* Year of Study 1 2 3 4 5

(please circle) Taught Course Research Qualification

(please circle) Full Time Part Time

Title of Course *(please state)* ....

Academic Staff: *(please circle)* Full Time Part Time

Academic Department *(please state)* ....

Non-Academic Staff: *(please circle)* Full Time Part Time

Other Library User: *(please specify status)* ....

INSTRUCTIONS

This questionnaire concerns the academic library **that you use most often.**

Please consider each of the statements below. The numbers shown alongside each one represent a scale indicating the following levels of agreement:

Completely 1   2   3   4   5   6   7   Completely
Agree   Disagree

You are asked to circle the number on the scale which indicates the extent to which you agree or disagree with each statement. Answer every question and try your best to avoid using the 'not applicable' (NA) choice.

Please circle the appropriate number

The library is responsive to user feedback	1	2	3	4	5	6	7	NA
Library staff are knowledgeable		1	2	3	4	5	6	7	NA
Shelves are poorly labelled		1	2	3	4	5	6	7	NA
Washroom facilities, for library users, are conveniently located	1	2	3	4	5	6	7	NA
Electronic search facilities are inadequate	1	2	3	4	5	6	7	NA
The physical environment is comfortable	1	2	3	4	5	6	7	NA
The library has too many rules and regulations	1	2	3	4	5	6	7	NA
Items are reshelved efficiently		1	2	3	4	5	6	7	NA
Levels of fines and other charges are fair	1	2	3	4	5	6	7	NA
Training in library use is satisfactory		1	2	3	4	5	6	7	NA
The library is clean and tidy		1	2	3	4	5	6	7	NA
I feel insecure in some parts of the library	1	2	3	4	5	6	7	NA
The location of subject areas, within the library, is unclear	1	2	3	4	5	6	7	NA
I am not allowed to borrow enough items at any one time	1	2	3	4	5	6	7	NA
The range of items is poor		1	2	3	4	5	6	7	NA
Access to library buildings, for disabled users, is satisfactory	1	2	3	4	5	6	7	NA
Documentation on using the library is poor	1	2	3	4	5	6	7	NA
There are too few seated places available	1	2	3	4	5	6	7	NA
Library staff are unhelpful		1	2	3	4	5	6	7	NA
Loan periods on key items are appropriate	1	2	3	4	5	6	7	NA
The range of subject areas is sufficient for my needs	1	2	3	4	5	6	7	NA
The catalogue system is hard to use		1	2	3	4	5	6	7	NA
Counter waiting times are acceptable		1	2	3	4	5	6	7	NA
The opening hours are acceptable		1	2	3	4	5	6	7	NA
Items are poorly labelled		1	2	3	4	5	6	7	NA
Up-to-date journals are readily available	1	2	3	4	5	6	7	NA

	Please circle the appropriate number							
The lighting is poor	1	2	3	4	5	6	7	NA
It is safe to leave personal items unattended	1	2	3	4	5	6	7	NA
Items are incorrectly located on the shelves	1	2	3	4	5	6	7	NA
Emergency evacuation procedures are unclear	1	2	3	4	5	6	7	NA
Interlibrary loans are hard to obtain	1	2	3	4	5	6	7	NA
The library contains sufficient items relevant to my studies	1	2	3	4	5	6	7	NA
There are insufficient group study areas with talking permitted	1	2	3	4	5	6	7	NA
Generally, I find the item that I seek in the library	1	2	3	4	5	6	7	NA
Adequate library aids are provided for special needs users	1	2	3	4	5	6	7	NA
Too many items have restrictions on borrowing	1	2	3	4	5	6	7	NA
Up-to-date books are readily available	1	2	3	4	5	6	7	NA
Photocopying facilities are poor	1	2	3	4	5	6	7	NA
The library is located appropriately	1	2	3	4	5	6	7	NA
There are too few quiet areas for private study	1	2	3	4	5	6	7	NA
The Information Technology equipment meets my needs	1	2	3	4	5	6	7	NA
There are enough library staff available	1	2	3	4	5	6	7	NA
Aisles between shelving are too narrow	1	2	3	4	5	6	7	NA
Private locker facilities are inadequate	1	2	3	4	5	6	7	NA
Refreshment areas, for library users, are conveniently located	1	2	3	4	5	6	7	NA
Aids to reach high shelves are readily available	1	2	3	4	5	6	7	NA
Overall, the quality of the library meets my expectations	1	2	3	4	5	6	7	NA

- Are there any issues that we have failed to raise which you think would help to improve the quality of your usual academic library? Please specify:

  ....
  ....
  ....

- We would like some constructive feedback which you feel might improve this questionnaire. Please indicate any changes that you feel would be beneficial:

  ....
  ....
  ....

- Finally, for our sampling purposes, please indicate when this questionnaire was completed:

Day of week: .... Date: .... Time: .... am / pm

Please check that you have completed all sections and then return the questionnaire

Many thanks for your help

Appendix 8

Distribution details and return rates for the *beta* instrument

Questionnaires were distributed by each of the six libraries according to the following schedule:

	Mon	Tue	Wed	Thur	Fri	W/end	Total
open–13.00	15	15	15	15	15	10	85
13.00–17.00	20	20	20	20	20	15	115
17.00–close	10	10	10	10	10	-	50
Total	45	45	45	45	45	25	250

The returns from each of the libraries were as follows:

University of Coventry	— returns 133,	return rate 53.2 per cent
University of Hertfordshire	— returns 175,	return rate 70.0 per cent
University of Napier	— returns 151,	return rate 60.4 per cent
University of Northumbria	— returns 119,	return rate 47.6 per cent
Robert Gordon's Institute	— returns 213,	return rate 85.2 per cent
University of Teesside	— returns 142,	return rate 56.8 per cent
Overall	— returns 933,	return rate 62.2 per cent

Appendix 9

Relative discriminative power of items for the *beta* instrument

Item	Rank Ordered Discriminative Power
The library is responsive to user feedback	22
Library staff are knowledgeable	15
Shelves are poorly labelled	36
Washroom facilities, for library users, are conveniently located	45
Electronic search facilities are inadequate	35
The physical environment is comfortable	19
The library has too many rules and regulations	33
Items are reshelved efficiently	4
Levels of fines and other charges are fair	10
Training in library use is satisfactory	11
The library is clean and tidy	13
I feel insecure in some parts of the library	20
The location of subject areas, within the library, is unclear	37
I am not allowed to borrow enough items at any one time	25
The range of items is poor	29
Access to library buildings, for disabled users, is satisfactory	47
Documentation on using the library is poor	24
There are too few seated places available	43
Library staff are unhelpful	9
Loan periods on key items are appropriate	23
The range of subject areas is sufficient for my needs	26
The catalogue system is hard to use	31
Counter waiting times are acceptable	2
The opening hours are acceptable	40

Items are poorly labelled	27
Up-to-date journals are readily available	6
The lighting is poor	18
It is safe to leave personal items unattended	7
Items are incorrectly located on the shelves	5
Emergency evacuation procedures are unclear	39
Interlibrary loans are hard to obtain	14
The library contains sufficient items relevant to my studies	17
There are insufficient group study areas with talking permitted	41
Generally, I find the item that I seek in the library	12
Adequate library aids are provided for special needs users	44
Too many items have restrictions on borrowing	21
Up-to-date books are readily available	8
Photocopying facilities are poor	38
The library is located appropriately	30
There are too few quiet areas for private study	42
The Information Technology equipment meets my needs	34
There are enough library staff available	3
Aisles between shelving are too narrow	1
Private locker facilities are inadequate	28
Refreshment areas, for library users, are conveniently located	46
Aids to reach high shelves are readily available	32
Overall, the quality of the library meets my expectations	16

Appendix 10

Cronbach's *alpha* showing reliability for selected items from the *beta* instrument

Item	Alpha if Item Deleted
The library is responsive to user feedback	.8620
Library staff are knowledgeable	.8614
Shelves are poorly labelled	.8678
The physical environment is comfortable	.8638
Items are reshelved efficiently	.8597
Levels of fines and other charges are fair	.8662
Training in library use is satisfactory	.8637
The library is clean and tidy	.8618
Library staff are unhelpful	.8624
Loan periods on key items are appropriate	.8659
The range of subject areas is sufficient for my needs	.8630
Counter waiting times are acceptable	.8609
Items are poorly labelled	.8623
Up-to-date journals are readily available	.8614
The lighting is poor	.8662
It is safe to leave personal items unattended	.8681
Items are incorrectly located on the shelves	.8631
The library contains sufficient items relevant to my studies	.8616
Generally, I find the item that I seek in the library	.8596
Too many items have restrictions on borrowing	.8659
Up-to-date books are readily available	.8605
There are enough library staff available	.8582
Aisles between shelving are too narrow	.8651

Reliability Coefficients
N of Cases = 799.0   N of Items = 23   Cronbach's *alpha* = .8683

Appendix 11

Factor analysis for selected items from the *beta* instrument

Determinant of Correlation Matrix = .0026689
Kaiser-Meyer-Olkin Measure of Sampling Adequacy = .89972
Bartlett Test of Sphericity = 4678.6473, Significance = .00000

Factor	Eigenvalue	Pct of Var	Cum Pct
1	6.22734	27.1	27.1
2	1.64031	7.1	34.2
3	1.31402	5.7	39.9
4	1.17164	5.1	45.0
5	1.09261	4.8	49.8
6	1.02114	4.4	54.2

Structure Matrix:

	Factor 1	Factor 2	Factor 3	Factor 4	Factor 5	Factor 6
STAFKNOW	.77774					
FEEDBACK	.74693					
TRAINING	.64010					
STAFHELP	.62661					
RELEVITS		-.85255				
RANGESUB		-.77479				
FINDITEM		-.74374				
UTDBOOKS		-.68118				
UTDJNALS		-.54490				
SHELABEL			.76451			
ITELABEL			.75392			
MISSHELV			.61835			
BORRREST				.74374		
LOANPERS				.72236		
FINEFAIR				.51505		
NUMSTAFF	.52700				-.64159	
WAITING					-.63926	
AISLES					-.59358	
SAFELEAV					-.59222	
RESHELVE					-.54970	
LIGHTING						.78282
LIBCLEAN						.67495
PHYSENV						.65018

Factor Correlation Matrix:

	Factor 1	Factor 2	Factor 3	Factor 4	Factor 5	Factor 6
Factor 1	1.00000					
Factor 2	-.34174	1.00000				
Factor 3	.26431	-.19074	1.00000			
Factor 4	.22812	-.11997	.11660	1.00000		
Factor 5	-.34225	.25816	-.18204	-.14556	1.00000	
Factor 6	.26082	-.20486	.14373	.10183	-.23533	1.00000

Appendix 12

The final instrument for measuring users' perceptions of academic library quality

USERS' PERSPECTIVES ON THE QUALITY OF ACADEMIC LIBRARIES

This questionnaire is designed to measure the quality of your academic library.

Please complete it, without discussion, by indicating your own view on each of the issues raised below. The numbers shown alongside each statement represent a scale indicating the following levels of agreement:

Completely 1   2   3   4   5   6   7 Completely
Agree   Disagree

You are asked to circle the number on the scale which indicates the extent to which you agree or disagree with each item.

	Please circle the appropriate number
The library is responsive to user feedback	1 2 3 4 5 6 7
The library staff are knowledgeable	1 2 3 4 5 6 7
The shelves are poorly labelled	1 2 3 4 5 6 7
The physical environment is comfortable	1 2 3 4 5 6 7
Items are reshelved efficiently	1 2 3 4 5 6 7
Levels of fines and other charges are fair	1 2 3 4 5 6 7
Training in library use is satisfactory	1 2 3 4 5 6 7
The library is clean and tidy	1 2 3 4 5 6 7
The library staff are unhelpful	1 2 3 4 5 6 7
Loan periods on key items are appropriate	1 2 3 4 5 6 7

The range of subject areas is sufficient for my needs	1	2	3	4	5	6	7
Counter waiting times are acceptable	1	2	3	4	5	6	7
Items are poorly labelled	1	2	3	4	5	6	7
Up-to-date journals are readily available	1	2	3	4	5	6	7
The lighting is poor	1	2	3	4	5	6	7
It is safe to leave personal items unattended	1	2	3	4	5	6	7
Items are incorrectly located on the shelves	1	2	3	4	5	6	7
The library contains sufficient items relevant to my studies	1	2	3	4	5	6	7
Generally, I find the item that I seek in the library	1	2	3	4	5	6	7
Too many items have restrictions on borrowing	1	2	3	4	5	6	7
Up-to-date books are readily available	1	2	3	4	5	6	7
There are enough library staff available	1	2	3	4	5	6	7
Aisles between shelving are too narrow	1	2	3	4	5	6	7
Overall, the quality of the library is excellent	1	2	3	4	5	6	7

**Please ensure that you have responded to all items
and then return the questionnaire
Many thanks for your help**

TOWARDS LIBRARY EXCELLENCE: BEST PRACTICE BENCHMARKING IN THE LIBRARY AND INFORMATION SECTOR

Penny Garrod
Margaret Kinnell

Introduction

Background

This report stems from research carried out at Loughborough University's Department of Information and Library Studies, with the help of funding from the British Library Research and Innovation Centre (BLRIC), for the period November 1994 to December 1995. The research team comprised: Professor Margaret Kinnell Evans, as Project Director; Penny Garrod as researcher; John Brockman, Quality Manager at the Ministry of Defence Headquarters Library, London, and Alan Gilchrist of Gavel Consultancy as consultants to the project. The study was complemented by other projects on quality, as described earlier in the Introduction to this volume.

The quest for excellence

The purpose of this project was to assess the relevance of benchmarking techniques to the library and information sector, and to evaluate levels of activity in, and current attitudes to, quality methods. Benchmarking is one of a range of quality management tools designed to help organizations improve their products and services, and to assist in the management of change (Bullivant, 1994). However, organizations which practise benchmarking usually do so as part of a quality management programme. Benchmarking is an acknowledged facilitator of learning; this process is not confined to learning through comparison with others, but extends to learning about the way one's own organization and processes function (Coopers & Lybrand, 1994). The concept of 'the learning organization' is a fundamental tenet of quality management, and therefore benchmarking, with its focus on interaction with other organizations, is perceived as a way of promoting a culture of openness, receptiveness to new ideas, and continuous improvement.

Quality management is growing in importance as organizations face up to the daily demands of an increasingly competitive market ethos. This trend is not confined to the commercial sector, as Oakland (1994) argues:

Whatever type of organization you work in—a hospital, a university, a bank, an insurance company, local government, an airline, a factory—competition is rife: competition for customers, for students, for patients, for resources, for funds.

The way to compete in this constantly changing and dynamic environment is to focus firmly on the 'customer'. However, to do this organizations have to determine who their customers are, and whether the use of the term 'customer' is apposite and acceptable to all parties, or whether an alternative, such as 'user', 'reader' or 'client', is preferred. The Total Quality Management (TQM) concept of the customer includes customers both external to and within the organization. Therefore all employees are customers because they interact with other workers within the organization in supplying a part of a product or service.

Quality management is exemplified by a mindset which places the needs of the customer before all other considerations. It is a proactive approach, and is user driven, but it is also a way of ensuring that dwindling resources are not wasted on tasks which add no value to the services on offer.

Successful companies have demonstrated that benchmarking can be a useful tool for implementing quality management. Rank Xerox is the company most commonly associated with the successful application of benchmarking techniques; in 1979 they established how their competitors had achieved success and then emulated them. According to one leading authority on quality, benchmarking is now widely credited with being one of the main factors responsible for improvements in company performance (Zairi and Hutton, 1995).

Two recent surveys revealed that benchmarking is growing in popularity with top European companies (Coopers & Lybrand, 1994; Coopers & Lybrand/CBI, 1993). In the first of these, which focused on the UK and drew its sample from the Times Top 1000 list of manufacturing and service companies, 67 per cent of respondents claimed to be benchmarking. In the European survey, carried out a year later, 78 per cent of UK respondents claimed currently to be benchmarking and 82 per cent of these reported the exercise to be a success. In other European countries, notably the Netherlands and Switzerland, its use was also widely reported at 72 per cent and 68 per cent respectively. It is noteworthy that in the UK survey 86 per cent of respondents stated that they had learnt lessons from benchmarking activities.

However, the Coopers & Lybrand findings focused on the activities of top companies alone. Their sample, of 105 UK companies, represents only a tenth of the Times Top 1000 list of companies. Their evidence therefore needs to be evaluated in the light of a report from the USA, which sees benchmarking as benefiting only the higher performing institutions (Ernst and Young/AQF, 1993). This report found that lower and medium performing organizations failed when benchmarking, because their choice of models for comparison was inappropriate. These models tend to be the 'best of the best', whose practices are ineffective when adopted by lower performing organizations. Bullivant (1994) warns us that benchmarking should be approached with caution as it is not an easy task, and it takes time to implement. The title of a recent Department of Trade and Industry (DTI) publication, 'Benchmarking, the challenge' confirms the view that benchmarking is not for the faint-hearted (DTI,1995).

Organizations seeking a route to excellence may therefore feel ambivalent about pouring scant resources into benchmarking, or other quality management activities. It may be universally acknowledged that quality management is a good thing *per se*; it may also be widely accepted that competition is rife, and that there is a perceived need for tools which assist hard-pressed managers to cope with constant change. However, the fact remains that quality management is better developed in manufacturing, production, or utility industries than it is in services (Wilkinson *et al.*, 1993). There may be doubt in the minds of many managers as to whether certain management techniques are worth the expenditure of time and effort required, especially where there is no guarantee of success in developing the business. In addition, criticisms of quality programmes have emphasized the perception of quality management as a sales gimmick or a management fad (Wilkinson *et al.*, 1993). In the library and information sector our findings indicate this perception to be a commonly held one.

Best practice in the library and information sector

Best practice has become a significant concept for library and information services (LIS), regardless of sector. In the academic sector, the opening up of higher education to a wider population and the growth of the 'new universities' have brought about an increase in demand whilst funding has been consistently squeezed. This has resulted in the increasing use of performance indicators and other measurement tools, which has received further impetus from the recommendations made in the Follett Report of 1993 (HEFCE, 1993). This report discusses two surveys which identify LIS as playing a fundamental role in the provision of quality education. A more recent publication develops the role of performance measurement in academic libraries, as a means to improved effectiveness (HEFCE, 1995).

A survey by Porter (1992) of quality initiatives in LIS found that most libraries which responded were involved in some aspect of quality assurance, but that this was not carried out in a formal or structured way, and there were few examples demonstrating how quality had been introduced. More recently, a study by EUSIDIC (the European Association of Information Services) focused on the particular problems of the information sector when trying to implement quality management programmes (Lester, 1994). These include the intangible nature of information itself, which presents difficulties when trying to assess quality.

Quality systems such as BS 5750 (now the international standard BS EN ISO 9000) have been appraised and deemed beneficial to libraries by Brophy (1994), Johannsen (1994), Ellis and Norton (1993), and Dawson (1993). However, this research project, in common with the Quality Management and Public Library Services project (see p.146) found that information professionals perceive the system to be too rigid and prescriptive to be of use to LIS, and that levels of adoption are very low.

In the public sector, central government policy has had a direct influence on library services, as described in the Background section in this volume. Local authorities now function more like private sector organizations. Public libraries may therefore be more motivated, or even driven, towards the adoption of quality management methodologies. They live with the constant threat of cutbacks, and need to demonstrate, with the help of modern management techniques, that they are offering services which are in line with customers' needs, and are cost-effective.

The position of special libraries was covered in a 1993 edition of the journal *Special Libraries*, and a BLRIC research project on the topic was published in 1995 (Webb, 1995).

Rationale

There is a need for LIS managers to develop a portfolio of techniques to implement quality management. Comparative performance is an important area for consideration, and is a natural extension of the current practice of performance measurement, which is carried out in many libraries. By comparing with others, LIS managers can evaluate the effectiveness of their service delivery, and emulate best practice. This type of exercise is becoming increasingly important, as both clients and funders evaluate services in terms of their quality and whether they represent value for money.

There is a high level of interest in the use of performance measures in the information sector. The first international conference on performance measurement was held at the University of Northumbria in the summer of 1995 and attracted 123 delegates, representing a wide variety of organizations (Wressell, 1995). In addition, the recommendations of the Follett Report (HEFCE, 1993), and the subsequent consultative report from the Joint Funding Councils' *ad hoc* group on performance indicators for libraries (HEFCE, 1995), advocate further use of performance measurement in libraries and offer a framework to identify overall library effectiveness.

Benchmarking involves the following basic procedures: measurement of key processes; identification of gaps in performance; comparison of these processes with other organizations; and establishment of best practice leading to improved performance. However, despite interest in quality management techniques, including performance measurement, there is little evidence of any formal comparative analyses of the processes which make up library services. In the light of the increasing use of benchmarking in the private sector (Coopers & Lybrand, 1994) and the findings of the Follett Report, it was considered vital to assess the relevance of benchmarking techniques to the LIS sector. This would be carried out within a quality framework, and one of the outcomes would be the drawing up of guidelines for use in the application of benchmarking in the LIS sector.

Research methods

Throughout this report organizations which took part in the benchmarking exercise have not been named in order to ensure confidentiality. For the same reason, comments which were added to the questionnaire survey, or made during the course of the telephone interviews, are not attributed to specific individuals.

Questionnaire survey

A questionnaire survey was undertaken to establish current levels of quality related activities in the library and information sector. All library and information services in the higher education sector, and a sample of 197 information units from the commercial/industrial sector, were surveyed. The mailing list for the academic sector was drawn from the database compiled by the Library and Information Statistics Unit (LISU), Loughborough University. The sample for the commercial sector was selected from the Aslib Directory (Reynard and Reynard, 1994) using a list of randomly generated numbers produced by the Loughborough University Computer Centre. The overall target group was 511 library and information services.

Telephone survey

Respondents to the questionnaire were asked to state whether they were prepared to take part in a follow up telephone interview. A sample of those who agreed to this were then interviewed, using a semi-structured approach. The aim was to investigate attitudes to benchmarking, and to ascertain whether interviewees felt benchmarking to be appropriate to the LIS sector. They were asked if they considered their LIS to be a model of best practice, which would merit comparison with others. The interviews produced some valuable qualitative data on organizational culture and the factors which influence organizations' ability to change.

Literature searching

Literature searching was an ongoing process for the duration of the project. New items on quality related issues are constantly being published, as the topic is highly dynamic and subject to constant review and criticism. Literature searching initially concentrated on identifying items for inclusion in a select bibliography on quality management, designed as an aid to library managers, which has now been published (Garrod and Kinnell Evans, 1995). It then progressed to a survey of previous research in the field, to supply data for an interim position paper. Searching in the area of quality management is made difficult by the proliferation of terms used—for example, performance measurement/performance indicators, quality management/total quality management, quality systems/quality standards, etc. This abundance of jargon-laden terminology and varied definitions represents one of the major barriers to the implementation of quality programmes. The field is rife with new theories—or, more accurately, old theories re-named, counter-theories, and new paradigms and conceptual models—and there is constant argument over semantics. This tends to discredit quality management, so that it is increasingly seen as 'just another management fad' (Brockman, 1992), and hence transitory and not worth pursuing.

'Demonstrator' projects

Action research was vital to the research methodology in order to test the practical application of benchmarking in a LIS environment, and thus evaluate its viability and utility to the sector. The findings of this aspect of the research were crucial to the identification of a suitable model of benchmarking, and to the production of guidelines on the implementation of benchmarking techniques. Many useful data were generated, which provided a unique insight into the type of problems which LIS might encounter when trying to implement benchmarking techniques.

Three 'demonstrator' projects were set up, consisting of library and information units which had volunteered to undertake a benchmarking exercise for the project. These organizations represent a cross-section of the academic, public and private sectors. All are actively involved in quality management programmes and are committed to a philosophy of continuous improvement. A profile of these participating organizations is given in Appendix A.

The procedure for the 'demonstrator' projects was as follows.

- Visits were made to each of the projects to obtain background information on the culture of the organization and the methods used to implement the quality programme. Interviews with key personnel were carried out and, where possible, meetings (e.g. of quality circles) were attended.

- Each 'demonstrator' was then invited to identify a key process for the benchmarking exercise, selected from amongst those which they perceived to be essential to the success of their particular unit or organization, and which impact on customer satisfaction.

- The sub-processes or procedures which made up the selected processes were mapped or documented, using flowcharts and lists of procedures, etc.

- Measurements were taken of those aspects of the process which were considered critical in determining customer satisfaction, e.g. the timeliness of an interlibrary loan, or the accuracy of an enquiry response. These are often referred to as critical success factors (CSFs). These measurements provided a snapshot of the process in terms of usage over a set period, and thus highlighted potential problem areas.

- Benchmarking partners were selected for the comparative exercise. Partners were identified through contacts of the benchmarking team during the course of the research process.

- Visits were arranged between demonstrators and partners, to allow for the exchange of information and ideas on the chosen processes. The researcher attended these meetings to observe proceedings and collect data.

- The issues raised throughout the process were identified as a means of developing the agenda for discussion in the project Workshop.

Workshop

A Workshop was set up at the end of the project to provide a forum for discussing the issues arising from the research findings. This took place at Burleigh Court Conference Centre at Loughborough University. The aim of the day was to develop guidelines on the use of benchmarking techniques in the LIS sector, and to focus on the role of training. The organizations which were involved in the benchmarking exercise on behalf of the project were able to contribute their experiences and thus provide a valuable source of data for use in the development of guidelines. Delegates were drawn from all sectors and included members of the Public Libraries benchmarking group (Mendelsohn, 1995; *Library Association Record*, 1995a) and a benchmarking group representing information units in the engineering sector (*Library Association Record*, 1995b).

Research findings

Introduction

This section of the report deals with the findings of the questionnaire survey and the follow-up telephone interviews. The aim of the questionnaire survey was to establish levels of formal activity in the field of quality in the LIS sector, and then to ascertain the nature of these activities. There was scope for comments on the questionnaire, and many of the qualitative data, especially those pertaining to attitudes to quality issues, were derived from these. The questionnaire was designed to complement that used in the Quality Management and Public Library Services project, and was adapted to suit the academic and industrial LIS sectors. John Sumsion, of the Library and Information Statistics Unit (LISU) at Loughborough University, assisted the project teams in its design. A copy of the questionnaire is shown in Appendix B.

The LIS which were targeted for the questionnaire survey, in both the academic and commercial sectors, for the most part form part of larger organizations. In the academic sector parent organizations comprised both the old and the 'new' universities (former polytechnics), together with colleges of higher education.

There was some confusion amongst the multi-site campuses, where a library was located at each site. The questionnaire requested information relating to policy, and thus individual libraries, belonging to one institution, were unsure as to whether they should complete the questionnaire, or whether one main or central university library should do this on behalf of all of them. With some institutions, especially those with a collegiate system, such as the Universities of Oxford, Cambridge and London, there is a high degree of autonomy at college level, and here responses from individual libraries were the norm. However, the degree of independence enjoyed by other multi-site institutions is less clear, and it is impossible to generalize. This, in itself, was an interesting finding and one which might merit further work. Responses were received from individual site libraries in some instances, whilst in others it was indicated that only one site had responded. It is also worth noting that there has recently been some movement involving the integration of colleges into other institutions, usually universities. Adjustments were therefore made to final figures. The total number of higher education institutions in receipt of the questionnaire, after adjustment, was 314. The response rate for this sector, after two mailings, was 73 per cent.

The sample group for the commercial sector consisted of 197 organizations randomly selected from the Aslib Directory of Information Sources (Reynard and Reynard, 1994). The response rate for this sector, after two mailings, was 30 per cent. In addition, 28 uncompleted forms were returned, representing 14 per cent of the total mailing. Reasons for non-completion included: the absence of a library and/or information service; outsourcing of the information service, resulting in the disbanding of the in-house information unit; and those who expressed the view that the questionnaire did not apply to their operations as they were small scale, or who simply judged the questionnaire to be irrelevant to their operations. The following responses indicate the type of problems and attitudes endemic to the commercial sector:

> We do not have a formal 'library and information service staff'—our office is a small team of seven, supplying information to member companies and outside enquiries.

> This is a single-handed, very small library. Many of the questions were not appropriate to the library operations in this situation.

> Please note our library is very small, out of date, and not really used by anyone. Our resources are not sufficient to contemplate any change.

> I run the information and library service single-handedly. It is a service provided for members [building materials producers] and the public alike. Quality is judged by myself—the way I look at it is that I give the type of service to the standard I would expect to receive myself. Hence, I find that I cannot answer many of your questions.

> I think much of what passes for 'quality' initiatives is bureaucratic, modish and a waste of management time.

Table 1 represents a breakdown of the response rate by sector.

Table 1: Response rates to questionnaire survey by sector

SECTOR	COMPLETED RETURNS (actual numbers & % of total mailing)	UNCOMPLETED RETURNS	TOTAL RETURNS	OVERALL PERCENTAGE RESPONSE RATE
ACADEMIC	229 (73%)	11	240	76%
COMMERCIAL	60 (30%)	28	88	45%
OVERALL % RESPONSE RATE	56.5%	0.08%	64%	

Policies and programmes

It was necessary first to establish to what extent formal quality policies and programmes existed at both organizational and LIS level in the target groups. This information would provide an insight into the extent to which strategic policy filters down to services and departments.

There was little disparity between the patterns of adoption in the two sectors, although as the response rate from the commercial sector was much lower than that in the academic it is less representative of that sector. The following figures are for the two sectors combined, but, where appropriate, separate data for the commercial sector alone are given. Just over a third of respondents were found to have a written policy on quality at the organizational level. However, when asked if a written policy on quality existed at LIS level, those replying in the affirmative were much lower at 11.6 per cent. Respondents were then asked to indicate whether they had a formal quality programme in place. Interestingly, the figures were slightly higher than those relating to written policy at LIS level, but considerably lower than those relating to written policy at organizational level. Table 2 shows the responses to these three interrelated questions for both sectors combined. The figures in square brackets represent the responses from the commercial sector alone in order to facilitate comparison.

Table 2: Existence of written policy on quality and formal quality programme: both sectors (commercial sector alone in square brackets)

QUESTION	YES %	NO %	IN PREP %
Organization: Is there a written policy on quality?	33.45 [27]	52.46 [45]	11.62 [11.66]
LIS: Is there a written policy on quality?	11.62 [10]	74.30 [70]	12.68 [11.66]
Do you have a formal quality programme?	14.08 [17]	65.85 [65]	18.66 [11.66]

In the academic sector one respondent indicated that, although there was no written policy on quality, the university had an institutional plan which embodied the institution's ideas on quality; the respondent added that the issue of quality was implicit in the library's written Operational Policy statement. Another example was of a policy being developed through the University Services Quality Programme. Despite the lack of an organizational policy on quality, one institution did have an Academic Quality handbook. Other variations included the existence of a statement which referred to the quality of service at 'Public Information Points', entitled 'PIPs Customer Care Policy Statement and Code of Practice'. These all reveal that quality related activities often do exist, but that they are not necessarily formalized or known as 'quality' policies and programmes.

These two comments originate from commercial sector respondents:

> We pride ourselves on the quality of our output, which is recognized by our customers. So as a small company we have no need of such a bureaucratic device as a written policy, overall or for internal information provision.

> Ours is a very small voluntary association. We would love to have the resources to implement 'best practice'. We are working towards that, I hope to get there in time...

When the responses were correlated for organizational and LIS level written policies on quality in both sectors, just under 10 per cent were found to have a policy at both levels. This suggests that just over 1.62 per cent of LIS have 'gone it alone' and implemented their own quality initiatives. When moving on to correlate those who claimed to have both a formal programme and a written policy at LIS level, 6.7 per cent were found to have both. The figure was slightly higher—at 10.92 per cent—for respondents with a formal programme and a written policy at organizational level. This reflects the trend noted earlier, i.e. that implementation levels are higher at organizational level. Of particular interest to the present research is the correlation between those LIS which have a written policy on quality with those which also claim to be using benchmarking techniques—1.4 per cent in total. As 7.4 per cent of LIS indicated in the questionnaire that they were using benchmarking techniques, this low figure suggests that 6 per cent of those using benchmarking techniques have no written quality on policy. As benchmarking is considered to be a quality tool, it would seem that those claiming to be using it are involved in quality initiatives, but that these have not yet been consolidated in written policies. Alternatively, some of those claiming to be benchmarking may be interpreting this to include comparisons made through statistics, such as those produced by SCONUL, rather than benchmarking through direct comparisons of selected processes with benchmarking partners.

Key players

Where a policy on quality did exist at LIS level, it was considered useful to identify who was involved in its development. Senior management were found to have been most heavily involved, although middle management and frontline staff also took part. The use of consultants was found to be very low, at 4.2 per cent. The following shows the responses for each of the five potential key players listed in the questionnaire:

- Senior management   31.34 per cent
- Middle management   22.89 per cent
- Frontline staff   19.37 per cent
- Clients   10.56 per cent
- Consultants   4.23 per cent

The level of involvement of senior management is commensurate with the philosophy of quality management, which states that a high level of commitment at senior level is essential if quality programmes are to be successful. However, empowerment is also a key issue for practitioners of quality management, and this is inextricably linked to the concept of ownership, in particular to ownership of processes. Despite this, only 19 per cent of frontline staff were found to have been involved in developing policies on quality. The term 'empowerment', however, like 'quality', is disliked and distrusted—the term 'participation' has been used instead to denote the type of creative involvement which is essential to the success of quality techniques (Minkoff, 1993). This term is perhaps more suited to a LIS environment.

Formal quality approaches

Having established who has a policy and/or programme on quality, the next step was to discover how this was being translated into action. Respondents were invited to state with which, if any, of six formal quality approaches or initiatives they were involved. Fifty per cent indicated that they were not involved in any quality initiatives.

BS EN ISO 9000

BS 5750, (now the international standard BS EN ISO 9000, but commonly referred to as ISO 9000), the formal system which was first published in 1979, is the British Standard for quality management systems. ISO 9000 has been adopted by more than 57 countries and there are more than 35,000 companies registered or working to the standard (DTI, 1994b). The system specifies procedures and criteria to ensure that products or services meet the customer's requirements. The word 'quality' in a BSI context is taken to mean fitness for purpose and safe to use; or, in the case of services, whether they are designed to satisfy the customer's needs (DTI, 1994b). Certification, by an accredited certification body, is a formal assurance that a supplier's products or services meet the specified requirements. The process of acquiring certification is through an assessment of the supplier's systems both in documentary form and in actual use. For the commercial sector, certification is an essential marketing tool, as purchasers look for assurance that their money will be well spent. It has been claimed that ISO 9000 will affect practically all businesses in the USA and Canada, and that it is a useful tool for the regulation of records management practices. It is also seen as an opportunity for records management professionals to play a key role in developing and managing quality programmes (Weise and Stamoolis, 1993).

There are only a few documented instances of the implementation of ISO 9000 in LIS, the most notable being the University of Central Lancashire library in 1992; their three-pronged approach has been described in the literature (Brophy *et al.*, 1993; Brophy, 1994). However, there have been many arguments adduced in its favour. In assessing the benefits of ISO 9000 for libraries, one study concluded that many of the objections to it are either based on 'myth', or are related to the way in which ISO is implemented (Johanssen, 1994). A working party, supported by Nordinfo, has recently prepared guidelines for the implementation of ISO 9000 in LIS (Erhvervs-Info Association, 1994). Another study has been published which is similarly convincing on the relevance of ISO 9000 to the LIS sector, with a guide through to certification offered to managers; Part 2 of the standard is felt to be appropriate to information services (Ellis and Norton, 1993). However, despite this handful of proponents of ISO 9000, we found that only 5.63 per cent of respondents were working towards it.

TQM

TQM is often regarded as a philosophy rather than a methodology. It requires a particular mindset, or what Oakland (1994) terms 'a problem-prevention mentality'. He advises organizations first to look at the problems that exist in key areas, and then to study the processes involved, using 'quality improvement teams' of trained staff. Their task would be to seek out, and correct, the causes of problems. Writing from a LIS perspective, TQM has been described as a change process, which affects all aspects of the management process, e.g. human resource management, recruitment, staff development and training, and systems and processes (Abbott, 1994). The Higher Education Quality Council's (HEQC) 'Guidelines on quality assurance' lists five guiding principles of TQM (1994). These could be helpful to any organization, irrespective of sector, and can be summarized as follows:

- Creating a climate of trust and individual responsibility

- Strong customer focus (rigorous analysis of customers is required)

- The use of hard data to support decisions and actions

- People-oriented: development of employee skills

- Continuous improvement—not 'business as usual'

Thirteen per cent of respondents to the questionnaire indicated that their LIS was involved in Total Quality Management. One respondent added that they were using a 'modified version of TQM'. Benchmarking would certainly have a role to play in a TQM culture, as it encompasses several of the guiding principles listed above (points 2, 3, 4, and especially point 5), just as performance measurement can provide supporting hard data to inform decision-making activities, and can also be used in benchmarking exercises (Abbott, 1994).

Investors in People

The brochure produced by Investors in People UK (1994) states:

> Business leaders, management gurus, politicians and academic researchers all agree that in a world where materials, technology and even know-how are widely available and easily transportable, the factor which makes the significant difference is people.

Investors in People (IiP) is a standard based on four key principles, three of which focus on staff training and development. The fourth principle is that senior management demonstrate commitment to developing all employees, in order to achieve business objectives. The scheme is delivered through the national network of Training and Enterprise Councils (TECs) in England and Wales, which can provide access to guidance and other support.

Around 19 per cent of LIS respondents indicated an involvement with IiP. Since the standard was only formally established by the DTI in 1991, this represents quite a high level of adoption. However, IiP can be implemented incrementally, so large organizations may select certain services or departments for implementation, with others, e.g. LIS, being included at a later date.

Other initiatives

Customer contracts were favoured by 12.68 per cent of respondents. One respondent indicated that they called these Service Level Agreements, another that they were developing a 'Service Charter'. An initial customer contract with the NHS was indicated by one respondent, with the intention of more widespread adoption at a later date. Another respondent from the academic sector went into greater detail, stating:

> The library has a Service Level Agreement with regard to services for postgraduate medical and dental education. The library has provided support/input to research assessment exercises; also to external audits of HEFCE teaching quality of University academic departments, where the rating to date for the library element has been excellent in each case.

Conclusion

The survey revealed that there is a trend for LIS, particularly in the academic sector, to use informal methods of ensuring the quality of services. These might include visiting other units to exchange ideas on a particular aspect of operations, or studying published statistics/league tables to establish how well other institutions are faring in relation to one's own. One respondent stated:

> We are concerned with quality, good service, etc., but provide that in an informal practical way.... the jargon of phrasing you use here scarcely seems relevant to a smaller library—you seem to be borrowing the worst aspects of the commercial world, and using them in ways that do not enhance the image of libraries...

This statement reflects the dislike of, and resistance to, what is seen as the increasing 'commercialization' of LIS, which has been voiced by many LIS professionals. Reactionary attitudes prevail, and there is a desire to preserve the 'intellectual' world of education from the influences of consumerism. This desire is inextricably linked to the perceived educational role of public sector and academic LIS, and the existence of a public service ethos which sees the world of business as inimical to that of libraries and learning.

Table 3 summarizes the responses relating to quality initiatives. If these results are compared with those of a survey undertaken on behalf of the Institute of Management in 1992 (Wilkinson *et al.*, 1993), one can gauge whether trends in the information sector are keeping pace with commercial practice. This listed 15 approaches to quality management and tried to assess which were most heavily used. Fewer than half of respondents to their questionnaire had achieved ISO 9000 certification. Customer satisfaction surveys were, however, used by 67 per cent of their target group, which reflects the market driven nature of TQM in the commercial sector. In the LIS sector, customer satisfaction surveys were found to be used by over half of respondents (57 per cent) to measure the quality of LIS service. Table 4 compares some of the findings from the two surveys where the questions coincided. The LIS figures are, for the most part, well below those of the commercial sector, even though the Institute of Management survey was undertaken four years ago, and had a low response rate (22 per cent).

Table 3: Quality initiatives with which the LIS is involved (both sectors)

QUALITY INITIATIVES— LIS (both sectors)	YES (%)
Investors in People	19.37
TQM	13.03
Customer contracts	12.68
Quality circles	8.10
BS 5750/ISO 9000	5.63
The Learning Organization	3.87
None	50.00

Table 4: Approaches to quality management: a comparison of findings with those of Wilkinson et al., 1993.

APPROACHES TO QM (%)	Quality and the Manager. (Inst. Management, 1992)	Best Practice Benchmarking: (Loughborough University, 1995)
TQM	36.0	13.0
Quality circles	40.0	8.0
Customer satisfaction surveys	67.0	57.0
Benchmarking	19.0*	7.4
Mission statement	69.0	35.5

* Competitive benchmarking stipulated here.

Management practices

The questionnaire listed seven different practices, identified by the research team as key to the development of an effective quality management programme, and asked respondents to indicate whether they had implemented any of them.

Staff appraisal schemes

Staff appraisal schemes are designed to help foster the development of individual members of staff and thus benefit the organization (Oldroyd, 1995). Ideally, they are for the mutual benefit of employer and employee, as they should facilitate the identification of training needs and focus on possible areas of improvement for the individual staff member. Schemes are usually formally documented and involve an annual interview in which an employee's needs are assessed and reviewed. Staff appraisals which contain these features play a vital role in the quality organization. They are geared to improving the effectiveness of all employees.

Staff appraisal schemes of some kind were found to be the most frequently used of the seven management practices listed. Almost 62 per cent of LIS had them in place, whilst a further 8 per cent indicated that they were preparing to implement them. The questionnaire did not, however, enable us to probe further into the details of the implementation of staff appraisal.

Team working

Teams are viewed as central to a commitment to learning and to the improvements which this produces. They also facilitate learning by providing an environment in which learning can be articulated and tested against the needs of the organization (Morgan and Murgatroyd, 1994). An important aspect of team working is that it often involves cross-functional working, which ensures that an organizational perspective is maintained when carrying out tasks. Team ownership of a process or programme also ensures continuity. Although quality 'champions' can enthuse and motivate others there is the risk that if they leave the organization commitment and momentum may cease.

Quality circles can also be viewed as a team working approach. In another section of the questionnaire under the heading 'Communication', respondents were asked whether 'quality groups' were used to communicate policies to LIS staff. Just under 9 per cent of respondents were found to use this method. Quality circles are formed voluntarily and meet on a regular basis to 'identify, investigate, analyze and solve their work-related problems' (DTI, 1994c).

Team working was found to be the second most favoured management practice, with over 53 per cent of respondents stating that work was carried out by teams.

Cost centres

Cost centres can give autonomy to departments and units and provide the means of improving local accountability. They can also help in planning for the future, as they facilitate the monitoring and allocation of resources. An in-depth study of applying the cost centre approach to academic libraries, published in 1989 (Revill, 1989), cites the Institute of Cost and Management Accountants' definition of a 'cost centre' as '...a location, function or items of equipment in respect of which costs may be ascertained and related to cost units for control purposes'.

An example of a cost centre operating within a library could be the photocopying service. Cost centres were found to be in place in over 33 per cent of responding organizations.

Performance indicators

Performance indicators have been the subject of much debate in the LIS sector for many years. Their use in the public library sector is well established, due to the Audit Commission's (1989) requirement that performance-related data be collected (see also pp.155-156, this volume). It has been argued that within the academic sector, they should be used within a quality framework (Winkworth, 1993; Abbott, 1994). One view is that, to be successful, performance indicators should involve staff as well as user viewpoints (Winkworth, 1993), whilst another, from experience of the Sports Council, is that performance indicators should provide the basis of a management information system (Hall, 1992).

Over 33 per cent of respondents stated that they were using performance indicators, with a further 22 per cent anticipating their use in the future. In the public library sector usage is much higher at 86 per cent (see pp.155-156, this volume), and they are being implemented as the basis of management information systems. Performance indicators represent hard data which are essential to the decision-making process.

Flatter management structures

'Leaner' organizations are fast becoming the norm for reasons of economy. Popular euphemisms for this include 'downsizing', and even 'rightsizing'. The trend is to encourage the exodus of older, and often more experienced, members of staff who are expensive to employ, and to redeploy or assimilate their work with that of others. Whole tiers of management, usually middle ranking executives, have been removed in cost-cutting exercises. Staff cutbacks could be one of the reasons for the distrust and fear expressed by some LIS staff in relation to quality management. In a quality environment flatter management structures should lead to better internal communications, with fewer errors through breakdowns in communication. Traditional hierarchical organizations, with many layers of management, have been criticized for their complexity and waste. Public services, such as the National Health Service and the Civil Service, were seen to be prime examples of bureaucratic, top-heavy organizations, which were both inefficient and ineffective. However, some public sector organizations have recently undergone privatization programmes, for example through the forming of NHS trusts and government agencies, and as a result have been subject to considerable change and rationalization.

The survey revealed that 26 per cent of respondents to the questionnaire had introduced flatter management structures. One more extreme aspect of this is that there were instances of libraries being run down and LIS staff being forced to seek employment elsewhere. One respondent commented that they had one part-time member of staff, and added: 'you can't get much flatter than that'. Quality, and its equation with the leaner organization, therefore has to be balanced against the reality that adequate staff numbers are needed if an effective service is to be provided.

Management information systems

Management information has been described as 'that data which needs to be collected and analyzed to ensure that the department is meeting corporate objectives in the most cost-effective manner' (Ward, 1987).

Management information systems (MIS) should offer managers access to a variety of data, which can be manipulated and analyzed to form the basis of strategic planning and help in the decision-making process. However, as the Follett Report noted, there are gaps in provision in library automation systems, one of which is the availability of management information (HEFCE, 1993). The reasons for this are partly to do with the limitations of the current generation of library automation systems, but the report also highlights the absence of a specification for an MIS, and recommends that a study be funded to develop one.

The respondents to the questionnaire were not using MIS to any significant extent. Twenty-eight per cent were currently using MIS, with a further 12 per cent indicating their intention to use them in future.

Management by function

Several respondents indicated that they did not know or understand what was meant by this term. One commented:

> Not clear what this means—we currently have managers responsible for specific library functions which cut across customer groups.

Management by function is the antithesis of line organization, which is based on hierarchies using a top down approach. Management by function is organized around what a department, group or unit actually does, and which departments it interacts with. In the case of LIS, management by function might consist of managing all the work to do with the acquisition and arrangement of stock under the function of bibliographic services. Over 18 per cent of respondents stated that they worked in this way. It is possible that this term was not widely understood, and that it is more widely used than the survey suggests.

Table 5 summarizes the usage results outlined above.

Table 5: Management practices in use

MANAGEMENT PRACTICE	YES: PRACTICE IN USE (%)	IN PREPARATION (%)
Staff appraisal	61.97	8.45
Team working	53.87	3.17
Cost centres	33.80	3.52
Performance indicators	33.80	22.18
Management information system	28.87	12.68
Flatter management structure	26.76	4.23
Management by function	18.66	1.41

Evaluating customer satisfaction

There are many ways of measuring and evaluating levels of customer satisfaction. As the needs of the customer form the axis around which all activities in a quality environment revolve, it was considered essential to determine which methods were currently being used by LIS. Six methods of measuring service quality were listed:

- Number of complaints received

- Number of compliments received

- Through existing performance indicators

- Customer satisfaction surveys

- Success against predetermined targets

- Greater value for money

Of the six methods, 57 per cent of respondents used customer satisfaction surveys. Surveys can be targeted at specific user groups or customers, e.g. part-time students, if there is concern about the level of service offered to them. However, one respondent felt that customer satisfaction surveys measured efficiency rather than the quality of service.

Existing performance indicators were the next most favoured method of evaluating customer satisfaction, and were found to be used by 44 per cent of respondents. Performance indicators enable comparisons to be made; these might be between different years or different sites and are a way of focusing on areas requiring further action (Abbott, 1994). Although performance indicators have a vital role to play in the production of hard data to support decisions, qualitative measures, based upon the subjective views of users, are also needed.

Counting the number of complaints and compliments received about the service is one way of finding out what customers think about it. Thirty-eight per cent of respondents favoured measuring complaints, whilst almost 35 per cent preferred to measure compliments. In the public sector customer complaints systems are a requirement of the Citizen's Charter (see p.158, this volume), but as yet there is no onus on academic or commercial LIS to monitor complaints. Recording actual numbers of complaints and compliments might be a worthwhile exercise, but it is the nature and content of these which is of more interest. Quantitative data on complaints and compliments need careful analysis, if serious and correctable faults in services are to be identified and rectified.

The remaining two of the six possible methods of measuring service quality were: success against predetermined targets and greater value for money. The former was found to be used by almost 28 per cent of respondents, and the latter by 17 per cent.

The most interesting data derive from the 'other' methods which respondents used. Many indicated that they had no formal methods in place, or stated that they did not measure their quality of service. Methods used included:

- book availability survey

- feedback from users via the library committee

- programmed contact between library staff and clients

- gossip

- occasional consumer surveys

- student course evaluation

- Annual Operating Statement

- through the college Quality Assurance Committee

- user focus/panel meetings

One LIS measured quality through the Christmas 'goodies' which they received, and through audits of various kinds. Another used an external consultant to assess quality. The general trend, noted in all these methods, was the use of customer feedback to measure quality; this was often obtained through various committees and user focus groups.

Training for quality

Training in the concepts, theories and practices of quality management is the key to successful implementation of quality programmes. In its 1992 survey (Wilkinson *et al.*, 1993) the Institute of Management stated:

> Effective training can make a positive contribution to the
> success of quality management, a conclusion which has

clear implications for the implementation of quality management, and which suggests that organizations need to
steer away from a 'cut-price' approach to quality.

However, they found that only 31 per cent of managers in the service
sector, who responded to their survey, were offered training in quality
tools and techniques by their organization. Those that had benefited from
training often commented that it had been 'too little, too late'. Slightly
higher levels of training were found to exist in primary industry (40 per
cent), manufacturing industry (51 per cent) and construction (38 per
cent).

Lack of training and education to support quality is one of the issues
affecting the development of quality management in Europe, and has
been identified in a 1994 European Union report (EC, 1994). This report
also found that small and medium sized organizations were ineffective
when adopting TQM, due to insufficient training.

The findings of the current benchmarking survey on training for
quality in the LIS sector were similar to those of the Institute of Management survey. An overwhelming 72.5 per cent of respondents stated
that staff at all levels received no training for quality at all. Fourteen per
cent of senior managers received some training in quality, as did 18 per
cent of middle managers and paraprofessionals.

A respondent from the academic sector, where training for quality had
been delivered, stated that they had taken part in Total Quality workshops
run by a large firm of management consultants. Another stated:

There is nothing specific on offer, though the university
has just engaged a management consultancy team to try
and appraise what training might be appropriate.

The use of a quality consultant, supported by 'tailored training', which
was organized by the consultant and the staff development officer, was
also the pattern in another institution. Other comments revealed LIS staff
being included in a college-wide quality training initiative, and the use
of advertised courses for senior managers. Follow-up seminars were
often organized, where the practices learnt on external courses were
discussed with a view to implementation.

One respondent felt that all training was geared to quality, and stated
that they had no specific training for quality in place. This reflects the
widely held view that quality is not something special to be treated
separately. Quality is regarded as being largely a matter of commonsense,

and the idea that staff need to be taught it is often perceived as patronizing and insulting. The use of external consultants, who are brought in to teach experienced library assistants how to answer the telephone, can be interpreted as demeaning; at the same time real training needs in relation to quality might be neglected.

Instruction might usefully include methods of delivering user education to the growing numbers of customers who lack basic research and study skills, and who cause considerable delays at service points. Good user education can help in the management of their expectations of the service, and it can improve relationships with frontline staff (Millson-Martula and Menon, 1995; McCarthy, 1995). In the late 1970s and early 1980s user education was a major topic for discussion and evaluation, and the then British Library Research and Development Department sponsored a series of international conferences on the subject (Fox and Malley, 1983). Perhaps the time has arrived for a reappraisal of user education in the context of the situation today. The growth in student numbers, many of whom come from a non-traditional educational background, coupled with diminished resources, means that LIS need to ensure that users are equipped with information seeking and retrieval skills.

Training in quality for staff needs to address poor communication between junior library staff and library management, so that difficulties faced at the point of delivery are discussed and tackled. In reality, procedures may be introduced which are wholly impractical, and which may make the job more difficult. Team working, involving all levels of staff, would go some way to addressing this problem, but in particular managers need to listen to frontline staff, not distance themselves, if the practicalities of delivering a quality service are to be addressed.

Evaluating effectiveness: measurement and comparison

Performance in the LIS sector has moved away from the concept of efficiency, which can be viewed as a simple ratio between input and output, towards one of effectiveness. Effectiveness is concerned with the quality of a service, or how 'good' it is (Orr, 1973). How 'good' a library is, in a quality context, is determined by the user not by the staff, and all measures of effectiveness must derive from the customer's standpoint.

Five methods of measuring and evaluating performance in LIS were listed in the questionnaire, and respondents were invited to state which, if any, they currently used. They were also invited to add any other, unlisted methods which they used. Feedback from users was found to be the method favoured by 81 per cent of respondents. This method should ensure that staff are made aware of what users actually want or need, rather than what they, the staff, believe they want or need (Parasuraman *et al.*, 1991).

However, equally widespread were usage statistics, which almost 79 per cent of respondents were found to be using. Usage statistics are basic number counts of transactions which occur within a prescribed timescale. Unlike performance indicators, which indicate a relationship between two or more variables (for example, the number of issues per registered user), usage statistics often substantiate what is already known, such as high volumes of issues. They may establish a need for more staff or other resources, but they are not an accurate measure of performance. Performance indicators, which were also listed, were found to be used by half as many respondents (42 per cent) to measure effectiveness.

Benchmarking

Benchmarking was used by almost 7.4 per cent of respondents. However, respondents were also asked if they compared any of their activities with those of other organizations as a measure of effectiveness, and 24.6 per cent replied in the affirmative. Many of these comparisons were carried out using performance indicators. One respondent listed these as: book purchasing per student; expenditure per full-time equivalent (FTE); and lending and reservations per student. Others used SCONUL published statistics as comparison tools, whilst informal visits to look critically at specific issues offer some the opportunity to compare their services with others. There was one outstanding example of benchmarking activity in the academic sector. The respondent was looking beyond the LIS sector at retail practice, in relation to the implementation of customer care, and had already effected comparisons with hotel services. In general the trend in LIS—where benchmarking has been used—is for participants to benchmark against institutions which are similar to themselves.

Communication within the organization

Effective communication between staff and management is a prerequisite of quality management; it can influence people's attitudes and behaviour, and thus prepare them to accept change (Oakland, 1994). Staff need to be kept informed of any quality initiatives and to be given a chance to contribute their ideas on how procedures can be improved.

There are various ways of doing this. There may be a formalized staff suggestions scheme, enabling staff, particularly process owners, to identify areas for improvement. The United Kingdom Association of Suggestion Schemes (UKASS) is a registered charity which provides access to a network of members involved in suggestion schemes.[1] Alternatively, there may be regular staff meetings, or team meetings such as a quality group, where problems can be discussed.

The survey revealed that staff meetings were used more than the other methods listed, with 70 per cent of respondents indicating their use. On-the-job training was found to be used by 54 per cent; whilst 40 per cent relied on managers 'walking the floor'. Appraisal schemes, which are a valuable training aid, were also found to be used by 40 per cent of respondents. Training courses, mission statements, and newsletters or bulletins were also offered as alternative methods of communicating quality. These methods were used by 37 per cent, 35 per cent, and 30 per cent of respondents respectively.

Perceptions of benchmarking

Qualitative information on attitudes to benchmarking was gleaned not only from comments added to the questionnaire but also at the telephone interview stage of the project. Interviewees were selected from a list of those agreeing to take part in this second phase of the survey. Twelve people were interviewed—six from each sector. An unstructured, interviewee-led approach was adopted. A copy of the interview questions is shown in Appendix C.

Interviewees were asked if they felt benchmarking to be relevant to the LIS sector; this question then led them to describe their own organization and the place of quality within it.

The private sector

The participants from the private sector represented a cross-section of industries. They included employees of an insurance company, a major bank, a materials technology research unit and a chamber of commerce.

---

1. United Kingdom Association of Suggestion Schemes (UKASS), St Nicholas, Hoe Court, Lancing, West Sussex BN15 0QX. Administrator: Susan M. Gwilliam.

The position of the LIS in each organization, in terms of usage and prestige, varied widely.

At one extreme, the library in the insurance sector had been disbanded as part of a cost cutting exercise. The holdings of the centralized corporate library had been dispersed to individual departments and, apart from the interviewee, library staff were no longer employed. Information requests were outsourced to information brokers, and secretarial staff had been made responsible for information collections. Online searching was carried out by an in-house qualified surveyor. The interviewee had been given a new job title, which better reflected her new support and secretarial role. Meetings, which took the form of 'team briefings', had taken place, but the interviewee had not had a voice in these, and her arguments for the preservation of the library had gone unheeded. Senior management had viewed the library as taking up valuable office space, so the stock had been distributed to departments according to its relevance to their particular area of work.

The interviewee did not understand the term benchmarking, but when it had been briefly explained, she voiced the opinion that in the light of the current situation within the organization there was 'little scope for such tools'. At present the organization had no system in place for evaluating the effectiveness of the current methods of obtaining information as outlined above.

Another interviewee managed a library which he referred to as a 'special library', although it currently forms part of a government agency. The information unit was in the process of 'soft privatization', which involved merging with a university, as part of a cost cutting exercise. In particular, the current site rent was exorbitant, but the library focused on an area which had been badly affected by the recession, so the whole issue of the 'soft privatization' of the library was politically sensitive. Plans for the future had included market testing and the introduction of Service Level Agreements, but both had been cancelled due to uncertainty about the future of the library. The use of teleworking had been considered, and there was already one person working from France using electronic mail. However, the interviewee felt that, as the manager of 17 staff, teleworking was not a viable option for him.

When asked about the use of benchmarking, this interviewee felt that it was relevant to the information sector, with the proviso that processes which are easy to monitor, e.g. interlibrary loans, were selected for the exercise. When asked if his information service documented and monitored key processes, he replied that this was carried out in order to justify funding. There was no use of customer feedback as a basis for improvement, as all current activities were motivated by the need to reduce expenditure, and planning was for six months ahead only. This manager, like the previous interviewee, voiced the opinion that his library was perceived to be occupying expensive space, and was expensive to maintain. It was therefore a prime candidate for a cost cutting exercise.

The interviewee in the Chamber of Commerce library explained that important processes, which were executed on a regular basis, had been identified and formally documented. Statistics relating to usage were maintained for monitoring purposes, but monitoring was not used as a basis for continual improvement. She felt that, having only one full-time and one part-time member of staff, the unit lacked time for monitoring and reviewing activities. Future plans included the targeting of 10–20 per cent of enquiries, in order to carry out follow-up telephone interviews, with the aim of assessing user satisfaction. Benchmarking was judged to be something which 'ought to be relevant', but 'might not be practical'. The interviewee felt that it needed to be done well, and would therefore require considerable time at the planning stage. She stated that her LIS was considered to be 'the best information provider in the county', and was an example of best practice. It could act as a role model to others.

Interviewees from the remaining organizations felt that benchmarking was of relevance to the LIS sector. Some stated that the aims of the participating organizations needed to be similar, otherwise the processes would differ, making comparisons difficult. One interviewee reinforced the popular belief that manufacturers, who had a tangible end product which was 'ready to go,' would make unsuitable benchmarking partners. She stated that library services, such as interlibrary loans, had many processes to go through before there was an end product. There was no recognition that products also have processes and procedures through which they have to go before they become 'the finished product'.

It has been noted that some managers in the information sector experience difficulty in relating LIS procedures to those of business and manufacturing industry. They perceive their operations to be 'different' from those of commerce and industry (Lester, 1994). Textbooks on benchmarking adhere to the notion that processes are comparable across sectors, but the latest DTI advice on benchmarking (1995) states:

> The benchmark performance can be based on other similar organizations (perhaps competitors), customer expecta-

tions, financial averages or a combination of all three. The best practices are the practices which will result in the benchmark performance.

This is a slightly moderated, or more cautious, statement about the choice of benchmarking partners. The DTI refers to organizations that are 'similar', or—as one interviewee referred to this—which share the same aims. The Royal Mail is concerned with document delivery and has many procedures or sub-processes which affect delivery times and, ultimately, the quality of the service offered. These can be compared to interlibrary loan procedures, where supply chains exist, and a document is transmitted from A to B having gone through several processes. However, benchmarking across sectors has yet to be widely demonstrated, so the efficacy and practicality of cross-sectoral benchmarking remains largely unproven.

The question which often arises, and which needs to be addressed, is: 'What's in it for me?'. Generalizations about the perceived benefits of benchmarking are not sufficiently convincing to LIS managers, who are currently operating under considerable financial constraints. They need practical examples of benchmarking working to the benefit of the LIS sector before they will be persuaded to embark on such a programme.

The academic sector

The range of responses from the academic sector in relation to benchmarking were much broader because of the higher response rate. An interviewee, who can be judged to be representative of many LIS professionals, admitted to being 'old-fashioned', believing firmly in the public service ethos. He felt that benchmarking was irrelevant to the LIS sector, and stated that society was 'rushing into all these measures, whether they are useful or not'. This viewpoint is understandable in an era of change and recession, when there is a tendency to seek quick solutions to what can be complex and perhaps insoluble problems. However, this same interviewee admitted to using measures to monitor key processes because 'there is little choice in having to do this, as the institution cannot stand outside what is happening in the rest of society'.

Another interviewee described the 'twinning' arrangement between the university and a US counterpart, in which staff visits were formally arranged. The aim of the visits was to gain knowledge of the host organization's strategy and, more specifically, of how a particular operation was carried out. The interviewee saw this exercise as being broader in approach than benchmarking, as it had a staff development role. The US host was acknowledged as being more technologically developed than its UK partner, and was also experienced in obtaining finance from private sources. It was therefore considered an example of best practice, and visits were a learning exercise at both the individual and the organizational level.

Concluding comments

Overall, there was found to be considerable interest in the use of benchmarking, but there was also much uncertainty surrounding its actual practice. Many respondents to the questionnaire failed to complete the ranking of benchmarking definitions. Some answered honestly, by stating that they did not know, or understand, what was meant by 'benchmarking', whilst others clearly indicated that they were not interested. One commented:

> At the moment I'm not sure what the term 'benchmarking' means at all, so my answer is sheer guesswork! I dislike the management jargon, although I don't disagree with the principles.

The ranking came at the end of the questionnaire and was probably perceived by many as not constituting a proper question, and therefore as optional. The definitions were all derived from authoritative texts on benchmarking, and ranged from the brief general statement

> Finding and implementing best practice,

to the particular:

> The continuous process of measuring products, services and practices against leaders, allowing the identification of best practices which will lead to superior practice.

The latter explanatory definition was preferred to the concise one, although ultimately it was a matter of personal preference.

Positive and negative aspects of quality programmes

Much has been written in textbooks on the potential of quality management to improve all aspects of an organization's operations. These include the empowerment of staff, leading to greater employee autonomy (Morgan and Murgatroyd, 1994), and greater user involvement which helps to justify to management the financial and human resources needed to provide services (Lawes, 1993). In many cases the actual benefits are not proven, but are subsumed in a long list of reasons for implementation. The reasons for introducing quality programmes are convincing, but hard evidence of the benefits to the LIS sector is needed before critical mass is reached. The expenditure of time and money may be seen as outweighing the actual advantages. Benchmarking techniques are still being tested, so it is too early to comment on the benefits of using this particular quality tool, not only in LIS but also in other organizations.

To try to gauge the benefits and disadvantages attached to quality management programmes, respondents to the questionnaire were invited to list the three major impacts—for good or bad—which had resulted from their quality programmes, where these had been implemented.

Positive aspects

The answers ranged from benefits on a macrocosmic level, such as improved understanding of LIS operations, coupled with an improved image of the LIS within the university, to the more in-depth housekeeping improvements, such as better access to bookstock due to the introduction of shelving rotas.

The ability of quality programmes to involve staff at all levels was noted by several respondents—some of whom commented on heightened levels of awareness of quality issues, and the adoption of a more positive attitude amongst staff. They felt that quality management encouraged the sharing of ideas, and the responsibility for dealing with them was shared with the university. Quality programmes helped in the identification of strengths and weaknesses, and led to better understanding of organizational culture and procedures. Better relationships with users had been achieved through containing, or managing, their expectations, whilst staff awareness of user needs had, in general, improved.

Other comments involved the structure or standards, which quality programmes imposed on the management of change and bringing about improvements. It was deemed a 'systematic method of improvement' by one respondent, whilst another stated that it 'rationalized systems and procedures'. The word 'culture' was used many times, implying that the quality process was one which involved re-thinking old ideas and attitudes. The term 'focus' was also popular, as respondents spoke of 'focusing university wide interest in value for money in library terms', and 'focusing on the customer and on improvement'. Quality management forces questions to be asked, such as 'why do we exist?' and 'why do we do that?', and reverses traditional 'business as usual' practices.

Negative aspects

A frequent comment from respondents was that quality programmes took up a considerable amount of time and, where staffing levels were considered to be below requirements, this placed additional strain on the workforce. One institution was attempting to produce a quality manual and found this difficult both to do and to sustain, due to the constant need for revision and the amount of time needed to do this well. Paradoxically, implementing quality was deemed to have an adverse effect on service quality in the short term. Other issues were related to general human failings, such as the tendency to talk about quality issues rather than act on them, and the slow pace at which attitudes changed, if at all. One respondent had avoided the term 'quality' altogether when introducing change, because of the 'level of cultural change necessary'. Interestingly, resistance to a quality initiative, in one instance, had been from professional staff, whilst support staff had been keen to implement change.

The need to focus on the worst aspects of the service was also felt to have a detrimental effect on staff and users. Staff could become 'disheartened', whilst users were 'inundated with questionnaires', and were considered to be suffering from 'questionnaire fatigue'. Users also became more demanding and critical of services once they became aware of their role in the quality of service provision.

Where service level agreements had been introduced, one respondent reported scepticism amongst users as to the ability of the LIS to deliver the services formally on offer.

Barriers to change

The research methodology provided ample opportunity to explore the problems that organizations face when implementing quality initiatives.

Some issues were found to be common to all organizations, irrespective of sector, whilst others might be considered especially pertinent to the information sector.

The first contact people have with quality management can colour their subsequent attitude to it. It is also argued that if quality programmes are enforced with little explanation as to their purpose and wider context, then people may feel suspicious of the motives behind the changes (Lester, 1994).

Language and semantics

During the course of the project certain phrases recurred, which sum up the apprehensions of many information professionals in relation to quality management. These are variations on: 'prescribed systems'; 'formal systems'; 'bureaucratic methods'; 'rigid systems'; and so forth. Many LIS staff perceive quality management to be the opposite of what it purports to be. Instead of being based on democratic principles, which aim to free the workforce and give them greater autonomy, they see quality as being prescriptive and rule bound. When questioned, one interviewee provided a valuable insight into this shared belief. She said that information professionals regarded themselves as intelligent, free-thinking individuals, who prided themselves on being apart from the common herd, and who questioned the validity of everything. What they did not want was a system—especially one which has connotations of the marketplace and the retail trade—imposed on them; what they did want was proof that quality management was not one in a line of 'management fads' (Brockman, 1992).

The whole language of quality management, like that of information technology (IT) before it, is treated by many with suspicion and/or derision. It smacks of exclusivity and arcanum. The profusion of terms, many of which mean the same thing, causes confusion, and promotes endless discussion on implied meaning. The language is often abstract and value-laden, as in 'good', 'quality', and 'effectiveness', and this adds to the problem. Little wonder that quality programmes are often criticized for stimulating conversation rather than action. The characteristics of the literature of quality management have been described as 'verbose, repetitious, anecdotal, and jargon-ridden' (Line, 1995).

Political implications

The research methodology also provided an opportunity to gather qualitative information which highlighted the barriers which exist in LIS in relation to quality management and its associated techniques, such as benchmarking. It became apparent that certain perceptions and beliefs prevail, which inform people's reactions to management initiatives. Woven into the problem with terminology, mentioned above, is the belief, or fear, that the language of quality management conceals or stands for something else. In an age of political correctness, language has become a powerful weapon, and it is often viewed with distrust. People look behind the facade of language, which speaks of improvements and empowerment, and perceive in its stead staff reductions and a heavier workload.

Secondly, many library personnel stated that they did not want libraries to be treated like supermarkets, where everything has a price but nothing is valued. This view is linked to commercial usage of quality techniques and the continued belief that quality is about products or other tangible objects, not about services. LIS staff also hold fast to the tradition of the educational role of libraries within society. This tradition is being undermined by consumerist ideology and government-led ways of working. Respondents expressed a genuine desire to preserve the ethos of the not-for-profit sector, despite the reality of demands for more accountability and business-like ways of working.

Organizational size

The view that quality programmes are the preserve of larger organizations is rife. Many respondents, from both sectors, stated that their information service was too small and under-resourced to consider implementing quality initiatives. They provided details of their staffing levels, which often consisted of one professional librarian, plus two or three part-time library assistants. They felt that, given their limited free time and low funding, there was little scope for change or innovation. In small information services the quality of the service is usually dependent upon the motivation of the staff; if they are enthused then everything will be done to provide a good service. This motivation, in turn, often depends upon the attitude of senior management at organizational level towards the information unit.

Cultural stasis

It has been argued that there is a need to establish new management styles and structures in libraries, to enable them to cope with the constant change and competitive ethos of the 1990s (Line, 1991). However, in some LIS, and/or their parent organizations, interviewees indicated that there was a low turnover of staff. One interviewee commented that this had resulted in no influx of new ideas and a stagnating organization replete with 'plateau performers'. Long-serving staff were thought more likely to retain traditional ideas about librarianship, and to be resistant to change. It was suggested that staff who wished to effect change may feel powerless to do so, until certain staff retire or move on; at the same time, concepts such as empowerment for junior staff may be viewed with fear and distrust by managers who already feel under threat.

Informal methods

Many respondents indicated that they were already using techniques and methods which focused upon the customer and the provision of effective services. Some preferred this method of working, and managers saw no need to formalize or 'bureaucratize' existing practice. As has already been noted, there is resistance to what are regarded as prescriptive ways of working; LIS managers prefer a selective approach, where they can adapt those management practices which they feel suit their particular organizational culture.

Theory into practice

Introduction

This Chapter details the action research component of the project, in which benchmarking techniques were tested by three 'demonstrator' library and information services. All three services form part of organizations where quality management has been implemented, and were therefore considered to be examples of best practice. The three will be referred to as organizations A, B and C. They comprised:

- Organization A—an academic institution

- Organization B—a pharmaceutical company

- Organization C—an NHS trust

A full description of the three participants can be found in Appendix A.

Before embarking on this exercise it was necessary to:

- examine the definitions and descriptions of benchmarking;

- identify the types of benchmarking, and evaluate their relevance to the LIS sector;

- evaluate the methodologies, models and techniques of benchmarking;

- identify a model which could be adapted to suit the information sector.

Definitions of benchmarking

There are various definitions of benchmarking, ranging from the general to the specific, many of which originate from well-known authorities on quality management (Camp, 1989; Bullivant, 1994). Some of these definitions were incorporated into the questionnaire as a ranking exercise, with the aim of gaining an insight into respondents' preferences and understanding of benchmarking terms. Many omitted to complete this part of the questionnaire; some stated that they did not know what the term 'benchmarking' meant, and would therefore be 'guessing' if they did complete the question. Amongst those that did complete it there was a preference for the more descriptive definitions. The following is a current description, originating from the CCTA (Government Centre for Information Systems), which defines the benchmarking process succinctly (1995):

> Benchmarking is a management technique to improve business performance. It is used to compare performance between different organizations—or different units within a single organization—undertaking similar processes, on a continuous basis.

To make this definition more acceptable to the library and information sector one need only substitute 'service levels' for 'business performance'. It was found useful, when dealing with a proliferation of benchmarking definitions, to focus on two key concepts: measurement and comparison. The aim of benchmarking is to document and measure a key process, and then compare the resulting data with those relating to similar processes in other organizations.

Types of benchmarking

Five main categories of benchmarking have been cited in the literature:

1. *Competitor*—comparing with leading organizations with similar products or services and adopting their approach. This method is suited to the with-profit sector, but the DTI also recommends its use by organizations providing the same services, but where there is no competition on a commercial basis, e.g. NHS trusts, government departments, and universities (DTI, 1995).

2. *Generic*—comparisons of business processes or functions that are very similar, regardless of industry (Oakland, 1994).

3. *Internal*—a comparison of internal operations by different departments within the same organization (Oakland, 1994).

4. *Functional*—comparisons to similar functions within the same broad industry, or to industry leaders (Oakland, 1994).

5. *Customer*—the aim of the improvement programme is meeting
   and exceeding customer expectations (DTI, 1995).

Generic benchmarking was selected for the project benchmarking
exercise, as it focuses on measuring and comparing key processes in
different organizations. Of the three LIS taking part in the benchmarking
exercise, two chose to benchmark their enquiry services, whilst the third
chose interlibrary loans. The benchmarking partners, which hosted visits
and provided comparative data, were also drawn from different sectors,
but again the same two processes were analyzed and evaluated to
facilitate comparison.

However, the fifth type of benchmarking listed above—customer
benchmarking—was recently identified by the DTI (1995), and may be
of particular relevance to the library and information sector:

> The benchmark is customer expectations. Customers de-
> velop their own benchmarks of performance when select-
> ing and judging suppliers. The improvement programme
> is aimed at meeting and exceeding customer expectation.

It is already common practice in the LIS sector to use customer
feedback and customer satisfaction surveys to measure the quality of
service provision. The findings of this project have revealed these
methods to be widespread. However, it also has to be acknowledged that
customer expectations can be unrealistic. In academic libraries they may
be unreasonably high, whilst in public libraries the converse may be
apparent. Despite these reservations, it would be worthwhile assessing
the development of customer benchmarking in the library and information sector. Customer benchmarking would merely formalize the customer feedback activities which are already in place, and could establish
optimum levels of service on the lines of charters already in use in many
public library services. However, it has yet to be established whether
these are considered desirable in the academic and private information
sectors.

Approaches to benchmarking

A number of authorities on benchmarking favour a stepped approach,
and many of their suggestions are variants on the Rank Xerox model of
benchmarking. One view is that benchmarking is similar to project
management, and therefore requires careful planning if it is to be effec-

tive. Bullivant (1994) suggests a twelve step approach to benchmarking (see Appendix D). The twelve steps fit into three stages—Planning, Analysis and Action—and represent a logical progression from selecting a process to reviewing progress.

Oakland (1994) also proposes a stepped (or staged) process, comprising fifteen steps, which are listed under the headings Plan, Analyze, Develop, Improve and Review. He states that these all focus on 'trying to measure comparisons of competitiveness'. Although this approach is predicated on matching one's competitors, he does add that the objective of benchmarking is to produce products and services that conform to the requirements of the customer.

An example of the stepped approach in practice can be seen in the 'strategic approach' to benchmarking adopted by the Royal Mail (DTI, 1994a). This comprises eight processes, which are laid out in a flowchart, including details of the required documentation at each stage of the process. It is significant that the Royal Mail selected a team to carry out this work and gave them special training. They also emphasize that an overriding criterion in their selection of benchmarking partners was that they should share a commitment to 'Total Quality' (DTI, 1994a).

In the LIS sector, an American information specialist offers a twelve step 'benchmarking methodology', which has been implemented in the technical library serving Sandia National Laboratories, New Mexico (Allen, 1993). Of all the stepped approaches it was felt that this offers a possible way forward for LIS. The first five steps are vital if the exercise is to be successful, and are listed here:

- identify the process to be benchmarked;

- establish management commitment to the benchmarking process;

- identify and establish the benchmarking team;

- define and understand the process to be benchmarked;

- identify metrics and collect process data.

The full twelve steps in the 'Sandia methodology' are listed in Appendix E. The author adds that there is no 'one right way' to benchmarking; it is merely a tool. She also points out that, at the time of writing (1993), it was too early to assess the relevance of benchmarking to the information sector, but she considers it important that information professionals become acquainted with the techniques involved and should be prepared to use them when, and if, required.

Identifying an appropriate benchmarking model

The generic model of benchmarking was selected as the most appropriate approach for the three demonstrator projects taking part in the project exercise. This approach ensures that those elements of a service which are crucial to customer satisfaction are identified and targeted for improvement. The generic model facilitates an in-depth scrutiny of the way operations are currently run, causing questions to be raised and identifying areas for improvement. It is therefore a learning process. The subsequent comparisons with other organizations enable participants to exchange ideas and analyze gaps in performance, with a view to implementing beneficial changes.

The organizations involved in the benchmarking exercise selected a process which they perceived to be critical to the success of their particular LIS—the enquiry service, selected by two, and interlibrary loans.

The following procedures represent the approach taken:

- Identifying a key process, critical to the success of the LIS.

- Documenting or mapping the sub-processes, which are carried out as part of this process. This might involve using existing documents, or producing flowcharts and lists of procedures.

- Taking measurements of those factors which are deemed critical to the success of the process, e.g. the speed of document delivery, or the relevance of a response to an enquiry. These would be elements of the service which the customer values.

- Analyzing the results of this exercise and identifying gaps in performance.

- Selecting benchmarking partners; arranging visits in order to compare the results of the exercise with other organizations using a similar process.

- Identifying 'best practice', i.e. methods used by benchmarking partners which can be adopted in order to improve one's own level of service.

Mapping the processes

Once the key process had been chosen by each of the demonstrator organizations, the next step was for these to be mapped or documented, so that each procedure in the operation was recorded.

In organization B detailed local instructions on the enquiry handling service were already in existence. These prescribed how each enquiry should be recorded, presented, and stored. Value is added at various stages in the procedure, e.g. in removing irrelevant references and summarizing the information. The procedures for follow-up, after the enquiry had been answered, were also detailed to facilitate monitoring the effectiveness of the service. The enquiry service had been subject to a quality audit over the past year—the results of this were circulated to relevant staff.

In organization A the interlibrary loans process was flowcharted. Reader input of interlibrary loan requests had been introduced in September 1994, via the LIBERTAS automated library system. Procedures prior to this arrangement were also flowcharted, so that comparisons could be made. The initial method of input was found to impact on the speed with which the request was processed, as requests posted off campus had to filter through to the appropriate member of the library staff via the internal mail system. Several checks are built into the process, which have been continued since the introduction of reader input of requests. These include amending, checking and approving the readers' self-service requests, and checking local stock to ensure the item is not available on site. An example of the type of data collected by organization A can be found in Appendix G.

In organization C the enquiry service provides patient related data and statistics to internal customers, e.g. the finance department, which is responsible for billing purchasers for services. Patient related data are also collected for statutory returns to the NHS Executive. It is not known if procedures are documented for the enquiry service as these were not made available to the research team.

Measuring critical success factors

Once the mapping exercise had been completed, the participating organizations then set out to identify those factors which they deemed to be critical to customer satisfaction, and hence to the success of the service. This would focus attention on improving those aspects of the service which were most valued by customers, and would lend structure to the exercise, given the compressed timescale of the project.

Enquiry services

In enquiry services the relevance and accuracy of the responses to the enquiries were deemed critical. These are difficult factors to measure, as user feedback tends to reveal general levels of satisfaction with the information provided. A list of critical success factors had been drawn up by one organization. This was written after consultation with key users of the service:

- Information is delivered on time

- Information is delivered in the format required

- Information is delivered in a consistent format that is easily recognized as being the work of Information Services

- The information that is delivered is relevant and answers the question

- Search results are of consistent quality

Interlibrary loans

The critical success factor for interlibrary loans was that of timeliness. The organization benchmarking interlibrary loans was an academic institution, where items are usually required as soon as possible to fulfil coursework commitments. Therefore the quicker the request can be satisfied, the higher the level of customer satisfaction.

Analyzing the results

Enquiry services

Detailed information on the procedures and routines used by organization B in their enquiry service was compiled by the process owner. This provided a document of their current methods for ensuring that the critical success factors, listed above, are addressed and monitored. In order to comply with the first of these factors, i.e. that information is delivered on time, deadlines have been set for response times. Urgent enquiries are responded to within 24 hours of receipt, and on the day of receipt if received by 1.00 p.m. Ninety per cent of enquiries are expected to be answered within five working days, or earlier, if agreed with the customer beforehand, and senior staff are given priority. All enquiries are logged onto a management information system (MIS), and statistics on turn around times, plus other key quantitative data, can be derived from this system for monitoring and reviewing purposes. Customer feedback is evaluated through studying the hardcopy search request forms, where details of the follow-ups are recorded. The other critical success factors listed above were measured in the quality audit of 1994.

Organization B stated that they had decided on their current method of measuring customer satisfaction after careful consideration of the alternatives. This method involves contacting the customer, by telephone or electronic mail, after a request for information has been completed. They are asked if they are satisfied with the information supplied. However, this method invariably produced a positive response, which led the LIS to question its effectiveness. Despite this drawback, the use of questionnaires or an evaluation form had been rejected in favour of the telephone call, as this was considered to be a quicker, more proactive approach.

Interlibrary loans

Quantitative data, which were collected over a period of one month in February 1995, provided a snapshot of the interlibrary loans service in operation at organization A. These data provided information on the following variables:

- Number of reader input requests, via the recently introduced self-service facility

- Number of staff inputs

- Date the request was input/date request sent

- Date item received

- Item supplier for each request

- Items passed to acquisitions for ordering

- Items found in stock/not requested

From these raw data certain trends were identified:

- The total number of inputs of requests was 771, and the average time taken to supply the item had been just over six days.

- This average reduced to five days, when 25 long-delayed requests were removed from the calculations. These 25 requests were deducted from the total because they each took over 25 days to be satisfied.

- Long-delayed requests represented only 3 per cent of the total, yet they extended the average supply time by one day.

The reasons for the delay in supplying the item warrant further investigation, but the data highlighted the dependence of LIS upon their suppliers, especially in respect of interlibrary loans, where the main supplier is the British Library Document Supply Centre (BLDSC). Nineteen of the 25 long delayed items were requests to BLDSC, which raised the question as to how levels of service can be improved when this interdependence exists. Organization A has six suppliers to choose from, each of whom is able to satisfy certain requests, but the majority are supplied by BLDSC. BLDSC handles large numbers of requests each day and has automated systems in place to improve document delivery times; nevertheless, due to the high usage of the system, some delays are inevitable. In addition, organization A commented on the obscure nature of some of the requests, which could impact on delivery times.

The interlibrary loan service at organization A does satisfy the criteria laid down in the Joint Funding Councils' consultative report on perform-ance indicators in libraries (HEFCE, 1995). This gives an example of a 'speedy and efficient interlibrary loan service' as one where 85 per cent of items requested are delivered within five working days. However, the authors add that timescales for the remaining 15 per cent of requests should be agreed with each customer. An undertaking to fulfil such an agreement would require library staff to identify obscure or difficult to acquire items in advance of transmitting the request, and then to consult with suppliers on expected delivery times. Table 6 summarizes the data extrapolated from organization A's log.

Table 6: Interlibrary loan usage and supply times at organization A for the period 31 January–28 February 1995.

DATA RECORDED		COMMENTS
TOTAL READER INPUTS	526	as percentage of total inputs: 68%
TOTAL STAFF INPUTS	245	as percentage of total inputs: 31.7%
TOTAL INPUTS	771	
TOTAL DAYS TAKEN TO SUPPLY ITEM	4900*	* includes delayed items
LONGEST TIME TAKEN TO SUPPLY ITEM	80 days	BLDSC
SHORTEST TIME TAKEN TO SUPPLY ITEM	2 days	BLDSC
AVERAGE TIME TAKEN TO SUPPLY ITEM	6.35 days	# Adjusted figure: 5 days
% SUPPLIED BY BLDSC	52.5%	
% SUPPLIED BY OTHER SUPPLIERS	38.04%	
% SUPPLIED BY: ORG A/ACQUISITIONS/IN STOCK	9.46%	

* Total of 3,863 days after removal of long delay items.
# This figure represents the adjusted average time taken after removal of long delay items (25).

Selecting benchmarking partners

The selection of partners is acknowledged as one of the most difficult aspects of benchmarking (Allen, 1993; Marsh, 1993). Organizations using competitive benchmarking techniques are likely to experience the most difficulty, due to concerns about confidentiality. Many companies exercise extreme caution when disclosing information or 'competitor intelligence', which might be used to their disadvantage. However, a collaborative approach is possible, whereby organizations that are not directly in competition, but which share common goals, form networks where they can share ideas on a regular basis (Marsh, 1993). This method of working would be ideally suited to LIS.

Existing league tables, such as those produced by SCONUL (1995), and the *Times Higher Education Supplement*, were found to be used by many LIS as comparative tools. These offer quantitative data on aspects of library services, such as expenditure on library staff, bookstock, seating and shelving, but they are not indicative of the quality of service, or the levels of user satisfaction. SCONUL statistics do provide some performance indicator related data, such as serial titles per 100 FTE students, but again these do not help with the identification and rectification of problems relating to specific processes. Benchmarking is interactive and operates on a human level, whilst league tables can be used at the desk, and do not require staff to leave the workplace. These factors need to be taken into consideration when trying to promote further use of benchmarking techniques.

Benchmarking partners were selected from organizations known to members of the benchmarking team. In addition they all satisfied one or more of the following criteria:

- Exemplifying best practice

- Involved in quality management programmes

- Holders of quality awards, e.g. ISO 9000.

The selected organizations were approached to determine their interest in benchmarking and their willingness to participate in the exercise. They were organizations which were not considered to be in competition with the demonstrator organizations. The procedures for the exercise were set out in a formal letter which was sent to benchmarking partners, together with contact details of the demonstrator organizations. Initial contact and arrangements for the visits were made by the demonstrator organizations at times which were mutually suitable to all involved.

The benchmarking visit

A meeting was set up between two of the demonstrator project organizations and a benchmarking partner who hosted the visit. The benchmarking partner will be referred to throughout as partner A. The aim of the meeting was to compare data and exchange ideas on the two processes selected for benchmarking purposes. The occasion was informal, and was led by the demonstrator organizations, with the researcher observing events.

Enquiry services

There were major differences between the types of enquiries being handled by organization B and partner A, and each served a different clientele. The LIS at organization B provides toxicological and other pharmaceutical information to employees of the company, whilst partner A deals with general enquiries from students and teaching staff. This influenced the procedures used and the degree of formality and documentation involved, and thus made it difficult to establish common points of reference. It became apparent, during the course of the meeting, that there might be more similarities between the commercial information service at partner A and the enquiry service at organization B. As a result, the member of staff responsible for the commercial information service at partner A was invited to the meeting, and a comparison of this service with that of organization B was carried out.

Best practice was then established, and there was agreement that the existence of the 'Local Instruction' documentation at organization B exemplified this. New methods for evaluating customer satisfaction were discussed, but no new and effective means of doing this were discovered.

Interlibrary loans

Partner A was in the process of implementing an in-house, user-input system for interlibrary loans. User-input of requests had been introduced at organization A a year earlier, so a direct comparison of the impact of this development was not possible. Various methods of improving procedures, using automated systems, were discussed. Problems with delivery times and reliance on suppliers were also discussed, but it was felt that little could be done to alleviate the problem of long-delayed items, especially when they were items of an esoteric nature. Best practice was established, although it was felt that further comparisons were warranted when user-input of interlibrary loans had been in place for a year at Partner A.

Conclusions

Types of benchmarking

From the various types of benchmarking described above, the generic approach was selected for the action research. This method can be applied incrementally, as it involves focusing on one process at a time, and it can be paced to suit organizational needs. However, rigid adherence to one type of benchmarking may not be feasible or productive. LIS may wish to consider the utility of 'customer' benchmarking as a way forward. Using customers' expectations as a benchmark would eliminate the problem of identifying suitable benchmarking partners. The organization would not need to search for examples of best practice, but would simply be responding directly to established customers' needs. However, organizations using this method would not benefit from the networking opportunities which benchmarking opens up, and they would be missing a chance to learn about other organizations' ways of working.

Timescales for benchmarking

Benchmarking is a time-consuming process; several interviewees, who had not been involved in benchmarking, thought that, to be successful, it needed considerable commitment in terms of time and effort. The research project was limited to a timescale of one year and this inevitably affected its outcomes. During the course of the research the 'demonstrator' organizations were undergoing considerable changes which also influenced the benchmarking exercise. The amount of time required to carry out a benchmarking exercise should not be underestimated. The DTI (1995) offers the following advice:

> Have a clear plan showing what is to be improved, where data will be found, the resources required and the timescale involved.

Owners of the process being benchmarked will certainly need to commit time and effort to the exercise, and senior management's guidance and advice will be needed throughout. The planning stage is vital, and considerable time needs to be spent thinking through the various stages of the exercise, and drawing up a plan and timescale for the project, before taking any action. This will save time and possible confusion later on. Planning the benchmarking exercise should ideally be carried out by a team, comprising senior management and the process owner(s), who should meet frequently to report problems and review progress.

Benchmarking partners

The identification of suitable benchmarking partners is difficult and may, in the case of LIS, be confined to those already known to the organization, who are willing to participate. The establishment of benchmarking groups or clubs is a possible solution, and there is already evidence of this happening in the public and commercial sectors. For the purposes of this research project, the organizations participating in the benchmarking exercise were all exemplars of best practice, and were therefore considered suitable partners. However, the result was that, although information was freely exchanged and participants did gain insights into the workings of the other organizations, the consensus was that little needed to be changed. Organization B did not discover a better method of evaluating customer satisfaction, and organization A was found to be delivering interlibrary loans in accordance with recently established guidelines (HEFCE, 1995), so they felt that they already exemplified best practice for these processes. It would be difficult to find instances of better practice within LIS, or where solutions to the problems encountered had been identified.

Benchmarking activities in LIS need to reach critical mass before suitable partners can be easily identified. A possible way forward would be to set up a database indicating which organizations had benchmarked certain processes, along with the outcomes of the exercise. This would both facilitate identification of partners and establish the 'best of the best'.

Quality management in the LIS sector: a cross-sectoral analysis

Quality in public libraries: a comparison

The Quality Management and Public Library Services project, reported earlier in this volume, ran parallel to the Best Practice Benchmarking project, and thus offered an excellent opportunity to compare the position of quality management across the public, private, and academic sectors of the library and information community. The questionnaire produced for the public libraries project was adapted for use in the benchmarking survey, thus enabling cross-sectoral comparisons to be made. The following observations were derived from comparing the data from the findings of both projects.

Written policies on quality and formal quality programmes

Local authorities with a written policy on quality totalled 26 per cent, slightly lower than the figure for organizations with a written policy in the academic/industrial sector (33 per cent). At LIS level, there was a correlation between local authorities with a written policy on quality, and LIS with a written policy on quality (26 per cent and 21 per cent respectively). However, in the academic/industrial sector the gap was much wider: only 12 per cent of LIS were found to have a written policy on quality, whilst 33 per cent of their parent organizations had a policy.

Further investigation at regional level revealed that local authorities in Northern Ireland were in the vanguard of quality management, with 40 per cent stating that they had a written policy on quality, whilst a further 20 per cent responded that they were preparing one. The higher levels of implementation of quality management in the public sector were attributed to the existence of quality 'champions', such as the newly appointed Chief Executives in six authorities, and Elected Members in three other authorities. In addition, there are political drivers, such as the

Citizen's Charter, and the Local Government Act of 1988, which aim to make public sector organizations more businesslike and customer-oriented, so that they operate like commercial organizations.

Involvement in quality initiatives

The adoption of the quality system BS 5750 (ISO 9000) was found to be even less evident in public libraries than in the academic/industrial sector; in the former only 3.5 per cent indicated that they had implemented it, compared to 5.6 per cent in the academic/industrial sector. However, Investors in People had been implemented by 26.5 per cent of public library respondents, and 19.4 per cent of academic/industrial sector respondents. Of the remaining initiatives there was little notable difference between the sectors: take-up of TQM, quality circles, customer contracts and the learning organization was correspondingly low. Of the four initiatives, the use of customer contracts was almost equal in all sectors. Table 7 summarizes the findings of both surveys in this respect.

Table 7: LIS involvement in quality initiatives: a comparison of the results of two surveys.

Quality Initiative	Public sector (% affirming use)	Academic/Industrial (% affirming use)
Investors in People	26.5	19.4
Customer contracts	13.5	12.7
TQM	10.0	13.0
Quality circles	8.0	10.0
BS 5750	3.5	5.6
Learning organization	2.0	3.9

Management practices

Performance indicators were found to be widely used in public libraries, where 86 per cent of respondents indicated their use. In contrast, only 34 per cent of the academic/industrial sector were using them. The role of the Audit Commission, by making it a requirement for public libraries to collect and report a range of performance data, is reflected in this high level of usage (see pp.155-156, this volume).

There were many other variations in management practices between the sectors. For example, the use of cost centres was higher in the public sector, and almost half of respondents in this sector indicated that they had introduced flatter management structures; in academic and industrial libraries figures for both were considerably lower. Figure 1 gives a breakdown of the findings in respect of management practices.

Measurement of service quality

Public libraries, in general, were found to be more proactive than their counterparts in the other sectors, when measuring service quality. The only exception to this was in their use of customer satisfaction surveys, which 25 per cent of respondents used as opposed to 57 per cent in the academic/industrial sector. Of the other methods listed (performance indicators, complaints, compliments, success against predetermined targets, and greater value for money) public library respondents indicated higher levels of use, as shown in Figure 2.

Training for staff on quality related issues

Both surveys revealed very low levels of training for staff on quality related issues, although, once again, public libraries were ahead of the academic and industrial sectors. The figures below in Table 8 represent the percentage of LIS which indicated that they had training on quality in place for various groups of staff.

Table 8: Categories of staff receiving training on quality issues: a comparison of the results of two surveys.

Training on quality issues	% Public Libraries	% Academic/Industrial
Senior managers	28.0	14.0
Middle managers	33.0	18.0
Paraprofessionals	31.0	18.0
No training	64.0	72.5

Figure 1: Quality management practices: a comparison of the two surveys

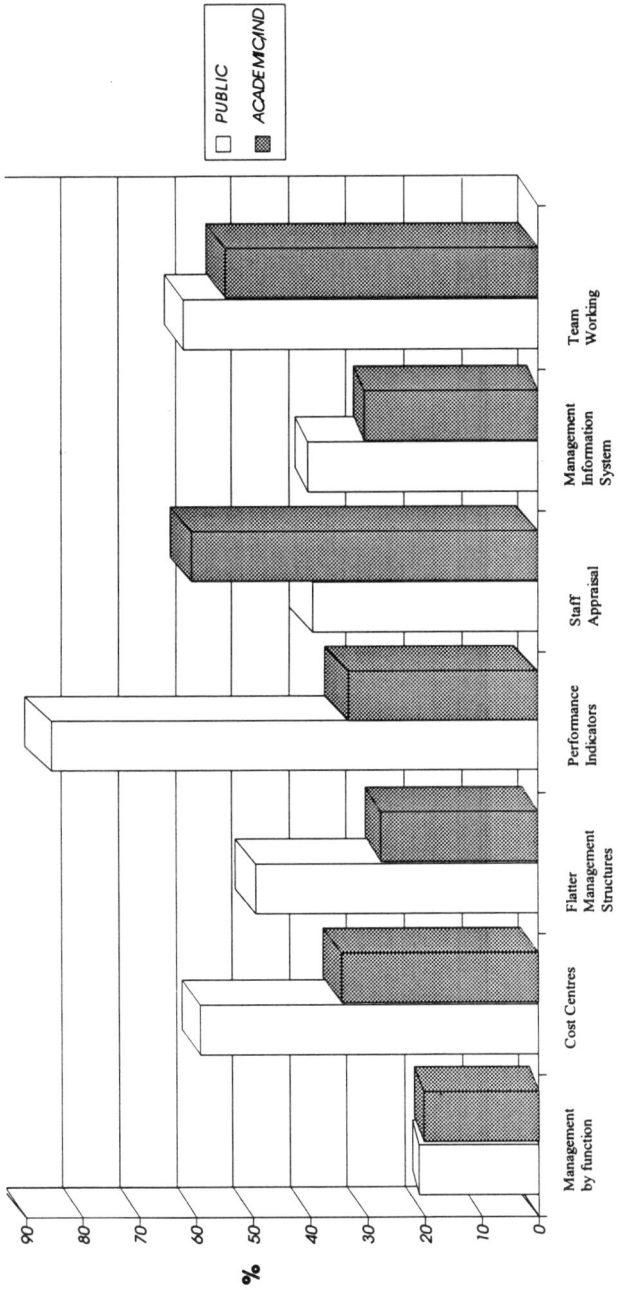

Figure 2: Methods used to measure service quality: a comparison of the two surveys

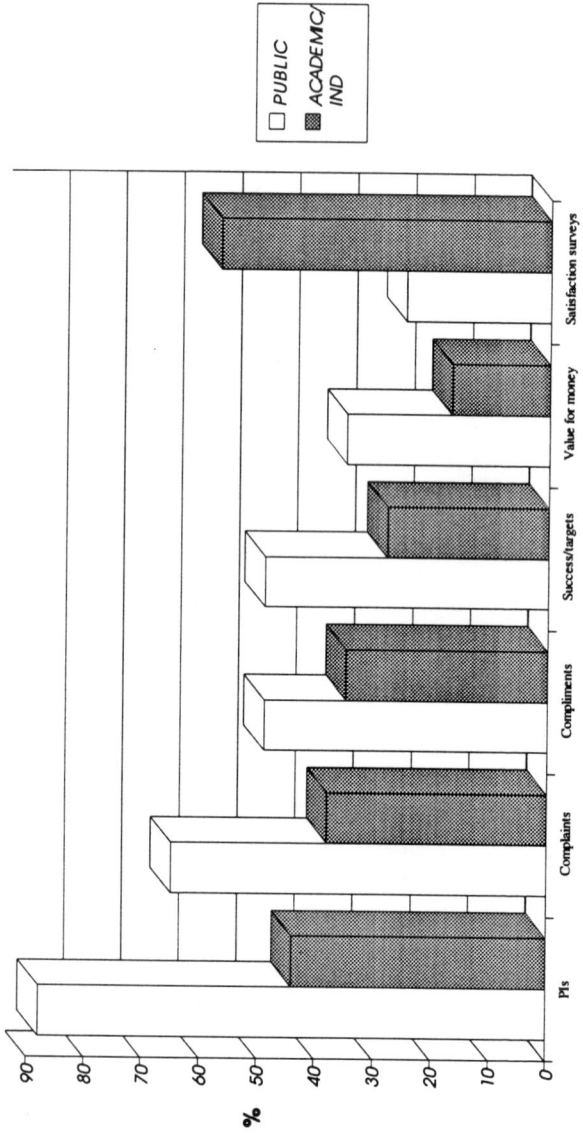

Communication with staff on quality initiatives and policies

Staff meetings were found to be the favoured method of communicating management initiatives and policies on quality. Respondents in both surveys indicated high levels of usage, with 89 per cent of public library respondents and almost 71 per cent of academic/industrial libraries claiming to use them. Eight other methods of communication were listed, where the trend, as before, was for public libraries to be ahead of their colleagues in the academic and industrial sectors. The one exception to this rule was the case of staff appraisal schemes, where the academic/industrial sector was ahead by 12.5 per cent. Training is essential if organizations are to be effective in implementing quality. Sixty-seven per cent of public libraries indicated that training courses in relation to quality were available to their staff; the figure for the academic/industrial sector was much lower at 37.7 per cent. Table 9 summarizes the comparative findings on the methods used for communication on quality matters.

Table 9: Methods used to communicate to staff LIS policies and initiatives relating to quality: a comparison of two surveys.

Communication with staff on quality issues: methods used	% Public	% Academic/Industrial
Staff meetings	89.0	70.8
Training courses	67.0	37.7
On the job training	66.0	54.0
Managers 'walking the floor'	60.0	40.0
Bulletin/newsletter	51.0	30.0
Team briefing	47.0	30.6
Mission statement	46.0	35.5
Appraisal scheme	28.0	40.5
Quality groups	9.0	8.8

The public libraries survey identified some of the disadvantages attached to implementing quality initiatives. These included the amount of time taken up in meetings, team working and producing documentation, which was perceived as slowing down the decision-making process. The cost of quality programmes was also thought to be prohibitive, at a time when financial constraints were in operation. Reports of 'initiative fatigue and cynicism' were also problematic. All of these negative aspects of quality were also noted in the survey of the academic and commercial sectors, although the positive comments far outweighed the negative ones, with managers in academic libraries reporting better staff morale, and increased levels of awareness of organizational goals and aims.

Benchmarking in public libraries: a comparison

At the time when the Public Libraries research project was being carried out, in 1995, the Public Libraries Quality Forum was prioritizing work on benchmarking in public libraries, and proposed a pilot study of benchmarking involving a number of authorities (see p.160 this volume). Since then Berkshire, Brent, Kent and Westminster library services have announced details of the first phase of their study (*Inquiries tests*, 1995; Mendelsohn, 1995). Each authority is to benchmark enquiry services, using a community library and a town centre library, with non-specialist reference staff. Comparisons with the other participating authorities can then be effected.

The Loughborough research team attended a meeting with representatives of the four participating authorities. The results of the exercise to date were discussed, revealing a very low completion rate for the questionnaire survey but, where questionnaires had been completed, a high level of satisfaction with the service. In the main, the results were considered to be invalid, due to customers' perception that the service was under threat and in need of their support, rather than criticism. It was also felt that the concept of benchmarking was hard to convey to staff, who failed to understand what was being done or the purposes behind it.

Quality in special libraries: a comparison

A study of the implementation of quality in UK special libraries was carried out with funding from BLRIC, in the period March to December 1994 (Webb, 1995). The term 'special libraries' here refers to libraries maintained by associations, business firms, museums, chambers of commerce, professional associations, government service, etc., as defined by UNESCO , 1993.

This study facilitates further cross-sectoral comparison in relation to quality management in the LIS sector. There are parallels between its findings and those of the benchmarking project. It noted that the take-up of quality in special libraries is lower than that of the employing organization as a whole—at both regional and national level. A correlation between an organization's size and its use of modern management techniques is also noted. Almost 50 per cent of larger organizations in the survey group had quality policies at both LIS and organizational levels. However, most of the respondents with a quality policy were found to be involved with ISO 9000 or TQM. Quality-related activities in libraries were not always part of formal quality policies, but where the parent organization had quality as part of the corporate culture, then the LIS could benefit by way of support and encouragement.

Benchmarking in special libraries: a comparison

A recent development in special libraries has been the setting up of a working party on benchmarking by the Special Libraries Committee (*In brief,* 1995). Libraries in the engineering sector are involved, and they are inviting other professionals in the special library sector to contribute their experiences of benchmarking. Developments such as this, and the current benchmarking activities within a group of public library authorities described above, demonstrate the interest in benchmarking as a tool for improvement. It can be expected that much will be learnt from the experiences of those LIS which are currently using benchmarking techniques and, once more practical experience is available, it will become possible to gain more evidence for the evaluation of the utility of benchmarking as a tool for the LIS sector.

Conclusions

Evidence from the two surveys suggests that the public sector is currently ahead of the private and academic sectors in quality related activities. The key driver has been the Government, whose policies and recent legislation have altered the way local authorities are managed. Local authorities now have to demonstrate their effectiveness in the provision of value for money, and are accountable to their 'customers'. Academic libraries have not been subject to the same pressure, and although funding does emanate in part from central government, they are further removed from direct control. Universities and colleges are more likely to be driven by internal 'champions' of quality, or as part of an organization-wide initiative. Several universities have been proactive in publicizing their quality-related programmes (Brophy *et al.*, 1993; Abbott, 1994; Winkworth, 1993). However, there is little evidence of more general activity and, as already noted, organizations may have written policies and programmes on quality, but these have not yet filtered down to libraries and information services.

In the private sector, respondents to the benchmarking survey mirrored experience in the academic sector, revealing little evidence of widespread activity in either quality management or benchmarking; only a handful of organizations seemed to be forging ahead with quality programmes.

Benchmarking: finding the right approach

Time management

Respondents to the questionnaire frequently commented on the time-consuming nature of quality management initiatives. They often felt that this time might be better spent on other tasks, or that more important matters were being neglected. Lack of time can be used as a justification for not accepting, or even attempting, quality, and can stem from having too narrow a view of what a job entails (Griffiths, 1991). It can also stem from impatience and a desire to see instant results. It has been argued that, in the context of continuing threats to their survival, organizations must be prepared to give up the 'quick fix' philosophy, to understand that commitment to continuous improvement implies that change is now the norm and stability has been relegated to the past (EFQM, 1994). Quality management is a gradual or organic process, involving cultural change and a holistic approach to management, which helps organizations to meet these threats.

Nevertheless, benchmarking is also a time-consuming process, requiring planning, team work, and frequent meetings, while visits to benchmarking partners take up valuable worktime. The whole process needs to be viewed as a learning experience, leading to raised levels of awareness, and a questioning of the way things are currently done, so that the organization can benefit in the long term.

Communications

Effective communication is essential for all quality management initiatives. Lines of communication may be adversely affected by a range of factors—for example, the location of a library or information unit in relation to the organization it serves. The availability of channels of communication, such as electronic mail and telephone answering machines, is also significant. Supply chains, both internal and external, depend on swift and effective communication. Delays and errors are often attributable to breakdowns in communication (Oakland, 1994):

> The essence of changing attitudes to quality is to gain acceptance for the need to change, and for this to happen it is essential to provide relevant information, convey good practices, and generate interest, ideas and awareness through excellent communication processes. This is probably the most neglected part of many organizations' problems, resulting in confusion, loss of interest and eventually in declining quality through apparent lack of guidance and stimulus.

The action research component of this project revealed problems with communications in some participating organizations. The benchmarking task was assigned to staff with no provision made for feedback or consultation with senior management on findings or progress. Staff often seemed unsure as to what to do, or how to do it. A gap existed between managers' perceptions of the level of understanding of staff, in respect of benchmarking activities, and what staff actually understood. It became apparent that the research team were expected to offer guidance on how to carry out benchmarking.

It is perhaps also true that there was some discrepancy between the demonstrators' perceptions of the role of the research team, and our own perceptions of our role. The aim of the research team was to be non-prescriptive, as many LIS staff had voiced a dislike for rigid, formally documented ways of working. The team also felt that the 'demonstrators' were best acquainted with their own procedures, and would prefer autonomy in the methods they used to document and measure their chosen processes. It was therefore important, if difficult, to establish a balance between being supportive and helpful, and being prescriptive and interfering. The team had to bear in mind that the organizations were volunteering for the exercise, and although it was anticipated that they would gain some benefit from it, there was constant awareness of constraints on their time and the inevitably pressured nature of the work, given that this was action research, rather than the development of a procedure to meet internal needs only.

Where a task, such as a benchmarking exercise, is delegated to a process owner or team, it is essential that they are able to communicate effectively with senior management throughout the exercise. Meetings should be set up in advance between senior management and staff carrying out the exercise, so that a reporting mechanism is in place, allowing assistance to be sought and problems solved. Formal quality circles may not be the appropriate forum for such discussions. Where these were in place they were found to involve all staff, and were not conducive to individuals' expressing needs or concerns on specific tasks. A small team, comprising process owners and a senior manager with a knowledge of benchmarking procedures, would provide the best mechanism for raising questions and discussing how to set about the task.

Formal versus informal approaches

Many respondents to the questionnaire and telephone survey indicated that they were involved in informal quality related activities. The questionnaire survey sought to establish the level of activity in formal quality programmes, and formal documentation of quality policies and programmes. The survey findings revealed that 74 per cent of respondents had no written policy on quality, whilst TQM had been implemented in 13 per cent of responding organizations. However, informal quality related activities are used and favoured by many LIS. Many respondents disliked the jargon of quality management and stated that they were concerned with quality, good service, etc., but provided this in an informal, practical way. Formal methods are frequently perceived to be theoretical, impractical, or 'bureaucratic'. One respondent stated that, although they had nothing formally in place, most quality related activities were done 'naturally'. The language and practice of quality management are associated with commerce and meet with resistance by some professionals in the academic sector purely because of this association. The ideas are often acknowledged as being sound, and are put into practice, but they are neither formal nor couched in quality management terms. Therefore, the spirit, if not the letter, of quality management is being obeyed in many cases, and levels of awareness of the need for best practice are high. Informal methods of evaluation, comparison and measurement, which respondents indicated they used in place of, or as well as, those listed in the questionnaire, included:

- Regular team meetings and 'brain storming' sessions
- Service Level Agreements; Service standards
- Student course evaluation

- Liaison (informally and formally—through Library Advisory Committee using performance indicators)

- Course review documents; annual course reports; external examiner reports; external and internal validation of courses

- Informal comparison of SCONUL/COPOL statistics

- Participation in university wide surveys

- Across the board comparison with a number of other universities

- Quality of service implicit in library's written Operational Policy Statement, although separate written policy on quality does not exist

- Charter Mark

- Information skills programme evaluated on regular basis

- Book availability survey

Many other methods were listed which are similar to the above, or to those listed on the questionnaire, but which are known by a variety of different names. Many academic LIS are using performance indicators to measure effectiveness. These include, for example: book purchasing per student; expenditure per full-time equivalent (FTE) student; and lending and reservations per student. Other institutions are collecting quantitative data on a whole range of activities, many of which are per FTE student. These help in targeting resources to best effect in times of constraint, and they provide supporting data within a quality framework (Abbott, 1994). Quantitative data, or metrics, are also required in benchmarking, whilst qualitative data can be gathered on site visits to other information units (Muir, 1993). These should comprise meaningful ratios, or performance indicators, between one variable and another, to indicate the relationship between them. Merely counting occurrences of transactions, e.g. the number of issues, will provide data which, in isolation, are of little use. However, linking the number of issues to the number of registered users provides meaningful proportional data.

The conclusion to be drawn from this is that, despite figures indicating low levels of activity in formal quality programmes, there is a high level of awareness of quality issues in LIS, and considerable evidence of informal activities, many of which are directly related to quality. A recent report on performance measurement (HEFCE, 1995) recommends that evidence of both formal and informal communication channels can exist to inform service provision. It states:

> Formal boards and committees may exist alongside informal subject-related links, suggestions boxes, and activities undertaken by Students Unions. Service level agreements and charter standards may also be in place. All these will provide assorted evidence of the effectiveness or otherwise of such liaison.

Confidentiality and the learning organization

The aim of the demonstrator projects was not only to test benchmarking techniques and evaluate their relevance to the LIS sector, but also for organizations from different sectors to meet and compare work practices and establish best practice. The informal visits and networking arrangements, noted above, involved like comparing with like—universities tend to compare themselves with other, potential competitor, universities. However, the involvement of commercial sector organizations in the benchmarking exercise highlighted new areas of concern. Confidentiality was considered a problem, with participants expressing a fear of exposing client and other confidential information to outsiders. They feared that this information might get into the hands of a competitor, who could make use of it to their detriment.

This once again highlights the misapprehensions which surround the benchmarking process. Information about individual procedures, in a particular process, are being compared, and there is no need for confidential information to be implicated. Benchmarking is about sharing information relating to the way things are done, and those who are apprehensive about sharing information, irrespective of its content, are perhaps not ready to participate in benchmarking. Visits can be conducted in meeting rooms away from the workplace if necessary, thus avoiding accidental exposure of confidential documents to outsiders.

The concept of the 'Learning Organization' is based on people, information and relationships. It depends on a network of partnerships and alliances and on a view of organizations as organic structures which continually change and grow (Chase, 1995). To do this, organizations need to cultivate an open minded approach and a macrocosmic approach to their business. They can do this by interacting with organizations which differ from their own, in terms of both culture and work practices. They can then learn to evaluate what they do and how they do it, within a broader framework, and perhaps adopt new ideas to improve their own practices. Benchmarking and other quality related activities cultivate this receptive, flexible mindset, which is so essential to survival in a rapidly changing environment.

Recommendations

Benchmarking

Benchmarking is of value to organizations which are already involved in quality programmes. It is a quality tool, and is therefore of most use where the culture and practices are already focused on achieving best practice. Where it is to be introduced, it is recommended that training be implemented first. This training should establish what benchmarking is in relation to the way in which it is to be implemented within the organization, and instil an understanding of what it involves and why it is being carried out. Without a contextual framework in which to set the benchmarking process, staff will be at a disadvantage when carrying out the necessary mapping and measuring stages of the process. If they understand the fundamental issues surrounding the exercise, then they will best be able to supply the data and documentation which are required to facilitate comparison. The training should also cover tools such as flowcharting and fishbone diagrams, which will help to establish current procedures, and identify problem areas.

There may be a need to be prescriptive—despite an expressed dislike of rigid ways of working. Benchmarking may need detailed procedures, or guidelines, on how to set about it. The Workshop on benchmarking, which was convened as part of the benchmarking project, aimed to provide practical guidelines on benchmarking procedures, and identify training requirements for LIS. The demonstrator organizations contributed to this event, bringing their practical experiences to bear on the outcomes.

The selection of suitable benchmarking partners is also problematic. This survey benchmarked organizations which were already considered examples of best practice—the corollary of which was that there was found to be little scope for change for the organizations involved. The exercise mostly served to establish that the demonstrator organizations were equal to, if not ahead of, the benchmarking partner with regard to enquiry services and interlibrary loans.

It is therefore felt that, although the concepts and ideology of benchmarking represent good management practice, the process is a difficult one, and the benefits may not be apparent for some time, if at all. Where benchmarking is felt to be most useful, especially in the LIS sector, is as a means of raising staff levels of awareness. The process of analyzing procedures and identifying gaps in performance can be a learning experience, which enables staff to distance themselves from a process, and view it in an organizational context. This awareness extends to outside organizations during benchmarking visits, and helps to foster a mindset which is receptive to new ideas and change. Benchmarking can therefore be perceived as an empowering tool, which, by focusing on process owners, enables paraprofessional staff to play a more proactive role in the identification of problems and implementation of change. It should also promote team working and better communication between junior and senior levels of staff—both of which are prerequisites of successful benchmarking.

The commercial emphasis on benchmarking against competitors, or world leaders, or the 'best of the best' may not provide a suitable framework for the LIS sector, particularly those in the academic sector, as the culture within the LIS is not, as yet, comparable with the with-profit sector. The benchmarking model shown in Figure 3 overleaf outlines the procedures which were followed for the action research component of the project; the model could be further adapted for use by the LIS sector, as benchmarking techniques are tested further.

Performance indicators

In accordance with the findings of the Follett Report (HEFCE, 1993), and the subsequent report on performance in academic libraries (HEFCE, 1995), performance measurement is a prerequisite to the 'effective academic library'. As a result of these two reports five areas of performance have been identified, which constitute a framework for the use of performance indicators in academic libraries. These are:

- Integration
- Quality of Service
- Delivery

Figure 3: Model of the benchmarking process used by the demonstrator organizations for the benchmarking exercise

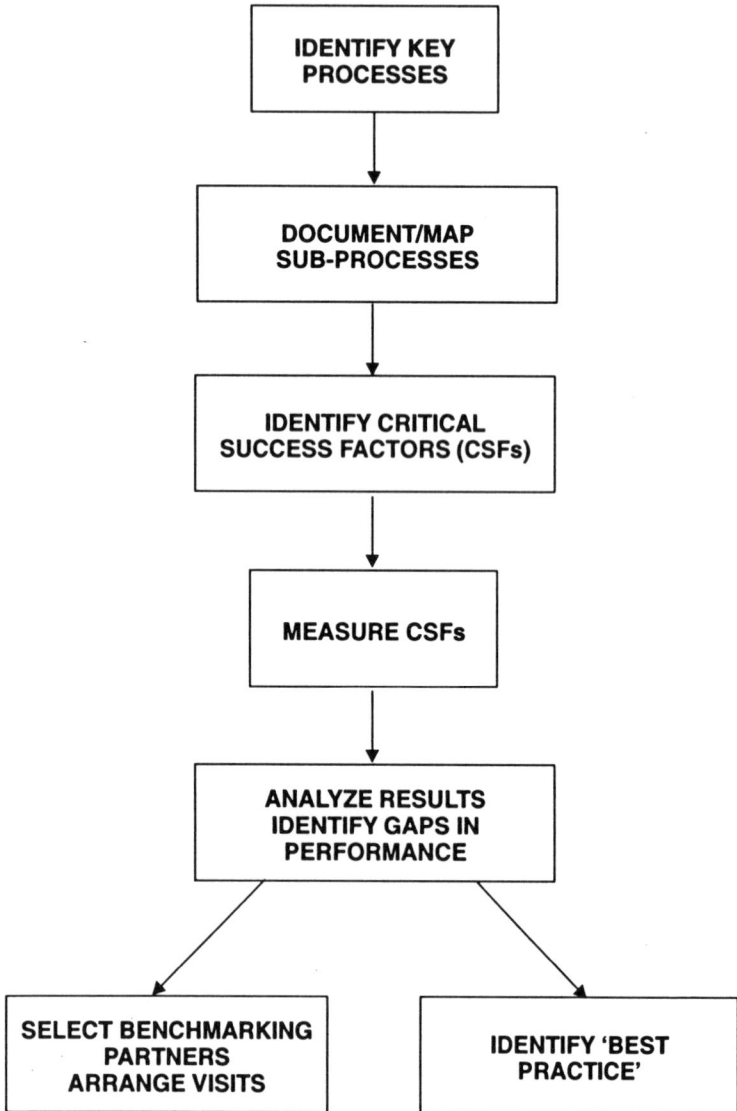

- Efficiency

- Economy

The proposed indicators comprise both hard statistical data and qualitative data. Almost half of libraries in the academic sector are already using performance indicators, whilst in public libraries over 80 per cent of libraries are using them. Their use should therefore be extended to those LIS which are not currently using them as they are designed to help institutions improve their performance; the indicators proposed in 'The Effective Academic Library' are designed to be applicable across the full range of institutions in the higher education sector (HEFCE, 1995).

Self-assessment

Self-assessment has been described as the first essential step in any change or improvement programme (Chase, 1995). Self-assessment enables an organization to review its current activities and results against a model of excellence, before embarking on any new initiatives. The Royal Mail has successfully used self-assessment at business unit level, thus demonstrating its application to the smaller organization or unit (Zaremba and Crew, 1995). It has national and international recognition as it is the basis for all the major quality awards. The European Quality Award is based on the European Foundation for Quality Management (EFQM) model; this model, which consists of nine criteria against which an organization can measure itself, offers a potential way forward for LIS irrespective of sector (see pp.40-41, this volume). The EFQM model of self-assessment focuses on customer and staff satisfaction, and its application to a service environment is immediately evident. Further research into the use, and/or adaptation, of the model to suit LIS requirements is therefore recommended.

References and bibliography

Abbott, C. (1994) Performance indicators in a quality context. *The Law Librarian*, 25(4), December, 205-208.

Allen, F. (1993) Benchmarking: practical aspects for information professionals. *Special Libraries,* 84(3), Summer, 123-130.

Audit Commission for England and Wales (1989) *Managing services effectively: performance review.* London:HMSO.

Brockman, J. (1992) Just another management fad? The implications of TQM for library and information services. *Aslib Proceedings*, 44(7/8), July/August, 283-288.

Brophy, P. (1994) BS: a curse or blessing? *Library Association Record,* 96(6), 320-21.

Brophy, P., Coulling, K and Melling, M. (1993) Quality management: a university approach 1992. *Aslib Information*, 21(6), 246-248.

Bullivant, J. (1994) *Benchmarking for continuous improvement in the public sector.* Harlow: Longman.

Camp, R. (1989) *Benchmarking. The search for industry best practices that lead to superior performance.* Milwaukee: ASQC Quality Press.

CCTA, The Government Centre for Information Systems (1995) *Benchmarking IS/IT. Improving value for money through comparisons.* London: HMSO.

Chase, R. (1995) *IFS Quality Newsletter.* October/November. Kempston: IFS International Ltd.

Coopers & Lybrand (1994) *Survey of benchmarking in Europe 1994.* London: Coopers & Lybrand. (Contact: Sue Cannon or Richard Archer on 0171 2133845).

Coopers & Lybrand/CBI (1993) *Survey of benchmarking in the UK.* London: Coopers & Lybrand and the Confederation of British Industry. (Contact: Sue Cannon or Richard Archer on 0171 2133845).

Dawson, A. (1993) Corporate libraries: the Taylor Woodrow experience. In *Total quality management, the information business, key issues '92.* Hatfield: University of Hertfordshire Press, 82-88.

DTI (1994a) *Managing in the '90s. Best practice benchmarking. An executive guide.* London: Department of Trade and Industry.

DTI (1994b) *Managing in the '90s. BS 5750/ISO 9000/EN 29000:1987. A positive contribution to better business.* London: Department of Trade and Industry.

DTI (1994c) *Managing in the '90s. Quality circles. An executive guide.* London: Department of Trade and Industry.

DTI (1995) *Managing in the '90s. Benchmarking, the challenge. A practical guide to business improvement.* London: Department of Trade and Industry.

EC (1994) Special feature: economic aspects of quality. In *Panorama of EU industry 94. An extensive review of the situation and outlook of the manufacturing and service industries in the European Union,* p.133. Luxembourg: European Commission.

EFQM (1994) *European Foundation for Quality Management, the case for joining.* Brussels: European Foundation for Quality Management.

Ellis, D. and Norton, B. (1993) *Implementing BS 5750/ISO 9000 in libraries.* London: Aslib.

Erhvervs-Info Association (1994) *ISO 9000 for libraries and information centres. A guide. Report of a project supported by Nordinfo.* (Translated from Danish). Arhus, Denmark: Foreningen Erhvervs-Info.

Ernst and Young/AQF (1993) *Best practices report. An analysis of management practices that impact performance.* New York: Ernst and Young and the American Quality Foundation.

Fox, P. and Malley, I. (eds.) (1983) *Third international conference on library user education. University of Edinburgh 19-22 July 1983. Proceedings.* Loughborough University of Technology, Loughborough: IN-FUSE.

Garrod, P. and Kinnell Evans, M. (compilers) (1995) *Quality management issues: a select bibliography for library and information services.*

FID Occasional Paper 10. British Library R&D Report 6220. The Hague: FID.

Griffiths, D. (1991) *Implementing quality with a customer focus*. Milwaukee: ASQC Quality Press.

Hall, S. (1992) Reviewing the performance of an information service. *Aslib Information*, 20(6), June, 248-249.

HEFCE (1993) *Joint Funding Councils' Libraries Review Group: report*. (The Follett Report). Bristol: Higher Education Funding Council for England.

HEFCE (1995) *The effective academic library. A framework for evaluating the performance of UK academic libraries*. Joint Funding Councils' *ad hoc* group on performance indicators for libraries: A consultative report to the HEFCE, SHEFC, HEFCW and DENI. Bristol: Higher Education Funding Council for England.

HEQC (1994) *Guidelines on quality assurance*. Birmingham: Higher Education Quality Council.

Investors in People UK (1994) Investing in people. How to get started. London: Investors in People UK.

Johanssen, C. (1994) Can the ISO standards on quality management be useful to libraries, and how? *Inspel*, 28(2), 227-239.

Lawes, A. (1993) The benefits of quality management to the library and information services profession. *Special Libraries*, 84(3), Summer, 142-146.

Lester, D.E. (1994) *The impact of quality management on the information sector. A study of case histories*. Luxembourg: EUSIDIC.

Library Association Record (1995a) In brief. *Library Association Record*, 97(11), November, 585.

Library Association Record (1995b) Inquiries tests. *Library Association Record*, 97(9), September, 477.

Line, M. (1991) Library management styles and structures: a need to rethink? *Journal of Librarianship and Information Science*, 23(2), June, 97-104.

Line, M. (1995) Needed: a pathway through the swamp of management literature. *Library Management*, 16(1), 36.

Marsh, J. (1993) *The quality toolkit. An A-Z of tools and techniques.* Kempston, Bedford: IFS Ltd.

McCarthy, C. (1995) Students' perceived effectiveness using the university library. *College and Research Libraries*, 56(3), May, 221-234.

Mendelsohn, S. (1995) Does your library come up to scratch? *Library Manager*, 8, June, 6, 8-9.

Millson-Martula, C. and Menon, V. (1995) Customer expectations: concepts and reality for academic library services. *College and Research Libraries*, 56(1), January, 33-47.

Minkoff, D. (1993) Quality: participation plus change. In *Total quality management, the information business, key issues '92*. Hatfield: University of Hertfordshire Press, 70-81.

Morgan, C. and Murgatroyd, S. (1994) *Total Quality Management in the public sector: an international perspective.* Buckingham: Open University Press.

Muir, H. (1993) *Developing benchmarking metrics. A librarian's guide.* Universal City: Library Benchmarking International.

Oakland, J. (1994) *Total Quality Management*, 2nd edn. Oxford: Butterworth Heinemann.

Oldroyd, R. (1995) Staff development and appraisal in an 'old' university library. *Librarian Career Development*, 3(2), 13-16.

Orr, R. (1973) Measuring the goodness of library services: a general framework for considering quantitative measures. *Journal of Documentation,* 29(3), 313-332.

Parasuraman, A., Zeithaml,V. and Berry, L. (1991) Understanding customer expectations of service. *Sloan Management Review*, Spring, 39-48.

Porter, L. (1992) *Quality initiatives in British library and information services.* British Library R&D Report 6105. London: The British Library.

Revill, D. (1989) Cost centres and academic libraries. *British Journal of Academic Librarianship*, 4(1), 27-48.

Reynard, K. and Reynard, J. (eds). (1994) *Aslib directory of information sources in the United Kingdom*, 8th ed. London: Aslib.

SCONUL (1995) *Annual Library Statistics 1993-1994*. London: SCONUL.

Special Libraries (1993) 84(3), Summer.

Ward, S. (1987) Management information needs: the industrial information service. In *Management information systems in libraries and information services,* ed. C. Harris, pp.50-66. London: Taylor Graham.

Webb, S.P. (1995) *Pursuing quality in special libraries. A study of current activities and developments in the United Kingdom.* British Library R&D Report 6214. London: The British Library.

Weise, C. and Stamoolis, P. (1993) ISO 9000: an opportunity for records management professionals. *Records Management Quarterly,* October, 3-8,10.

Wilkinson, A., Redman, T. and Snape, E. (1993) *Quality and the manager.* Corby, Northants: Institute of Management.

Winkworth, I. (1993) Performance indicators and quality assurance. *Aslib Information,* 21(6), June, 250-251.

Wressell, P. (ed.) (1995) *Proceedings of the first Northumbria international conference on performance measurement in libraries and information services.* 31 August – 4 September 1995. Longhirst Management and Training Centre, Northumberland. Newcastle-upon-Tyne: Information North.

Zairi, M. and Hutton, R. (1995) Benchmarking: a process-driven tool for quality improvement. *The TQM Magazine,* 7(3), 35.

Zaremba, D. and Crew, T. (1995) Increasing involvement in self-assessment: the Royal Mail approach. *The TQM Magazine,* 7(2), 29-32.

Acknowledgements

We should like to thank our funders, the British Library Research and Innovation Centre, for making this research possible. Particular mention should go to Isobel Thompson, whose support throughout the project was much appreciated.

We should also like to extend our thanks to the consultants to the project, Alan Gilchrist of Gavel Consultants and John Brockman of the Ministry of Defence Headquarters Library, for their contribution over the year.

Our special thanks go to the organizations which took part in the benchmarking exercise, both the 'demonstrator' projects, and those who acted as benchmarking partners. Considerable effort and time were expended by individual members of staff, in order to give a practical basis to the research and thoroughly test benchmarking techniques. Their willingness to share information with other organizations and to host visitors made the exercise a success.

We should also like to thank all those library and information units which completed and returned the questionnaire. Additonal thanks must go to those who took part in the follow-up telephone interviews. Their comments provided valuable insights into organizational culture and how it influences service delivery, and highlighted some of the problems which currently confront many information units.

Appendix A

Demonstrator projects: profile of participating organizations

Organization A—an academic LIS

The LIS at organization A serves a college which forms part of a university. The main subject coverage is science and technology, and, in addition to supporting the teaching and research activities of the college, the LIS has a wider role as a national information resource. The library building is located on the periphery of the college, remote from the main *loci* of activity, which means that it can be overlooked or regarded as difficult to access. However, the library building does house a bookshop, a coffee shop and a recreational library, so users are able to obtain refreshments and take a break from studying without leaving the premises.

The college is committed to quality and has both vision and mission statements. The college recently had to submit an invitation to tender in order to renew its contract. In order to win the contract the college management felt that they had to ensure that stakeholders recognized and acknowledged that their services represented 'good value for money', and offered a 'good product package'. Staff development is rated highly, and the development programme is in process of being adapted, using feedback from the staff and from a consultant whose advice was sought in 1994.

There is a strong customer focus in the LIS and a quality council meets regularly (approximately every three weeks). There are quality improvement teams for many functions and activities, including: accommodation; collections management; development and strategy; disaster planning; and interlibrary loans. Teams are also formed as and when a need is identified; an example of this was the formation of a user feedback team in 1995. Weekly progress meetings serve as a reporting mechanism which keep staff informed of new initiatives.

Financial constraints are not a problem at organization A, and this impacts on quality and students' perception of the service offered by the LIS. For example, students are allowed 200 interlibrary loan requests a year, of which 30 can be current at any one time.

The quality context

The university, of which organization A forms a part, has a Total Quality Management programme. The commitment to quality dates back to involvement with quality assurance in the 1970s, and therefore the current drive towards quality has a long, well-established history. The LIS has an overall policy on quality, whilst other departments at the college have separate policies; for example, the estates department has ISO 9000 accreditation. Copies of mission and vision statements are circulated to staff throughout the college; students, however, were not thought to be aware of their existence, as they had a 'student charter' which acted as their statement of service entitlement and standards. Senior management at organization A changed every two years, so overall policy was subject to change—according to the personal management style of each new incumbent of the post. The current senior manager was both supportive of the LIS and committed to quality management, and this had affected both the morale and operational methods of the LIS.

Organization B—a LIS in the pharmaceutical industry

Organization B is a pharmaceutical company with a large research and development (R&D) department, which is information intensive. The LIS provides an information service to R&D staff, which is seen as vital to the organization's goals and objectives. The purpose of R&D is to generate new scientific information and knowledge, which allows the company to manufacture and market its products. The company invests heavily in IT, and uses its network infrastructure as a means of sharing corporate information, generated as a result of R&D activities. Published information is also imported by electronic means. A wide area network (WAN) links the worldwide research centres of the organization, and there are plans to expand capacity to support image and compound document transfer. Electronic mail is used, and there is access to the Internet, although a 'firewall' exists for security purposes. All professional staff have a personal computer in their offices, or have access to one in their laboratories.

Top management at organization B perceive quality management, with its association with standards and regulation, as incompatible with the innovative and creative nature of the pharmaceutical industry. The company has a mission statement, which makes reference to the ethical nature of the organization's work; this means that prescription-based, rather than 'over-the-counter', drugs are produced. There are quality programmes in existence, such as 'Good Laboratory Practice', and 'Good Management Practice', for which guidelines have been produced. However, there is no single document detailing set practices. The Department of Health and the Food and Drug Administration (FDA) carry out inspections to check for falsification of clinical trials—a procedure which is highly regulated as quality is critical.

LIS used to be integrated with IT, and during this period quality management was introduced to the LIS by an IT manager. The programme was low key, consisting of a lecture and workshop on quality management, and there was no user input to the data gathering. A benchmarking exercise was carried out as part of this programme, which focused on interlibrary loans. The LIS maintains a commitment to the provision of a quality service, and is proactively seeking ways of improving the service to users.

The enquiry service at Organization B was identified as a key service. It provides current and accurate information which R&D staff depend upon to carry out their work. There are 30 information scientists who cover all areas of expertise, of which competitor intelligence is a growth area for enquiries. In particular, LIS management was looking for new ways of determining levels of customer satisfaction with the enquiry service, whilst generally focusing on potential areas for improvement. The aim of the enquiry service is to 'add value' to the online search process, so that information is tailored to meet individual needs. Information is selected and presented in an easily readable format, which is aimed at saving users' time, and which therefore ensures more effective use of R&D staff time.

In 1994 a quality audit of the enquiry service was carried out. The subsequent report revealed trends and highlighted areas for improvement. In particular, the report noted that follow-up procedures—to evaluate user satisfaction—were inadequate, or were not being adhered to as laid down in the local instruction. The benchmarking exercise involved comparing the procedures for answering enquiries at organization B with those of the benchmarking partners, whilst identifying ways of evaluating customer satisfaction with the service.

Organization C—an information service in an NHS trust

The trust was formed under the NHS privatization programme and it administers a large hospital, with an Accident and Emergency (A&E) unit, which provides health services to a large, multicultural city. At the time of the research project the trust was undergoing a programme of business process re-engineering (BPR), and the hospital site was also the subject of large-scale rebuilding and re-allocation of accommodation. The effect of these factors had to be taken into account in the benchmarking exercise. It was hard to locate various departments, due the disruption caused by the building works and the re-housing of various units. The rate of change was found to cause confusion and to exacerbate existing internal communication problems.

Quality at organizational level

Quality standards exist in the Patient's Charter, and also in contracts with purchasers. There is also the issue of administrative and clinical quality, which is subject to medical and clinical audit. The trust is currently in process of implementing Kings Fund accreditation, a quality system similar to ISO 9000 but specifically aimed at the health sector. A mission statement broadly asserts an intention to provide customers with the best health care possible.

The information service

The information service is responsible for managing patient-related data within the patient services branch of the trust. An information systems strategy was produced in October 1994 which states that the aim of the information service is to equip hospital staff with the skills and tools they need to use information effectively and to cope with change. It also states an intention to deal with ongoing problems such as 'legacy systems' and quality of data. Staff are to be provided with integrated clinical workstations on a desktop basis, and there is a plan to implement a hospital information system (HIS) which will improve patient care. The HIS has the following aims: ensuring that staff are better informed; the sharing of information with external agencies; provision of a digital medical record system; reducing paperwork; provision of automatic audit of performance of processes; and, finally, ensuring there is a secure and efficient information flow using an open systems approach. The information service selected the enquiry service for the benchmarking exercise as this had been identified as a problem area due to the undefined method of dealing with enquiries. Enquiries take two forms: external enquiries, which are channelled through a help desk; and internal enquiries, which are channelled through the information service.

Appendix B

Project questionnaire

QUALITY MANAGEMENT AND PERFORMANCE EVALUATION IN LIBRARY AND INFORMATION SERVICES

POLICY & PLANNING

1. Does your organization have a written policy on quality?

Yes   No   In preparation

2. Does the Library and Information Service have a written policy on quality?

Yes   No   In preparation

3. Do you have a formal quality programme in place?

Yes: in place   In the process of being set up   No

4. Which of the following initiatives is the Library and Information Service involved with? (Please tick as appropriate)

Total Quality Management   Customer contracts
Quality circles   The Learning Organization
BS 5750   Investors in People
Other (please specify)   None

....
....

5. Who was involved in developing the policy on quality for the Library and Information Service? (Please tick as appropriate)

Frontline staff   Senior management
Clients   Middle management
External consultants

6. Has your Library and Information Service implemented any of the following?

	Yes	No	In preparation

Management by function
Cost centres
Flatter management structure
Performance indicators
Staff appraisal
Management information system
Team working

7. How is the quality of your service measured?

Number of complaints received
Number of compliments received
Through existing performance indicators
Customer satisfaction surveys
Success against predetermined targets
Greater value for money
Other (please specify)

....

....

PERSONNEL & TRAINING

8. Is there a specific person or team responsible for quality within the Library and Information Service?

Yes   No   In preparation

If yes, please give job or team title

....

9. Do you have a training programme designed to enhance the knowledge and skills of staff in relation to quality within the Library and Information Service?

Training for Senior Managers
Training for Middle Managers
Training for Paraprofessionals
No specific training in quality is offered

[We would be grateful if you could send us examples of course outlines that you may have.]

METHODS USED TO MEASURE AND EVALUATE PERFORMANCE

10. Which of the following methods does your Library and Information Service use to measure and/or evaluate performance? (Please tick as appropriate)

Usage statistics
Performance indicators
User feedback
Cross charging
Benchmarking
Other (please specify)

....
....
....

11. Is your Library and Information Service comparing any of its activities and/or functions with those of other organizations as a measure of effectiveness?

Yes   No   In preparation

If Yes, please list the activities and/or functions being assessed in this way.

....
....
....

COMMUNICATION

12. How are specific policies and initiatives on quality communicated to staff of the Library Service? (Please tick as appropriate)

Staff meetings   Mission statement
Training courses   Team briefing
Quality groups   On the job training
Appraisal scheme   Bulletin/newsletters
Managers 'walking the floor'

13. Does the Library and Information Service operate a formalized suggestions scheme for staff?

Yes   No   In preparation

14. How is the Library and Information Service's attitude to quality communicated to users? (Please tick as appropriate)

Handouts	Suggestions scheme
Posters	Interface with frontline staff
Complaints scheme	In-house newsletters/publications
Meetings with users	

GENERAL

The concept of 'benchmarking' has become significant as the value of quality management principles and practices has become recognized in library and information services, in common with business organizations.

As part of its remit for the British Library this project aims to identify the activities and perceptions relating to benchmarking in the Library and Information sector. Please help us with this task by answering the following question relating to benchmarking:

15. Please rank the following definitions of the term 'BENCHMARKING' on a scale of 1 to 6 according to your understanding of the term. The definition which, in your opinion, offers to best description should be ranked number 1 and the least preferred should be ranked 6.

(a) Finding and implementing best practice   ____

(b) A structured approach for learning from others
and applying that knowledge   ____

(c) The search for best industry practices that will
lead to superior performance   ____

(d) Benchmarking is a systematic and continuous
measurement process...which will help the organization
take action to improve its performance   ____

(e) Benchmarking is a positive, proactive process to
change operations in a structured fashion to achieve
superior performance   ____

(f) The continuous process of measuring products,
services and practices against leaders, allowing the
identification of best practices which will lead to
superior performance   ____

16. If you have implemented quality initiatives, what have been the three major impacts for good or bad?

....

....

....

A number of Library and Information Services will be invited to take part in a follow-up telephone interview. If you are willing to take part in this follow-up discussion, please indicate by ticking the box.

If yes, who would be the most appropriate person to contact in the first instance?

....

Name/Title of person completing questionnaire:...

Address:...

....

....

Tel. No. ....

Fax No. ....

THANK YOU FOR YOUR TIME AND COOPERATION

Appendix C

Follow-up telephone interviews

The following questions formed the basis of follow-up telephone interviews to ascertain the degree of 'benchmarking type' activities carried out in selected LIS. Respondents were asked to say whether the statements were true for some or all of their activities, or whether none of the statements applied.

A process is the transformation of a set of inputs, which can include actions, methods, operations, manpower and materials, into outputs that satisfy customers' needs and expectations in the form of information, library materials or other services.

Lead-in question: Do you think that benchmarking is relevant to the LIS sector? Can you state your reasons for answering in this way?

- Have key processes within the LIS been *identified*? (Key processes are those top priority activities which the LIS must carry out particularly well in order to achieve its main objectives, or even to survive).

- Are these key processes formally *documented*?

- Are appropriate measures used to *monitor* key processes?

- Is *monitoring* used as a basis for improvement in key processes?

- Is *feedback* from customers used as a basis for improvement in key processes?

- Is an *improvement and review* mechanism in place with *targets* for improvement?

- Are key processes *systematically managed for continuous improvement*?

- Are key processes *benchmarked* against *best practice elsewhere in the LIS sector?*

- Are key processes regularly *examined* and modified if required?

- Are these key processes a *role model* for other LIS?

Appendix D

The 'stepped' approach to benchmarking: John Bullivant's 12 steps to successful benchmarking

PLAN

- Step 1   Select subject area
- Step 2   Define process to benchmark
- Step 3   Identify potential benchmarking partners
- Step 4   Identify data required

ANALYSIS

- Step 5   Collect the data and select benchmark partners
- Step 6   Determine the gap compared to benchmark
- Step 7   Establish difference in process
- Step 8   Target future performance

ACTION

- Step 9   Communication and commitment
- Step 10   Adjust targets and develop corrective improvement plan
- Step 11   Implementation and monitoring
- Step 12   Review progress and recalibrate

Bullivant, J. (1994) *Benchmarking for continuous improvement in the public sector*. Harlow: Longman, p.7.

Appendix E

The 'stepped' approach to benchmarking: Ferne C. Allen's 12 steps to benchmarking

- Step 1   Identify the process to be benchmarked
- Step 2   Establish management commitment to the benchmarking process
- Step 3   Identify and establish the benchmarking team
- Step 4   Define and understand the process to be benchmarked
- Step 5   Identify metrics and collect process data
- Step 6   Identify rank and implement internal process improvements
- Step 7   Identify benchmarking partners
- Step 8   Collect process data from benchmarking partners
- Step 9   Analyze benchmarking partners' process data and compare against internal process data
- Step 10   Site visits, interviews, and reanalyze data.
- Step 11   Implement improvements and monitor results.
- Step 12   Continue to conduct benchmarking of this process, or other aspects of this process, as appropriate.

Allen, F. (1993) Benchmarking: practical aspects for information professionals. *Special Libraries*, 84(3), Summer, 123-130.

Appendix F

Demonstrator project interviews: Questions asked to gain overview of the organizations' quality culture

General quality management issues

- Does the organization have an overall policy on quality?
- Does it produce a mission statement?
- How is this communicated:
  - » To staff?
  - » To users?

- Critical Success Factors:
  - » Are these derived from the mission statement?
  - » Are they measurable?
  - » Is a target set?
  - » Who is responsible for achieving it?

- How is the level of service/service quality reviewed?
  - » User surveys? Suggestions box? Other?
  - » Has usage increased? How was this measured? Were statistics kept?

- Staff training/development/involvement:
  - » Do staff undergo regular training?
  - » Is training reviewed on a regular basis?
  - » Is there a staff appraisal scheme?
  - » Are staff involved in management meetings/informal discussions affecting service quality?

Appendix G

Survey of interlibrary loan transactions at organization A

Table overleaf: Example of the type of data collected during the month of February 1995

Notes:

1.   Input by: relates to reader input (R) or staff input (S)

2.   In stock: where item is found to be in stock request is passed to the Issue Desk (I/Desk)

3.   New supplier: relates to a potential supplier—currently being evaluated by checking the requested item against their database

4   Supplier of document

Request No.	Input by (1)	Form Recd	Date Input	In Stock (2)	Passed to	New Supplier (3)	Date sent	Days before trans	Libs tried	Recd	From (4)	Days taken	Comments
17631	R		2.2.95	N		N	2.2.95	0	1	9.2.95	BL	5	
17632	R		2.2.95	N		N	2.2.95	0	1	14.2.95	BL	8	
17633	R		2.2.95	Y	I/Desk	-	2.2.95	0	0	2.2.95	In stock	0	In stock
17634	S	30.1.95	3.2.95	N		N	9.2.95	4	2	23.3.95	other via BL	6	
17635	R		2.2.95	N		N	2.2.95	0	1	10.2.95	BL	6	

Index

Page-numbers in **bold** type denote main references; *fig* ;and *table* denote figures and tables respectively.